KEY CONCEPTS IN
DEVELOPMENT
GEOGRAPHY

KEYCONCEPTS
IN HUMAN GEOGRAPHY

The *Key Concepts in Human Geography* series is intended to provide a set of companion texts for the core fields of the discipline. To date, students and academics have been relatively poorly served with regard to detailed discussions of the key *concepts* that geographers use to think about and understand the world. Dictionary entries are usually terse and restricted in their depth of explanation. Student textbooks tend to provide broad overviews of particular topics or the philosophy of Human Geography, but rarely provide a detailed overview of particular concepts, their premises, development over time and empirical use. Research monographs most often focus on particular issues and a limited number of concepts at a very advanced level, so do not offer an expansive and accessible overview of the variety of concepts in use within a subdiscipline.

The *Key Concepts in Human Geography* series seeks to fill this gap, providing detailed description and discussion of the concepts that are at the heart of theoretical and empirical research in contemporary Human Geography. Each book consists of an introductory chapter that outlines the major conceptual developments over time along with approximately twenty-five entries on the core concepts that constitute the theoretical toolkit of geographers working within a specific subdiscipline. Each entry provides a detailed explanation of the concept, outlining contested definitions and approaches, the evolution of how the concept has been used to understand a particular geographic phenomenon, and suggested further reading. In so doing, each book constitutes an invaluable companion guide to geographers grappling with how to research, understand and explain the world we inhabit.

Rob Kitchin
Series Editor

KEY CONCEPTS IN

DEVELOPMENT
GEOGRAPHY

ROB POTTER
DENNIS CONWAY
RUTH EVANS
SALLY LLOYD-EVANS

Los Angeles | London | New Delhi
Singapore | Washington DC

First published 2012

SAGE Publications Ltd
1 Oliver's Yard
55 City Road
London EC1Y 1SP

SAGE Publications Inc.
2455 Teller Road
Thousand Oaks, California 91320

SAGE Publications India Pvt Ltd
B 1/I 1 Mohan Cooperative Industrial Area
Mathura Road, Post Bag 7
New Delhi 110 044

SAGE Publications Asia-Pacific Pte Ltd
3 Church Street
#10–04 Samsung Hub
Singapore 049483

Library of Congress Control Number: 2012930731

British Library Cataloguing in Publication data

A catalogue record for this book is available from the British Library

ISBN 978-0-85702-584-5
ISBN 978-0-85702-585-2 (pbk)

Typeset by C&M Digitals (P) Ltd, Chennai, India
Printed in Great Britain by Ashford Colour Press Ltd.
Printed on paper from sustainable resources

CONTENTS

ABOUT THE AUTHORS

Rob Potter is currently Head of the School of Human and Environmental Sciences and Professor of Human Geography at the University of Reading. His research and teaching interests span development geography and development studies; urban geography; return migration; transnationality and issues of identity. He is the founding Editor-in-Chief of the interdisciplinary journal *Progress in Development Studies*, published by Sage. Rob Potter was elected to the Academy of Social Sciences in 2006 and in 2007 was awarded the degree of Doctor of Science by the University of Reading, in recognition of his contributions to the fields of Geographies of Development and Urban Geography.

Dennis Conway is Professor Emeritus of Geography at Indiana University, Bloomington, Indiana. His research interests span population geography, development geography and urban geography. Current research focuses are on Caribbean small island development, transnational migration and return migration, and alternative tourism genres such as 'slow tourism'. He retains interest in globalization's geo-economic dimensions and agency interactions, and is collaborating with a Nepalese colleague of long-standing in GIS-research on contemporary Nepal's environmental and developmental landscape transitions.

Ruth Evans is a lecturer in Human Geography, Department of Geography and Environmental Science, University of Reading. Ruth's research and teaching interests focus on culture and development in Sub-Saharan Africa, in particular, how children, youth and families negotiate caring relations, poverty and social vulnerabilities. Her book *Children Caring for Parents with HIV and AIDS: Global Issues and Policy Responses* (The Policy Press, 2009, co-authored with Saul Becker) discusses children's caring roles in the global North and South. Recent research explores time-space practices of caring in youth-headed households in Tanzania and Uganda and inheritance, food security and the intergenerational transmission of poverty in Senegal and Ghana.

Sally Lloyd-Evans is a lecturer in Human Geography, Department of Geography and Environmental Science, University of Reading. Sally's teaching and research interests in development cut across traditional

North-South divides through a focus on globalisation, labour markets and livelihoods from gender and social justice perspectives. She has recently published on cities and urban livelihoods, micro-enterprise and the informal economy in the Caribbean, and the social inclusion of Muslim workers in the UK labour market. Sally is currently engaged in participatory research with local civil society and voluntary organisations in Berkshire on issues surrounding gender equality, diversity and community engagement.

ACKNOWLEDGEMENTS

We would like to thank Robert Rojek for asking quite persistently that we consider taking on this book project. This occurred at a complex and busy time and Robert was patient in waiting for a final response. Thereafter Sarah-Jayne Boyd helped to keep us on track throughout and, near to completion, she was ably joined by Sophie Hine. Katherine Haw became part of the team at the production stage and ensured smooth passage of the manuscript. All four helped in many ways, for example, in answering queries and checking points of detail and not least by showing real enthusiasm for the project. Closer to home, Christine Jones of the School of Human and Environmental Sciences at the University of Reading provided support in a number of ways, most particularly in assisting with the final preparation of the bibliography, for which we are very grateful.

INTRODUCTION

A Highly Unequal World: Poverty and Inequality

We live in a world characterized by major contrasts and differences. Although those who live in the rich countries of the world may not have reason to think about it every day, grinding poverty and poor living conditions are two of the major characteristics of the globe, not affluence and wealth. On the other hand, within the rich countries of the world the early twenty-first century has come to be characterized by a small minority of the population earning vast salaries, owning and controlling inordinate resources, and living implausibly and – to some at least – unacceptably affluent lifestyles. In a nutshell, these few observations represent the central topics of concern of *Key Concepts in Development Geography*: the global incidence of mass poverty and wide inequalities.

At one end of the spectrum we witness the worlds of celebrity, fame and success, where sportsmen and women, entertainers, and successful business people and bankers can command incomes that run into multiple millions of pounds or dollars per annum, that is multiple thousands of pounds or dollars per week. In some parts of the media we are bombarded on an almost daily basis with images of megastars and celebrities, and in many quarters of the media, an overwhelming emphasis is placed on conspicuous consumption. At the other extreme, a recent study carried out by the World Institute for Development Economics Research (2006) on behalf of the United Nations showed that 50 per cent of the world's total population owned total assets of less than $2,200 and collectively accounted for only one per cent of the world's total wealth. As we shall see later in this book, over half the world's population is currently to be found living on just over US$2 per day or less.

The same study undertaken by the World Institute for Development Economics Research (2006) showed that, viewed in terms of the standards of rich countries, you did not have to own very much in the way of resources to be part of the richest population group on earth. Their investigations showed that owning assets worth US$500,000 or more, or about £350,000 plus, put you into the richest one per cent of people on the planet. This top one per cent was in control of some 40 per cent of the world's total wealth. The percentage distribution of the world's elite wealthiest one per cent was: the USA (37 per cent), Japan (27 per cent), UK (6 per cent), France (5 per cent), Germany (4 per cent), Italy (4 per cent), the Netherlands (2 per cent) and Canada (2 per cent). The rest of the world's countries accounted for only 13 per cent of the richest people on earth.

These massive contrasts in the basic human condition at the global level are exemplified by economic events over the last few years. Notably, the economic and banking crashes and linked recession experienced in the wealthy global North since 2008 have been directly linked to huge profits, million pound pension payments and bonuses made to some of those who are already astoundingly rich. In the meantime, this disastrous economic downturn has seen the world's poor majority getting relatively poorer, especially those living in the poor world or global South. In addition the huge profits made in the rich world or global North by banks and other financial institutions are the direct outcome of speculation on the world's money markets, with such speculation – along with all other forms of neoliberal deregulation (the freeing-up of markets) – being the prime mechanism in creating global economic instability, and thus poverty. Understanding the global system requires an understanding of the underpinnings of these key issues and concepts, and this is exactly what *Key Concepts in Development Geography* seeks to provide for the interested student.

This book follows closely the rationale provided for the Key Concepts in Human Geography series as a whole, offering upper level students a comprehensive introduction to this vital and increasingly important area of the discipline dealing with global inequalities and the incidence of global poverty. It may be argued that in the past, development geography and the cognate multidisciplinary area of development studies showed signs of being treated as the 'Cinderella' of the discipline of geography in particular and the social sciences in general – that is, an area the importance of which has been generally downgraded. The current pace and depth of globalization and the spread of the canons of the free market or neoliberal order in a world which is becoming markedly more unequal – and many would say

2

unjust – means that it is vital to include development-related work at the core of the curriculum.

The Nature and Scope of Development

So what exactly is implied by the word 'development'? Following the account above it can be ventured that, at a basic level, development is about improving the life conditions that are faced by the global majority, and specifically this means reducing existing levels of poverty and inequality at the world scale. A more detailed working definition of development might be adopted that stresses development as attempts to reduce poverty and world inequalities in an effort to guide the world to a situation of betterment and improvement over time (see Kothari, 2005; Potter et al., 2008). For example, the issues surrounding what development means and how it can be assessed and measured are the specific concerns of Section 1 of this book.

Although systematic efforts to improve conditions for the poor, disadvantaged and excluded majority may be said to date from the 1940s, from the dawn of civilization, presumably, some members of society have endeavoured to guide change in ways that might help improve the lives of members of the general population, and in that direct sense were trying to guide development and improve human welfare (Potter and Conway, 2011). The essence of development is that there is a poor world and there is a rich world, and it is implicit that it is the responsibility of the latter to assist the former. In other words, there is a pressing ethical need to equalize the highly disparate conditions that currently exist in the poor and rich worlds. The key concepts and ideas behind this pressing task represent the focus of this book.

Development, however, is also a practical subject and nations, international agencies, non-government organizations (NGOs) and community-based organizations are all involved in the policy-related process of trying to promote development on the ground. Combined, the practice of development and the concepts that underlie such practice give rise to what is referred to as the broad arena of 'development studies'. Development studies represents theoretical, empirical and policy-related studies concerning how development has been, and should be, implemented. Development studies has its origins in the 1940s, when

3

development became an overt aim of Western or advanced states – those of Europe and North America.

The Cross-Disciplinary Field of Development Studies

The rise of development studies as an academic subject that can be studied at university dates from the 1960s. In a review of the history of the field, Harriss (2005) puts its origins in the work of a number of mainly British economists and other social scientists who were unhappy with the insights that were being provided at that time by existing social science subjects, notably traditional or classical economics. These traditional approaches emphasized the importance of quantitative paths to the study of societies and economies. These approaches were seen as reflecting a positivist orthodoxy in the social sciences at that time, which stressed the importance of hypothesis testing and statistical verification as the paramount sources for knowledge.

4

At this juncture the 'new universities' were being established in the United Kingdom and were premised on the idea of 'doing things differently'. In particular, the new universities were keen to promote multi- and interdisciplinary studies that cut across the boundaries of traditional disciplines. Changes in both thinking and practice at this point were also closely linked with the growth of radical Marxist approaches in the 1960s (Harriss, 2005; Kothari, 2005). The Institute of Development Studies was established at the University of Sussex in 1966 and represented a founding institution. Seven years later in 1973 the first undergraduate teaching programme in the field opened at the University of East Anglia. Development studies has spread as an academic discipline to other universities such as Oxford, Manchester, Bath, SOAS London, LSE and Birmingham among others, and has remained quite strongly British. In the words of Harriss (2005: 18): '(d)evelopment studies has been, institutionally, a distinctively British and to a lesser extent other European field of study'. Of course, as we shall see in several chapters of this book, over the years, scholars from developing countries have made fundamental contributions. However, the field still means relatively little in the USA, for example, although similar issues are studied in cognate fields such as international relations, politics, economics and, of course, geography.

It can be argued that rather than being either inter- or multidisciplinary, development studies is cross-disciplinary in nature in that it serves to bring together a large number of fields in the study of poverty and inequality. This is represented in graphical summary form in Figure 1. Following what we said earlier in the chapter, the core concern of development studies may be seen as the existence and seemingly inexorable deepening of global poverty and inequality. In its early stages, 'breakaway' economists were strongly involved in the rise of development studies. Reflecting this in the core discipline, a distinct sub-discipline within economics can be recognized that is now conventionally referred to as 'development economics' (Figure 1). Geographers, with their strong tradition of regional and area studies, represented another area of involvement and interest (Figure 1). In the same way as in the case of economics, the rise of 'development geography' can be recognized.

Other mainstream social science disciplines such as politics and sociology also contributed to the rise of development studies and equally came to be characterized by home disciplinary patches, known respectively as the sociology of development and the politics of development (Figure 1). Attesting to the truly cross-disciplinary character of the field, subjects such as demography, international relations, anthropology and history, and urban and regional planning should also be identified as making a distinct contribution to development studies (Figure 1).

5

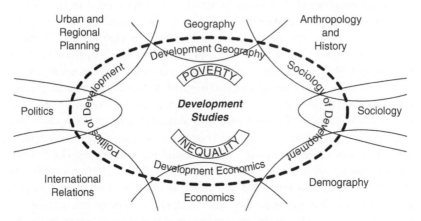

Figure 1 The cross-disciplinary field of Development Studies

Development, Development Geography and Development Studies

This book aims to present the key concepts involved in development studies and practical development policy to geographers taking courses broadly defined as development geography or development studies. But, given the cross-disciplinary nature of the field, the volume should also prove useful for all those students taking components of the various disciplines shown in Figure 1 that focus on the development process, as well as other subjects which are not shown on the figure for reasons of space (for example, the fields of law, gender studies and so on).

In a recent essay, Potter and Conway (2011) summarized the evolution of thinking about development in relation to the advancement of geography as a discipline since the 1940s and the emergence of development studies as a field in the 1960s. Presented in summary terms, such an account is useful in that it serves to stress the similarities and differences in focus that have characterized development practice, development geography and development studies over the last sixty years or so. In doing this, it provides a broad-brush introduction to many of the concepts and ideas that are considered in the main body of this book. We shall now briefly summarize events on a decade-by-decade basis.

The 1940s

The modern roots of development practice can be traced to the period immediately following World War II and to the inaugural speech made by United States President Truman in 1947. In this speech Truman effectively stated that it was the responsibility of rich nations such as the United States and those of Europe to develop poorer countries in their own image. In this period, during which development was emerging, geography was characterized by forms of development-oriented enquiry which might be described as 'colonial', 'military', 'tropical' and 'regional' geographies. Interest in the 'great overseas' had been stimulated initially by consideration of the countries making up the British Empire under colonialism. Then, between 1939 and 1945, a number of British geographers travelled to countries such as Singapore, Egypt, India and Ceylon (present-day Sri Lanka) as part of their wartime military service. The main statement on development came with the publication of the French geographer Pierre Gourou's (1947) text

6

Tropical Geography. Of course, aspects of development had always formed part of the bread and butter of the discipline, in the guise of regional geography; however, as already noted, there was no separate field of development studies per se at this juncture.

The 1950s

The decade of the 1950s was strongly involved with post-war reconstruction and economic development. The ultimate goal was seen as being the application of the historical-development experience of the rich nations in the development of the poorer nations. During this period development policy came to be strongly associated with traditional (classical) economic theory. This was largely based on classical and neoclassical economic theory and emphasized the importance of 'liberalizing', or freeing-up world trade at the global level. At the national level, the approach mainly advocated concentrating development around natural growth poles. At this time, underdevelopment was regarded as an initial state beyond which Western industrial nations had managed to progress. It was envisaged that the experience of the West could assist other countries in catching-up, by sharing capital and technology. Thus, the approach was very much a Western one and was very top-down. In the academic field of geography, the period was associated with the spread of what is still referred to as the 'new geography'. This was based on the search for generalized explanations of the real world by means of the development of models and the use of quantitatively-derived generalizations and laws.

7

The 1960s

The 1960s saw the emergence of radical political perspectives within both society as a whole as well as within mainstream social science subjects, albeit to a greater or lesser extent. A major development was the emergence of what came to be called 'dependency theory', which had its roots in Latin American and Caribbean development. Dependency theory essentially argued that the global pattern of Western-dominated development had served to keep the poor world poor, rather than serving to aid its accelerated development. Dependency theory thereby represented an almost complete rebuttal of classical and neoclassical economic approaches to the challenges of development. It argued that less-developed countries would do better to de-link from the developed world and to follow an alternative development path. Despite this radical ferment in the wider social sciences in the 1960s, by contrast, it was the quantitative revolution that was coming to full fruition in the academic field of geography. But by this time the seeds were already being sown for the development of cross-disciplinary development studies, as already noted in terms of the establishment of the Institute for Development Studies at the University of Sussex in 1966.

The 1970s

It was the early 1970s that saw the emergence of more radical approaches in the field of geography. A landmark publication was David Harvey's *Social Justice and the City* in 1973. The analyses of Harvey and others gave rise to an increasing acceptance of political-economic, or structuralist approaches in human geography by the mid-1970s. Such an orientation was more encouraging to the emergence of a distinct development geography as a sub-discipline, although the term itself was little used at that stage. In a further series of developments, dissatisfaction with the quantitative revolution gave rise to avowedly humanistic approaches in the field of geography, which stressed the subjectivity of phenomena and knowledge. At the same time, alternative and more humanistic-orientated approaches were coming to influence thinking about development practice in what is often referred to as the emergence of 'another development'. This was anchored in a growing critique of urban-based, top-down, centre-out neoclassically inspired development policies. It was at this very juncture that, as already noted, the first development studies undergraduate degree programme was introduced at the University of East Anglia in 1973.

8

The 1980s

In the 1980s development practice and policy were broadly characterized by the rise of what can be referred to as the 'New Right' in Europe and 'Neoconservatism' in the United States. This is also referred to as the rise of the neoliberal agenda, the strong view that liberal free trade and unregulated free markets should be left to make economic decisions and that they would do so rationally and effectively. Thus the New Right sang the praises of the unrestrained power of the unregulated free market. In Britain, full-blown neoliberalism came in the form of

Margaret Thatcher's 'popular capitalism', and in the United States it was witnessed by President Reagan's 'Reaganomics'. Both Thatcher and Reagan pushed for the extension of private-market inspired controls into the public sector. While development studies can be seen to have started to consolidate as a field during the 1980s, and despite the emergence of common concerns between geography and development studies at this time, the focus of geography remained firmly in the fields of cultural and historical geography and the accent was placed mainly on Europe and North America. Surveys carried out at the time showed that what could be recognized as development geography was at best taught by one specialist member of staff in the majority of British geography departments (Potter and Unwin, 1988; Unwin and Potter, 1992).

The 1990s

Postmodernism emerged as an alternative paradigm for the social sciences at the start of the decade. The approach was associated with the rejection of meta-theories and meta-narratives – that is, the big explanations and big ideas that had come to be associated with modernizing as the inevitable and invariant path to development and change. Instead, postmodernism suggested that emphasis should be placed on a wide range of possibly discordant and even contradictory views, voices and discourses. Thus, 'development' was one of the very meta-narratives that was to be questioned, giving rise to what have been referred to as 'anti', 'post' and 'beyond' development stances. In particular at this juncture the question asked was whether the 'development mission', as posed in the 1940s, 1950s and beyond, could ever have been successful given its essentially Eurocentric stance and origins in Western experience and thought. In short, the move toward a distinctly postmodern turn might be interpreted as having given rise to doubts, uncertainties and reflections in both development studies and development geography. In that sense, the 1990s can be seen as having given rise to something of a greater degree of possible commonality between geography and development studies as academic fields. However, there is a critical, alternative interpretation of postmodernity, one that argues it is nothing more than the next logical stage in the progress of modernity. Such a view sees postmodernity as the latest manifestation of late capitalism, seeing individual and group choice being hailed and promoted in an essentially free market setting.

9

The 2000s

Potter and Conway (2011) argue from the point of view of geography as an overall discipline, that, since the turn of the new millennium, matters seem to have been changing for the better and that there have emerged some grounds for optimism, both within the discipline and the development establishment more generally. Thus, there have been definite signs of a more positive view of development-related issues in geography as a discipline, albeit born out of the pressing global developmental–geo-political crises the world currently faces: '(t)he world is now so deeply unequal that the need for a truly global geography has never been greater' (Potter and Conway, 2011: 607). There are the signs that the geographical study of critical development-oriented issues is starting to become more valued and central to geography as a whole. This certainly needs to be the case in the twenty-first century, as an era that faces the pressing realities of the global financial crisis, the other geographical realities of unregulated and unruly globalization, transnationality, global conflict, and environmental change – in particular, climate change.

10

Structure and Scope of this Book

As already noted, *Key Concepts in Development Geography* aims to foster an understanding of the pressing development issues that are being faced globally, in the twenty-first century, among those studying development geography, development studies and cognate fields. It seeks to do this by means of twenty-four concise and carefully presented essays, each of around 2,500 words. Although standard format textbooks have their place – and there are now some well-established ones in the field of development geography (Willis 2005; Potter et al., 2008; Chant and McIlwaine, 2009; Williams et al., 2009) – it is increasingly appreciated that undergraduates often find particularly useful, relatively short and focused essays that present the key issues they seek to understand. This has been demonstrated by the publication of a number of successful companion volumes and readers (see, for example, Chari and Corbridge, 2008; Desai and Potter, 2008); but where these seek to be highly comprehensive, rather than being limited to key themes and ideas, they too become rather large, expensive and over-inclusive for mass purchase within the undergraduate market.

The text of this book is divided into five clear sections. The first two deal with the basic concepts that form the foundations of development geography: the first with the nature and meanings of development and the second with the theory and practice of development. Thus, Section 1 covers key concepts such as the definition and measurement of development, the spatial nature of development issues, the definitions and measurement of poverty and the Millennium Development Goals as a framework for future progress in development. Section 2 covers key concepts such as modernity, postmodernity and post-structuralism, radical development theory, neoliberalism and globalization, the development imperatives of global institutions and sustainable development. In Section 3, the focus is placed on work and employment, covering the vitally important topics of rural livelihoods, industrialization and the New Division of Labour, the informal sector, the digital economy and global trade, aid and regulation. This is then followed in Section 4 by a focus on the interconnections between people, culture and development. In this, key concepts such as gender, households, children, youth and development, health, disability, sexualities and ageing are examined in relation to the process of development and change. In order to round off the volume, a number of cutting-edge contemporary issues in development are reviewed in Section 5 – ranging from human rights and culture, issues of transnationality and diaspora, to civil society and social capital, and to the call for Tobin-type taxes to tackle speculative trading on global markets – and in so doing, to raise money for core aspects of development, such as universal primary education.

Section 1
Understanding
Development

INTRODUCTION

This first section of *Key Concepts in Development Geography* seeks to provide a basic overview of the key concepts that underpin the field. In so doing, it deals with the basics, examining the concept of development and the closely associated issue of the meanings that have been attributed to development. One of the key themes of this section of the book is that, in both theoretical and practical terms, thinking about development has changed markedly over time. A further lesson is that at any given time concepts of development tend to be diverse, reflecting the prevalence of different social, economic, political and even moral viewpoints.

The meanings that have been attributed to development are specifically overviewed in Chapter 1.1 and at the outset it is stressed that, however it is defined, development is something that has to be conceptualized at the global level. This is because development issues involve both poor and rich countries as well as poor and rich people and groups, and the need is to move the former in each case to a more advantageous situation. This account stresses that the origins of international development lie within what is known as the Enlightenment Period. This transition in thought occurred from the eighteenth to nineteenth centuries and emphasized a general belief in science, rational thinking and ordered principles of progress and advancement. It is then explained how the modern or contemporary conceptualization of development came about in the late 1940s and that early approaches to development were almost universally based on the quest for economic growth and increasing prosperity. But starting from the 1960s onward, successive critiques emphasized that wider conceptualizations of development were required, involving attempts to enhance social well-being and to promote self-esteem and basic human freedoms. In other words, it was increasingly recognized that the qualitative aspects of peoples' lives are as important as material issues and benefits.

There are, of course, pressing reasons to want to be able to measure levels of development in order to compare places and to see whether change and betterment have occurred over time. Thus, Chapter 1.2 demonstrates that the measures of development that have been employed have closely reflected the various concepts of development which have been advanced and used over the years. From the 1960s the measures of Gross Domestic Product (GDP) and Gross National Product (GNP) per capita have been used to assess broad levels of economic or material development. By the 1980s, as other conceptualizations of development were increasingly being advanced, the Human Development Index (HDI) was introduced by the United Nations and this incorporated the three aspects of longevity, knowledge and standard of living. Finally in this chapter, the move toward multidimensional measures of development – including aspects of gender, social welfare and human rights – is considered.

The fact that the world is such a manifestly unequal place is the focus of Chapter 1.3. That the world is becoming less and not more equal is a vital point to appreciate, especially as there are strong arguments that wide inequalities in society can be linked with the occurrence of various forms of social malaise and to social conflict. The chapter then considers the global spatial expression of such wide inequalities, charting, for example, the origins of the Third World in the geopolitics of the post-colonial era. Although it is recognized that critiques of the concept of the Third World appeared from the early 1970s, giving rise to dichotomies such as developed and developing nations, the global North and the global South, and rich and poor countries, there is a valid argument that a disadvantaged, marginalized and poor 'Third World' exists whatever we chose to call it.

This consideration of global inequality leads directly to an examination of the concept of poverty in Chapter 1.4 and this is particularly important as many analysts argue strongly that poverty reduction must be seen as the principal focus of development practice in the contemporary world. The chapter reviews the various broad definitions and associated measures of povery that have been advanced and employed. At the simplest level poverty can be defined as a lack of income and thus the lack of goods and services that can be obtained in the marketplace. But just like development itself, there is a mounting argument that poverty is best conceptualized and measured as a multidimensional phenomenon, covering non-economic factors such as health, education, housing, quality of life, environmental quality and basic freedoms, among others. The Human Poverty Index developed out of the Human Development Index by the UN in the 1990s represents an effective multidimensional measure of poverty, although in 2010 it was superceded by the Multidimensional Poverty Index.

16

Bringing together the concepts involved in defining development together with the concepts involved in measuring levels of poverty and development through time are the Millennium Development Goals (MDGs), and these are reviewed in Chapter 1.5. The MDGs represent a set of agreed international development targets by means of which it is intended that the world should move towards a more equitable pattern of development by the year 2015. A total of eight main Millennium Development Goals together with 18 associated targets and 48 variables were identified in 2000. Consideration of progess made since around 1990 indicates that while some progress has indeed been made, the overall situation can be described as patchy at best and, in particular, little or no progress has been made in respect of sub-Saharan Africa. This remains one of the most pressing issues to be faced in the arena of global development and change and again emphasizes the extreme inequality that characterizes the world in which we live.

17

1.1 MEANINGS OF DEVELOPMENT

Introduction: The *Rough Guide* Definition of Development

> International development is the journey the world must take in order for poor countries to become prosperous countries. At the very least it's about making sure that the most basic things that we take for granted can also be taken for granted by everyone else in the world. People in all countries should have food on their plate every day; a roof over their heads at night; schools for their children; doctors, nurses and medicines when they are sick; jobs which bring money into the home. International development – sometimes called global development – describes the collective efforts of all countries which are working to free people from poverty. (Wroe and Doney, 2005)

The quotation above is taken from *The Rough Guide to a Better World*, which was produced by Rough Guides and the Department for International Development (DFID), the UK Government agency for development. The extract first emphasizes that international development is something that has to be pursued by the world as a whole. It continues by highlighting the desirability of poor countries becoming prosperous ones, stressing that incomes and standards of living are important components of development. The definition then suggests that development involves making sure people have the basic things they need, like food, housing, schools, health care and jobs. Finally, freeing people from the grip of poverty is seen as a vital task of development.

The quotation witnesses that a major use of the word 'development' is at the global scale. The principal division of the world is between so-called relatively rich 'developed nations' and the relatively poor 'developing nations'. Overcoming this divide is frequently understood to involve stages of advancement and evolution. At the simplest level developed countries are seen as assisting the developing countries by means of development aid, in an effort to reduce poverty, unemployment, inequality and other indicators of 'underdevelopment'. A key part of this is making sure that the basic needs of the people are being met. All of these aspects of development are alluded to in the Rough Guide/ DFID definition.

But in day-to-day terms what exactly is meant by 'development'? Have views of, and attitudes toward, development changed markedly over the years? Who is development for? Do global institutions, national governments, non-governmental organizations (NGOs), firms and individuals understand the word 'development' to mean much the same thing? These issues are the focus in this chapter.

The Modern Origins of the Process of Development

The origins of the modern process of development lie in the late 1940s. The so-called 'modern era' of development is often directly linked to a speech made by the then United States President, Harry Truman in 1949 (Potter et al., 2008). In this, Truman employed the term 'underdeveloped areas' to describe what was soon to be referred to as the Third World. In his speech, Truman made clear what he saw as the duty of the developed world or 'West' (see Chapter 1.3) to bring 'development' to such relatively underdeveloped countries.

Colonialism may be defined as the exercise of direct political control and the administration of an overseas territory by a foreign state (see also Chapter 1.3). Thus, effectively Truman was emphasizing a new colonial – a neocolonial – role for the USA within the newly independent countries that were emerging from the process of decolonization. Truman was encouraging the so-called 'underdeveloped nations' to turn to the USA and the West generally for long-term assistance, rather than to the socialist world or 'East', based on Moscow and the USSR.

The genesis of much of development theory and practice lay in the period between 1945 and 1955 and what is referred to as the period of high modernism. Modernism may be defined as the belief that development is about transforming 'traditional' countries into 'modern, Westernised nations'. For many Western governments, particularly former colonial powers, such views represented a continuation of the late colonial mission to develop colonial peoples within the concept of trusteeship (Cowen and Shenton, 1995). Trusteeship can be defined as the holding of property on behalf of another person or group, with the belief that the latter will better be able to look after it themselves at some time in the future. At this stage there was little recognition that many traditional societies might, in fact, have been content with the way of life they already led.

The Origins of Development in the Enlightenment

The origins of modern development, however, undoubtedly lay in an earlier period, specifically with the rise of rationalism and humanism that was held to have occurred in the eighteenth and nineteenth centuries. During this period, the simple definition of development as change became transformed into the idea of more directed and logical forms of evolution. Collectively, the period when these changes took place is referred to as the Enlightenment.

20

The Enlightenment generally refers to a period of European intellectual history that continued through most of the eighteenth century (Power, 2003). In broad terms, Enlightenment thinking stressed the belief that science and rational thinking could progress human groups from barbarianism to civilization. It was the period during which it came to be increasingly believed that by applying rational, scientific thought to the world, change would become more ordered, predictable and meaningful.

The new approach challenged the power of the clergy and largely represented the rise of a secular (that is a non-religious) intelligentsia. The threads that made up Enlightenment thinking included the primacy of reason/rationalism; the belief in empiricism (gaining knowledge through observation); the concept of universal science and reason; the idea of orderly progress; the championing of new freedoms; the ethic of secularism; and the notion that all human beings are essentially the same (Hall and Gieben, 1992; Power, 2003).

Those who did not conform to such views were regarded as 'traditional' and 'backward'. As an example of this, the indigenous Aborigines in Australia were denied any rights to the land they occupied by the invading British in 1788, because they did not organize and farm in what was seen as a systematic, rational Western manner. It was at this point that the whole idea of development became directly associated with Western values and ideologies. Thus, Power (2003: 67) notes that the 'emergence of an idea of "the West" was also important to the Enlightenment ... it was a very European affair which put Europe and European intellectuals at the very pinnacle of human achievement'. Thus, development was seen as being directly linked to Western religion, science, rationality and principles of justice.

In the nineteenth century, the ideas of the natural scientist Charles Darwin on evolution began to emerge, stressing gradual change towards something more appropriate for future survival (Esteva, 1992). When combined with the rationality of Enlightenment thinking, the result became a narrower but 'correct' way of development, one based on Western social theory. During the Industrial Revolution, this became heavily economic in its nature. But by the late nineteenth century, a clear distinction seems to have emerged between the notion of 'progress', which was held to be typified by the unregulated chaos of pure capitalist industrialization, and 'development', which was representative of Christian order, modernization and responsibility (Cowen and Shenton, 1995; Preston, 1996).

It is this latter notion of development that began to characterize the colonial mission from the 1920s onwards, equating development in overseas lands with an ordered progress towards a set of standards laid down by the West. Esteva views this as amounting to 'robbing people of different cultures of the opportunity to define the terms of their social life' (Esteva, 1992: 9). Little recognition was given to the fact that 'traditional' societies had always been responsive to new and more productive types of development. Indeed, had they not been so, they would not have survived. Furthermore, the continued economic exploitation of the colonies made it virtually impossible for such development towards Western standards and values to be achieved. In this sense, underdevelopment was the creation of development, as would later be argued by dependency theorists such as André Gunder Frank (see Chapter 2.2).

21

Conventional Development: 'Authoritative Intervention' and Economic Growth

In his speech of 1949, President Truman stated directly that the underdeveloped world's poverty is 'a handicap and threat both to them and more prosperous areas ... greater production is the key to prosperity and peace. And the key to greater production is a wider and more vigorous application of modern scientific and technical knowledge' (Porter, 1995).

Enlightenment values were thus combined with nineteenth-century humanism to justify the new trusteeship of the neocolonial mission, a mission that was to be accomplished by authoritative intervention, primarily through the provision of advice and aid programmes suggesting how development should occur (Preston, 1996). Clearly, the 'modern notion of development' had a long history.

It is, therefore, perhaps not too surprising that, in its earliest manifestation in the 1950s development became synonymous with economic growth. One of the principal 'gurus' of this approach, Arthur Lewis, was uncompromising in his interpretation of the modernizing mission, 'it should be noted that our subject matter is growth, and not distribution' (Esteva, 1992: 12). In other words, increasing incomes and material wealth were seen as being of far more importance than making sure that such income was fairly or equitably spread within society. During the second half of the twentieth century, therefore, the development debate came to be dominated by economists.

The prominence and influence of development economics in the 1950s and 1960s have clear repercussions on the way in which underdeveloped countries were identified and described, a point covered in Chapter 1.3. The earliest and, for many, still the most convenient way of quantifying underdevelopment has been through the level of Gross National Product (GNP) per capita pertaining to a nation or territory. This can broadly be seen as measuring income per head of the population and its method of calculation is explained in Chapter 1.2.

Wider Definitions of Development: Social Well-being and Freedoms

Classical economic-inspired approaches thus dominated development thinking in the 1940s and 1950s, based on concepts such as modernization theory, and top-down development. Little changed until the 1960s when, in the wake of the Vietnam War and a number of other developments, radical dependency approaches were advanced (see Chapter 2.2). The approach argued that the development of the West had acted as an inhibitor of development in the emerging developing world. The 1970s then witnessed another counter movement, one that argued that development should be based on local resources rather than economic efficiency – giving rise to development from below, rural-based development, and eco-development, something that would later become sustainable development.

Accordingly, the 1970s and 1980s saw the appearance of a whole series of social indicators of development, including those relating to health, education and nutrition. The argument that development is more than economic growth was advanced on a number of fronts. The main issue is that even with growth and the provision of more goods and services, it depends how these are distributed between different members and groups of the society. This emerging view was reflected in the derivation of the Human Development Index (HDI) as an overall multidimensional measure of development (see Chapter 1.2). In this, income is still included as a measure of standard of living, but as one of three major variables: the other two measuring health (life expectancy) and knowledge/education (literacy, educational enrolment).

Eventually, such social indicators were broadened to incorporate measures of environmental quality, political and human rights and gender equality. This has recently been fully explored by the Nobel Laureate in economics, Amartya Sen (1999), in *Development as Freedom,* where he argues that 'Development consists of the removal of various types of unfreedoms that leave people with little opportunity of exercising their reasoned agency' (Sen, 1999: xii). In this view freedom is defined in terms of certain human and civil rights that must be guaranteed for all. Above all, people must have the opportunity to be fit, healthy and educated. For Sen (2000) development consists of the removal of various types of unfreedoms that leave people little choice and few real opportunities. Sen's emphasis is on the need for instrumental freedoms – those that will make a difference to peoples' lives.

The need for an understanding of the multidimensional nature of development had in fact been clearly outlined by Goulet in his book *The Cruel Choice: a New Concept on the Theory of Development* (1971). In this he recognized three components of development, these broadly equating with the economic, followed by personal and wider societal freedoms:

- **Life sustenance** is concerned with the provision of basic needs. No nation can be regarded as developed if it cannot provide its people with housing, clothing, food and education. This is, of course, closely related to the issue of distribution within society. It is perfectly possible for a poor country to be growing fast, yet its

distribution of income to be widening. Such a nation may have grown, but has not developed, as only the elite will have got richer.
- **Self-esteem** is concerned with feelings of self-respect and independence. Being developed means not being exploited/controlled by others – for example, as is the case under colonialism. Similarly the International Monetary Fund and the World Bank dominate economic policymaking in many developing countries. Also multinational corporations often exercise a strong controlling influence.
- **Freedom** refers to the ability of people to determine their own destiny. People are not free if they are imprisoned on the margins of subsistence, with no education and no skills. Expansion of the range of choice open to individuals is central to development. The majority not the elite must have choice.

In the words of Chant and McIlwaine (2009) '(i)n short, development comprises multidimensional advances in societal well-being, many of which defy precise determination'.

24 Anti-development stances

Criticisms of development have been voiced ever since the 1960s. But there are long antecedents to anti-(Western) developmentalism, stretching back to the nineteenth century. Anti-development is sometimes also referred to as post-development and beyond-development (Corbridge, 1997; Blaikie, 2000; Nederveen Pieterse, 2000; Schuurman, 2000, 2008; Sidaway, 2008).

In essence, the theses of anti-developmentalism are not new since they are essentially based on the failures of modernization. Thus, anti-developmentalism is based on the criticism that development is a Eurocentric Western construction in which the economic, social and political parameters of development are set by the West and are imposed on other countries in a neocolonial mission to normalize and develop them in the image of the West. Nederveen Pieterse (2000: 175) has commented that 'Development is rejected because it is the "new religion" of the west'.

In this way, the local values and potentialities of 'traditional' communities are largely ignored. The central thread holding anti-developmentalist ideas together is that the discourse or language of development has been constructed by the West, and that this promotes a specific kind of intervention 'that links forms of knowledge about the Third World with the deployment of terms of power and intervention, resulting in the mapping and production of Third World societies' (Escobar, 1995: 212). Thus, Escobar argues, development has 'created abnormalities' such as poverty, underdevelopment, backwardness, landlessness and has proceeded to address them through what is regarded as being a normalization programme that denies the value of local cultures. Here the anti-developmentalist in general, and Escobar in particular, places great emphasis not only on grassroots participation but more specifically on new social movements as the media of change.

Usefully the anti-development movement has brought about a re-emphasis on the importance of the local in the development process, as well as the important skills and values that exist at this level. It also reminds us of what can be achieved at the local level in the face of the 'global steamroller', although few such successes are free of modernist goals or external influences.

KEY POINTS

- The *Rough Guide to a Better World* stresses that development is something that has to be pursued by the world as a whole, in both material and wider terms.
- The origins of what we understand as international development lie in the Enlightenment period, which occurred in the eighteenth and nineteenth centuries and stressed a belief in science, rationality, and ordered progress. It was thus a very European view of progress.
- The modern idea of development came about from the late 1940s and the so-called era of modernity.
- Early views of development emphasized economic growth and prosperity. From the 1960s onward, wider definitions involving social well-being and freedom were increasingly stressed.
- There have always been critics of the development mission, and they are today voiced in the form of 'anti-development'.

25

FURTHER READING

The Rough Guide/DFID *Rough Guide to a Better World* provides an interesting and generally very accessible starting point for the interested reader (Wroe and Doney, 2005) and is downloadable from the DFID website (www.dfid.uk.gov). Helpful wider academic accounts are to be found in Sylvia Chant and Cathy McIlwaine (2009) *Geographies of Development in the 21st Century: an Introduction to the Global South* (Chapter 1) and Rob Potter et al.'s (2008) *Geographies of Development: an Introduction to Development Studies* (Chapter 1). A somewhat more advanced treatment is provided in Chapters 1 and 2 of *Rethinking Development Geographies* (2003) by Marcus Power.

1.2 MEASURING DEVELOPMENT

Following Chapter 1.1, given that development is something that does – or does not – happen over time and across territories, it is inevitable that scholars and practitioners have sought to find methods to measure its progress. It also follows from Chapter 1.1 that the approaches used to measure development have reflected very closely the principal conceptualizations of development as a process that have gained prominance at various times. Thus in the 1950s through to the early 1980s development was generally measured in terms of economic growth and, in particular, the growth of production and income. In the late 1980s through to the 1990s, changes in the way development was being envisioned were directly recognized in the promotion of wider indices of human development and change.

This trend toward recognizing the multidimensional nature of development was continued from the 1990s through to the start of the twenty-first century, whereby wider sets of factors, reflecting more subjective and qualitative dimensions of development, have increasingly been referred to. These have included wider measures of social welfare and human rights. Accordingly, these three approaches are used in this chapter to review measures of development, specifically: (i) measuring development as economic growth: GDP and GNP per capita; (ii) measuring development as human development: the HDI; and (iii) measuring development in wider terms including human rights and freedoms.

Measuring Development as Economic Growth: GDP and GNP per capita

In the simplest definition, this approach uses 'income' per head of the population as a measure of development – suggesting that the higher the income of a country or territory, the greater its development. The approach sees development as being essentially the same thing as economic growth. During the era of unilinear development models and theories, the growth of GDP/GNP was taken as the surrogate measure of development. More accurately, in this approach the standard of living of a country is used as a summary measure of development (Thirlwall, 2008). The GDP/GNP of a territory is directly affected both by the number of people working within a country and their overall level of productivity.

- **Gross Domestic Product (GDP) per capita** – measures the value of all goods and services produced by a nation or a territory, whether by national or foreign companies. When calculated, the national total is divided by the total population, to give the value of goods and services produced per head of the population.
- **Gross National Product (GNP) per capita** – this is Gross Domestic Product to which net income derived from overseas is added. In other words, income which is generated abroad is added, and payments made overseas are subtracted. This total is also then divided by the total population. In recent years, international organizations like the World Bank have increasingly referred to this as Gross National Income (GNI) per capita.

28

Through time from the 1950s, GDP, GNP/GNI have been used as measures of development. Figure 1.2.1 shows the global distribution of GDP

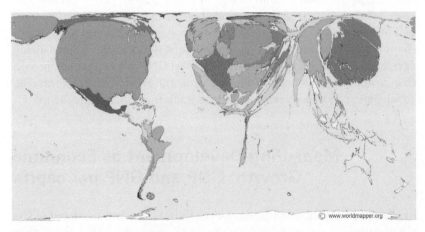

Figure 1.2.1 Gross Domestic Product by country (size of country shows the proportion of world wealth accounted for by that country).

Source: Worldmapper map number 169 © Copyright SASI Group (University of Sheffield)

around 2009 and demonstrates just how unequal the world is in terms of a clear North versus South split. The measure has been popular as it makes possible the international comparison of living standards by using per capita incomes, customarily measured in United States dollars. Employing such an approach, the basic causes of poverty of any given nation are seen as the low productivity of labour that is associated with low levels of physical capital (natural resources) and human capital (for example, education) accumulation and low levels of technology. The economic growth of countries is measured by the increase in output of goods and services (GDP/GNP) that occurs over a given time period, normally a year (Thirlwall, 2008).

Measuring Development as Human Development: the HDI

Development, however, is far wider than the growth of income alone. First, GDP/GNP take no account of the distribution of national wealth and output between different groups of the population, or between different regions. Further, such income-based measures do not take into acount the wider well-being of people, which includes more than goods and money.

29

In the 1980s, it was increasingly recognized that non-economic factors are involved in the process of development. Reflecting this, in 1989, the United Nations Development Programme (UNDP) promoted the Human Development Index (HDI) as a wider measure of development. HDI data were published for the first time in 1990 in the inaugural *Human Development Report 1990* (UNDP, 1990). In the original HDI the emphasis was placed on assessing human development as a more rounded phenomenon. There was still a measure of economic standing, but this was only one of three principal dimensions identified:

1 **A long and healthy life** (longevity) – originally measured by life expectancy at birth in years.
2 **Education and knowledge** – initially measured by the adult literacy rate and the gross enrolment ratio (the combined percentage of the population in primary, secondary and tertiary education).
3 **A decent standard of living** – originally measured by Gross Domestic Product per capita in US dollars, as outlined above.

In the HDR 2010, the formula was changed somewhat and the manner in which the basic HDI is now calculated is shown in Figure 1.2.2A. The three dimensions of health, education and living standards are translated into four indicators, and these are summed to give a single Human Development Index. In the case of all the indicators, the measures are then transformed into an index ranging from 0 to 1, to allow equal weighting between each of the three dimensions.

Since 1990, the *Human Development Report* has been published by the UNDP every year. Within these reports, the HDI has been used to divide nations into what have come to be referrred to as high-, middle- and

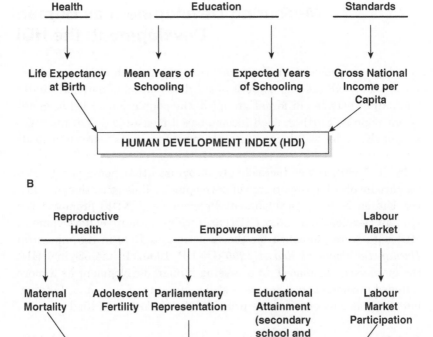

Figure 1.2.2 Calculating (A) the Human Development Index (HDI) and (B) the Gender Inequality Index (GII)

low-levels of human development. Recently, the classification has been extended to also include a 'very high' human development category. It should be stressed that the HDI is a summary and not a comprehensive measure of development. For example, over the years since its introduction various methodological refinements have been tried by the United Nations, including the Human Poverty Indices 1 and 2, the Gender-related Development Index and the Gender Empowerment Measure. These are all variations on the basic Human Development Index. In each case, additional variables were brought in to reflect the revised index. HPI 1 and HPI 2 are explained in Chapter 1.4, along with the recent development of the Multidimensional Poverty Index (MPI). In 2010, the Gender Inequality Index (GII) was introduced, looking at disparities existing between males and females over the dimensions of reproductive health, empowerment and participation in the labour force, as shown in Figure 1.2.2B.

The Worldmapper depiction of global HDI around 2009 is shown in Figure 1.2.3. The imbalance between the global North and South is shown once more, but this time it is somewhat less pronounced than in the case of GDP. Some of the features of the HDI are shown if we look at the HDI scores and associated data for a selection of countries, as displayed in Table 1.2.1. These data have been taken from the *2009 Human Development Report* (UNDP, 2009). It is noticeable that within the 'very high' human development category, Qatar shows the highest

31

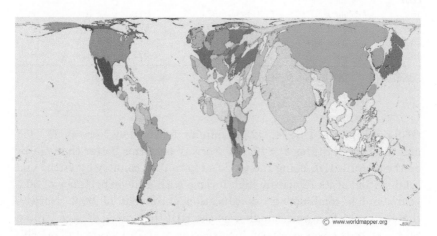

Figure 1.2.3 Human Development Index (size of country shows the proportion of world human development accounted for by that country).
Source: Worldmapper map number 173 © Copyright SASI Group (University of Sheffield)

Table 1.2.1 Human Development Index Scores 2009 and Component scores for a selection of Countries classified as Very High, High, Medium and Low Human Development nations

HDI Rank (Group)	Country	HDI value	Life expectancy at birth in years	Combined gross enrolment ratio in education %	GDP per capita US $	Difference between GDP and HDI rank
Very High						
1	Norway	0.971	80.5	98.6	53,433	4
2	Australia	0.970	81.4	114.2	34,923	20
13	United States	0.956	79.1	92.4	45,592	−4
21	United Kingdom	0.947	79.3	89.2	35,130	−1
33	Qatar	0.910	75.5	80.4	74,882	−30
37	Barbados	0.903	77.0	92.9	17,956	11
High						
39	Bahrain	0.895	75.6	90.4	29,723	−9
51	Cuba	0.863	78.5	100.8	6,876	44
64	Trinidad/Tobago	0.837	69.2	61.1	23,507	−26
66	Malaysia	0.829	74.1	71.5	13,518	−5
Medium						
87	Thailand	0.783	68.7	78.0	8,135	−5
96	Jordan	0.770	72.4	78.7	4,901	11
129	South Africa	0.683	51.5	76.8	9,757	−51
Low						
160	Malawi	0.493	52.4	61.9	761	12
169	Liberia	0.442	57.9	57.6	362	10
181	Afghanistan	0.352	43.6	50.1	1,054	−17
182	Niger	0.340	50.8	27.2	627	−6

Source: UNDP 2009: Human Development Report, 2009, Table H, pp 171–175

GDP per capita at US$74,882 per annum, followed by Norway $53,433 and the United States at $45,592. Norway performs better than Qatar on the overall HDI, being the world's top ranked country by virtue of a combination of its relatively high income with a life expectancy of 80.5 years and a combined gross education enrolment of 98.6. Norway thereby ranks four places higher on the HDI than on GDP. The United States records lower scores on life expectancy at 79.1 years and on educational enrolment (92.4) and, therefore, a lower rank on HDI than on income (–4). The high income of Qatar is offset by a somewhat lower life expectancy at 75.5 years and an educational enrolment of 80.4 per cent. Qatar, therefore, shows a 30 place differential between its HDI rank and its GDP rank. Australia, the nation with the second highest HDI score in the world, is shown to be characterized by the reverse: it has a higher HDI rank than income rank by some 20 places. Barbados has a much lower GDP per capita at $17,956 than other countries in this class, but is ranked 37 in the world on the HDI by virtue of its enhanced rates of literacy and educational enrolment, both of which are higher than those recorded by Qatar. An argument that is quite often put forward is that countries which show relatively high incomes along with marked inequalities in income distribution (that is, high inequalities), often show lower levels of life expectancy and a range of social problems (see Chapter 1.3).

This is further implied when we look at the 'high' human development category. Nations here generally show life expectancies of between 69 and 76 years and educational enrolments of 60–90 per cent. Cuba is an interesting case, however, having a very low GDP per capita for this class at $6,876 per annum; however, its very good health and educational records are reflected in a life expectancy of 78.5 years and a gross educational enrolment of 100.8 – levels more typical of a very highly developed nation. Thereby, Cuba's HDI rank is some 44 places higher than its rank according to GDP per capita.

Turning to the 'middle' human development group of countries, the case of South Africa shows a reverse situation to that of Cuba. South Africa shows a massive 51 difference in rank according HDI as opposed to GDP per capita. While its GDP per capita is relatively high for the category, standing at $9,757, it records a life expectancy as low as 51.5 years, again pointing to massive socio-economic inequalities.

As would be expected, there is a greater overall agreement between GDP per capita and life expectancy and educational enrolment in respect of the 'low' human development grouping. The terrible reality is that virtually all the nations falling into this category are to be found in Africa. For the nations in this group, life expectancy at birth hovers around 50 years and is as low as 43.6 years in the case of Afghanistan. Gross educational enrolment levels of around 50 per cent are also typical of this category and are as low as 27.23 per cent in the case of Niger, the world's least developed nation according to its overall HDI score.

33

Measuring Development in Wider Terms Including Human Rights and Freedoms

In Chapter 1.1 the ideas of Goulet (1971) and Sen (1999), stressing the importance of self-esteem and freedoms as components of the development equation, were outlined. Such views represent specific recognition that wider aspects of development are vital, particularly those that relate to the quality of people's lives, their freedom from various inequalities, and the attainment of human rights and basic freedoms.

In Chapter 1.5 the Millennium Development Goals (MDGs), designed to steer the world to enhanced levels of development, are explained and reviewed. For each of the goals there are associated targets and detailed indicators. The indicators can be employed in order to assess the progress of nations and regions towards the goals and targets, and thereby represent measures of the wider dimensions of development, covering issues such as:

(i) Eradicating extreme poverty and hunger – measured by the percentage of the population living on less than $1 or $2 per day (now $1.25 and $ 2.50 per day)
(ii) Achieving universal primary education
(iii) Promoting gender equality and empowering women
(iv) Reducing child mortality
(v) Improving maternal welfare
(vi) Combatting diseases

National reports covering progress towards the MDGs are available on the UNDP website. The 94-page Report for India 2009, for example, shows in considerable detail the mixed success achieved by that nation on the 12 targets that apply to it.

In terms of basic human rights, an interesting approach is to chart the extent to which countries have ratified the six major human rights conventions and covenants (for example, the Rights of the Child, Against Torture, etc.; see Potter et al., 2008). In like vein, as noted above, the *United Nations Human Development Report 2010* introduced the HDI-derived Gender Inequality Index (GII) (see Figure 1.2.2B). The statistics input to the GII include the national female and male shares of parliamentary seats and educational attainment. The GII also includes female participation in the labour market. Thereby, the GII represents a direct effort to measure the progress made by countries in advancing the standing of women in wider political and economic developmental terms.

KEY POINTS

- Measures of development have closely reflected the various paradigms of development that have been advanced and embraced over the years.
- GDP and GNP per capita have been used since the 1960s as measures of economic growth.
- The HDI was developed by the United Nations in the late 1980s to reflect three major dimensions of human development – longevity, knowledge and standard of living.
- The HDI can be adapted and rendered as a strongly gendered measure of development.
- Wider sets of dimensions, including those involved in the MDGs, can be used to measure the multidimensional nature of development, including social welfare issues and human rights – as in the Gender Inequality Index.

35

FURTHER READING

Wider aspects of the assessment and measurement of development are covered in Chapter 1 of Rob Potter et al.'s (2008) textbook, *Geographies of Development: an Introduction to Development Studies*. Further summary treatments are to be found in *Geographies of Development in the 21st Century* by Sylvia Chant and Cathy McIlwaine (2009) and *Theories and Practices of Development* by Katie Willis (2005), in both cases in the introductory Chapter 1. For the view of a development economist on issues of measuring development, a readable account is offered in 'The development gap and the measurement of poverty', Chapter 2 of Tony Thirlwall's (2006) *Growth and Development: with Special Reference to Developing Economies*. For the HDI etc., see http://hdr.undp.org/en/statistics/indices/gdi_gem/.

1.3 SPACE AND DEVELOPMENT

WHY SPACE MATTERS

An Unequal World

While there is a strong argument that in the realm of social policy the focus should be on poor people rather than poor places, this has to be evaluated against the remarkable degree to which the world can be divided into rich and poor areas, cities, regions, nations and continents. Additionally, all the available evidence shows that the world is continuing to get more uneven and unequal. Inequality across space can be seen as one of the major characteristics of the world in which we live, both within and between countries. In short, space matters as part of the development equation.

Around the world, a high proportion of people still face conditions that can only be described as far from acceptable. In August 2008, the World Bank presented a major overhaul of their estimates of the incidence of global poverty. What used to be measured as US$1 a day was then changed to $1.25 a day. Some 1.4 billion people live at or below this level – representing 21.7 per cent of the world's population (Table 1.3.1). This means that more people are living in poverty than was previously believed – as this was estimated at 984 million with the old measure of $1 in 2004; however, almost half the world's population – some 3.14 billion people – live on $2.50 a day or less (Table 1.3.1). The table also reveals that around 80 per cent of the world's population currently lives on US$10 a day or less, amounting to a staggering 5.15 billion people in total.

The proportion of the world's population living on US$1.25 fell by some 25 per cent between 1981 and 2005, as indicated in Figure 1.3.1A. During the same period, China's poverty fell from 85 per cent to 15.9

Table 1.3.1   Percentage of world population living at different poverty levels 2005

Poverty line $ US per day	Percentage of world population below the poverty line	Number (billions)
1.00	13.6	0.88
1.25	21.7	1.40
1.45	26.6	1.72
2.00	40.2	2.60
2.50	48.6	3.14
10.00	79.7	5.15

Source: United Nations Development Programme, 2009

per cent. Indeed, China accounted for nearly all the world's reduction in poverty during this period. Excluding China from the figures, world poverty fell by only 10 per cent (Figure 1.3.1B).

Such statistics point squarely to the fact that inequality and highly skewed distributions of wealth and assets characterize the modern world. In 2004, a minuscule 0.13 per cent of the world's population controlled 25 per cent of the world's assets. At the same date, the

37

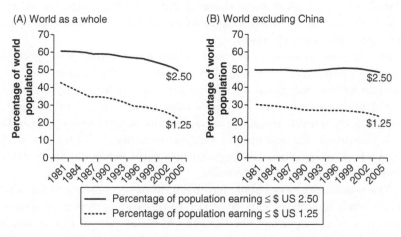

Figure 1.3.1   Proportion of the population living on less than $US 1.25 and 2.50 for (A) the World and (B) the World excluding China, 1981–2005

Table 1.3.2 Income inequality in selected world regions

Region	Ratio of the earnings of the richest to the poorest 20 per cent of the population
Latin America and the Caribbean	20
Sub-Saharan Africa	18
Middle East and North Africa	10
East Asia and Pacific	9
High Income Nations	8
Europe and Central Asia	6
South Asia	5

Source: World Bank Development Indicators, 2008

wealthiest 20 per cent of the world's population consumed 76.6 per cent of the world's goods. And more than 80 per cent of the world's population lives in nations where income differentials are widening.

The same is true at the continental scale within the developing world, as shown in Table 1.3.2 and based on World Bank data. Inequality in high-income nations stands at around 8, measured by the ratio of the earnings of the poorest versus the richest 20 per cent of the population. This ratio is as high as 20 times in the case of Latin America and the Caribbean, and high in sub-Saharan Africa (18 times); other areas are also high, such as the Middle East and North Africa (10 times) and east Asia and the Pacific (9 times).

In addition, available data and evidence show that with greater equality, important variables like educational attainment and life expectancy are enhanced. As income and wealth inequality increase, health and social problems rise, as do the incidences of mental ill-heath, drug use, child mortality, levels of imprisonment and homicide rates (in rich countries). For example in relation to homicide levels, the USA shows high inequalities and high murder rates, while Japan, Norway and Denmark illustrate the reverse.

There is a strong argument that inequalities increase social tensions at all levels in society. This gives rise to the argument that as well as having a minimum wage, for the sake of social cohesion there needs also to be a maximum wage. For example, it has recently been argued that the CEO or head of an organization should earn no more than, say, 20 times the lowest paid worker.

The Emergence of the Third World in the 1950s and 1960s

The term that has most commonly been employed to refer to spatial contrasts in development at the global scale is the 'Third World'. As with the word 'development', the term goes back beyond 1949, although not much further. The origins of the term were political, largely centring around the search for a 'third force' or 'third way' as an alternative to the Communist–Fascist extremes that dominated Europe in the 1930s. In the Cold War politics of the immediate post-war years, this notion of a third way was revived initially by the French Left, who were seeking a non-aligned path between Moscow and Washington (Worsley, 1979). It was this concept of non-alignment that was seized upon by newly independent states in the 1950s – led in particular by India, Yugoslavia and Egypt – and culminated in the first major conference of non-aligned nations, which was held in Bandung in Indonesia in 1955. Indeed, at one point 'Bandungia' appeared to be a possibility for their collective label.

It was a sociologist, Peter Worsley (1964), who played a major role in the popularization of the term 'Third World', principally via his book of that title. For Worsley the term was essentially political, labelling a group of nations with a colonial heritage from which they had recently escaped and to which they had no desire to return under the guise of new forms of colonialism, or 'neocolonialism'. Nation building was, therefore, at the heart of the project. For a while in the 1950s and 1960s, this Afro–Asian bloc attempted to pursue a middle way in international relations.

39

In economic terms, however, it was a different story. Almost all newly independent states lacked the capital to sustain their colonial economies, let alone expand or diversify. Most remained trapped in the production of one or two primary commodities, the prices of which were steadily falling in real terms, unable to expand or improve infrastructure and their human resources. Once Worsley had identified the common political origins of the Third World in anti-colonialism and non-alignment, he cemented this collectively through the assertion that its current bond was poverty. By the late 1960s the term Third World was in widespread use, even by its constituent states, in forums such as the United Nations (Potter et al., 2008). Conceptually, therefore, the world was firmly divided into three clusters, namely the West, the Communist bloc and the Third World.

Critiques of the Third World in the 1970s

By the early 1970s, the rather loose combination of political and economic features that constituted the Third World had already attracted criticism. The French socialist Debray (1974: 35) argued that it was a term imposed from without rather than within, although more developing nations were beginning to use the term. Anti-developmentalists consider this to be a critical point in the development process, a time when the Third World was beginning to recognize its own underdevelopment, adopting Western evaluations of its condition. Many other critics, however, also felt the term was derogatory since it implied that developing countries occupied third place in a hierarchy of the three worlds.

The main cause of the doubts that emerged during the 1970s was related to the growing political and economic fragmentation of the Third World. Ironically, perhaps the biggest impetus to the break-up of the Group of 77 non-aligned nations came from within, when the nations making-up the Organization of Petroleum Exporting Countries (OPEC) raised the price of their oil massively in 1973–74, with a second wave of price rises in 1979 following the fundamentalist revolution in Iran. Initially conceived as a political weapon against the West for its support of Israel, the oil price rise had a much greater effect on the non-oil-producing countries of the developing world, many of which were following oil-led industrial and transport development programmes. The result was a widening income gap between developing countries.

This was further reinforced by the new international division of labour in the 1970s in which capital investment – via multinational corporations and financial institutions – poured out of Europe and North America in search of industrial investment opportunities in developing countries. Most of this investment was highly selective and cheap labour alone was not sufficient to attract investment: good infrastructure, an educated and adaptable workforce, local investment funds, docile trade unions and the like were also important. The result was that investment focused on a handful of developing countries (specifically, the four Asian tigers, plus Mexico and Brazil) where GNP per capita began to rise rapidly, further stretching relative economic and social contrasts within the Third World.

40

The Third World in the 1980s

Nevertheless, during the 1980s a growing critique of the term 'Third World' began to emerge from the new right-wing development strategists who argued that the Third World is merely the outcome of Western guilt about colonialism, a guilt which is exploited by the developing countries through the politics of aid. In the eyes of the so-called New Right, virtually all developing countries are tainted with socialism and their groupings have invariably been anti-Western and therefore anti-capitalist, a view which has effectively been taken to task by John Toye (1987). Ironically, many Marxists also found it difficult to accept the term Third World because they regarded the majority of its constituent countries as underdeveloped capitalist states linked to advanced capitalism. Thus, in their eyes there were only two worlds, capitalist and Marxian socialist, with Marxian socialism subordinate to capitalism. Unfortunately, there was little agreement among Marxists as to what constituted the socialist Third World.

The notion of two worlds perhaps represented the most concerted challenge to the three-world viewpoint and, indeed, most of the semantic alternatives that we currently use are structured around this dichotomy, namely Rich and Poor, Developed and Underdeveloped (or less developed), North and South. And such perspectives led to the notion of dualism. The North–South labelling, in particular, received an enormous boost in popularity with the publication of the Report of the Independent Commission on International Development Issues (1980), known as the Brandt Report. As many critics have noted, the Brandt Report set out a rather naive and impractical set of recommendations for overcoming the problems of underdevelopment, relying as it did on the governments of the South to pass on the recommended financial support from the governments of the 'North' (Potter and Lloyd-Evans, 2009).

From a developmental perspective, one of the Brandt Report's major defects was its simplistic subdivision of the world into two parts based on an inadequate conceptualization of rich and poor. Some critics have claimed that this amounted to spatial reductionism of the worst kind, apparently undertaken specifically to divide the world into a wealthy, developed top half and a poor, underdeveloped bottom half – North and South, them and us – although the terms did no more than rename pre-existing spatial concepts. However, the labels North and South do seem

41

to be used with disturbing geographical looseness, since the South includes many states in the northern hemisphere, such as China and Mongolia, whereas Australasia comprises part of the North.

Although attention in recent years has focused on growing contrasts within the Third World itself, it has also masked the more important fact that global contrasts too are continuing to widen. In particular there has been much concern that a large number of countries, particularly in Africa, have not only failed to exhibit any signs of development but have actually deteriorated, saddled as they have been with the spiralling debts of poverty and harsh structural adjustment programmes. In this context, convergence theory could be seen as a myth. Indeed, it is arrogant to assume that the process of economic and cultural transfer is one way. The West has not merely exported capitalism to the developing world, capitalism itself was built up from resources transferred to the West from those same countries. Similarly, acculturation is not simply the spread of Gucci and McDonald's around the world; in almost every developed country, clothes, music and cuisine, together with many other aspects of day-to-day living, are permeated with influences from Asia, Africa, Latin America and the Caribbean such as bamboo furniture, curries and salsa music.

42

The Third World by Another Name?

If the Second World no longer exists, can there be a Third World? In this sense, there is little justification for retaining the term, particularly since the early commonality of non-alignment and poverty has also long been fragmented. Many commentators in the 1990s, particularly those who form part of the anti-development school, suggested that it is time for the term to be abandoned. Sachs (1992: 3), inelegantly but forcefully, stated that 'the scrapyard of history now awaits the category "Third World" to be dumped'. Yet despite such strong condemnation the term persists in common usage, even by some of those who have criticized its overall validity.

So why is the term still in use? Perhaps, as Norwine and Gonzalez (1988) have remarked, some regions are best defined or distinguished by their diversity. Despite the variations in the nature of the Third World that we have noted, most people in most developing countries continue to live in grinding poverty with little real chance of escape.

This is the unity that binds the diversity of the casual labourer in India, the squatter resident in Soweto, or the street hawker in Lima. All are victims of the unequal distribution of resources that the world manifestly exhibits. And this expression is strongly spatial in character – space matters in development.

Further, it still holds true, that there is a unity provided by colonization and decolonization. The same sort of view gives rise to the argument that 'the Third World is *SIC*', that is, it is the outcome of the forces of Slavery, Imperialism and Colonialism. It is for these sorts of reasons that some commentators still approve of the use of the term Third World, in that it stresses the historical–political and strategic commonalities of relatively poor, primarily ex-colonial countries. Virtually all Third World nations, with the notable exceptions of Thailand, Iran, parts of Arabia, China and Afghanistan, share a history of colonial rule and external domination. Thus a case can be made, on the grounds of history, for the continued use of the collective noun 'Third World'.

In this sense, in the words of Norwine and Gonzalez (1988: 2–3) the concept of the Third World is an 'extremely useful figment of the human imagination ... The Third World exists whatever we choose to call it. The more difficult question is how can we understand it and change it according to priorities set out by its own inhabitants'. Most of those students of development who continue to use the term Third World must realise, therefore, that it is not simply a semantic or geographical device, but a concept that refers to a persistent process of exploitation through which contrasts at the global, regional and national levels are growing wider.

43

KEY POINTS

- We live in a highly unequal world and it is becoming more, rather than less, unequal.
- There is a strong argument that inequalities lead to a reduction in social cohesion within society and that, further, they are linked to the generation of social conflicts.
- The origins of the label 'Third World' were originally essentially geo-political, denoting what were mainly former colonial nations.
- Critiques of the concept of the Third World appeared from the early 1970s and gave rise to new forms of dichotomous thinking, not least Rich and Poor, Developed and Underdeveloped and North–South.

- There is an argument that the Third World exists whatever we choose to call it. Other descriptors include Poor countries, former colonies and non-aligned nations.

FURTHER READING

The Global Issues website, 'poverty around the world', offers a useful introductory account to statistics summarizing the major inequalities that characterize the contemporary world: www.global.issues.org/article/4/poverty-around-the world. Interested readers will also benefit from consulting the Worldmapper website for a wide array of maps showing all too clearly global inequalities. For more academic treatments consult Sylvia Chant and Cathy McIlwaine's *Geographies of Development in the 21st Century: an Introduction to the Global South* (2009), where spatial meanings and connotations are covered in the first part of Chapter 1; and Potter et al.'s *Geographies of Development* (3rd edition), has a section covering 'Spatialising development: the Third World/Developing World/Global South/Poor Countries', in Chapter 1 (pp. 22–32).

1.4 DEFINING AND MEASURING POVERTY

Poverty: Basic Concepts and Definitions

In recent years, numerous commentators have emphasized that poverty reduction and poverty alleviation strategies must be placed at the very core of development practice. For example, in the early 1990s, the World Bank's policies were regarded as giving rise to what was described as the 'New Poverty Agenda'. In the same context, in 1999 'Poverty Reduction Strategy Papers' were introduced as a vital policy instrument in respect of 'Heavily Indebted Poor Countries'.

The simplest conceptualization of poverty is that it represents a lack of money and income. Proponents of this view point to the high correlation that generally exists between income and other measures of social and economic well-being, such as health and education. But just like the definition of development itself, while income and money are important components, poverty needs to be seen as multidimensional. White (2008) notes that as well as income and consumption, factors such as health, education, social life, environmental quality, and political and spiritual freedoms are all vital components of poverty and that deprivation in respect of any one of these may be regarded as giving rise to poverty.

As noted by White (2008), studies have shown that relatively poor people themselves often assess dimensions other than income as being of considerable importance in assessing poverty levels. A well-known study carried out by Jodha (1988) showed how the welfare of poor Indians had increased by measures they themselves viewed as important. These improvements included wearing shoes and occupying accommodation separate from livestock. However, surveys showed that during the same period as these improvements had been occurring the incomes of the poor had actually fallen, showing clearly how factors other than income have a direct bearing on poverty. As UNDP (2009) has stressed, viewed in this manner, poverty means that opportunities and choices basic to human development are not available to those experiencing it. Such a view links to the definition of poverty as a lack of power and access in the marketplace, including education, employment, housing and health. The occurrence of a number of linked disadvantages gives rise to the concept of cumulative or multiple deprivation, where lack of power in one arena leads to a consequent lack of power in others.

Absolute and Relative Poverty, Entitlements and Vulnerabilities

In Chapter 1.3 we noted that, while globally the average level of poverty is reducing, the difference between the incomes of the rich and the poor is getting wider. This represents a situation where while absolute poverty is decreasing, relative poverty is increasing.

Viewing poverty purely in terms of income suggests economic growth as the route to poverty reduction. If a multidimensional view is taken, then poverty alleviation requires targeted social policies. A good example of this relates to changing views of poverty. Sen (1984) argued that to understand poverty, malnutrition and starvation, it is necessary to think in terms of what may be referred to as entitlements. These refer to the resources that the poor can access to withstand short- and long-term food crises. Entitlements include income, ownership of wider resources, and access to public goods such as health care along with other basic services (Thirlwall, 2006; Chant and McIlwaine, 2009). Malnutrition involves a lack of access to food, but this does not depend solely on whether food is available. It is also a reflection of people's entitlements to food. Groups may go short of food not because food is unavailable, but because their entitlement to it has been impaired. From this perspective, famine results from a rapid decline in the entitlements of various groups to the local food supply.

Sen cites the example of the Great Bengal Famine in 1948, which mainly affected fishermen, agricultural labourers and transport workers. In this famine, demand for the services of these workers declined while, at the same time, the demand for labour in urban areas was serving to push up the price of the staple foodstuff: rice. This illustrates people can become too poor to afford the food that is actually available. At the global level, there has always been enough food to feed the people of the world, but this has not been true locally – that is, entitlements have not been met, representing a situation of food insecurity. These conditions etch out a situation where the vulnerabilities of certain poor groups become all too apparent. In other words, the vulnerable poor sometimes face famine even when food is plentiful.

Measuring Poverty

GNP/GDP per capita as measures of goods and production per head of the population can be taken as aggregate measures of income poverty within particular territories or nations. However, the most straightforward measure of income poverty is the headcount. This is the percentage of the population that falls below a stipulated poverty line. To calculate this, the poverty level or line first has to be defined.

We can now look at income poverty for broad continental divisions of the developing world (see Table 1.4.1). In this the frequently employed poverty measure of the percentage of the population living below an income of US$1.00 per day is used as the poverty line. The headcount figures show that nearly 50 per cent of the population of sub-Saharan Africa is living below this poverty line and that the region has shown no real improvement since 1990. On the other hand,

47

Table 1.4.1 Percentage of the total population living on less than $1 per day, 1990, 1999 and 2005 by major region in the developing world

Region	1990	1999	2005
Sub-Saharan Africa	57	58	51
Southern Asia	49	42	39
South-Eastern Asia	39	35	19
Eastern Asia	60	36	16
Latin America and the Caribbean	11	11	8
Western Asia	2	4	6
Comm. of Ind. States of S Asia	3	8	5
North Africa	5	4	3
Transition Countries of SE Europe	0.1	2	1
Developing Regions	*42*	*31*	*25*

Source: United Nation Development Programme, 2009

the poverty headcount for Eastern Asia has declined markedly since 1990, to its present level of less than 16 per cent, having stood as high as 60 per cent in 1990.

A specific measure of some of the wider aspects of multidimensional poverty is provided by the Human Poverty Index (HPI), developed by the United Nations Development Programme (UNDP) as an extension of the HDI since the 1990s and used through to 2010. Accordingly, the HPI concentrated on measuring deprivation with respect to the three essential elements used to assess the original HDI: a long and healthy life, knowledge and a decent standard of living (see Figure 1.4.1).

First, the health dimension was measured by the probability at birth of not surviving to 40 years of age. Secondly, education was measured by the adult literacy rate. Thirdly, the income component was measured

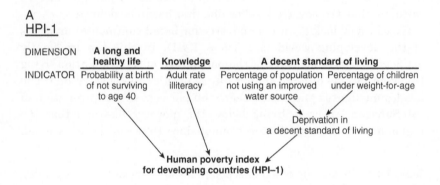

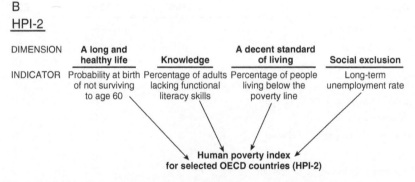

Figure 1.4.1 Calculating (A) the Human Poverty Index 1 (HPI-1) and (B) Human Poverty Index 2 (HPI-2)

by the unweighted average of the percentage of the population without access to safe water and the percentage of underweight children for their age group. This was referred to as the HPI-1 and it was used for developing countries (see Figure 1.4.1A). The HPI-2, shown in Figure 1.4.1B, was used in relation to developed nations. A long and healthy life was measured by the probability at birth of not surviving to the age of 60. To this were added a measure of functional literacy, the percentage of the population that exists below the poverty line, and the long-term unemployment rate. Together these variables provided a wider measure of the multidimensional aspects of poverty.

The nations of the world are shown proportional to their scores on the Human Poverty Index in Figure 1.4.2, reproduced from the Worldmapper series. The extreme concentration of poverty in Africa, the Indian sub-continent and, to a lesser extent, parts of Asia, is clear from this figure. Figure 1.4.3, which summarizes the global incidence of girls not attending primary school, shows an even stronger rich world–poor world division (see also Chapters 1.2 and 1.3).

In July 2010 it was announced that the HPI, used in annual *Human Development Reports* since 1997 would be supplanted by a new measure, the Multidimensional Poverty Index (MPI). The MPI has been developed by the UNDP in conjunction with the Oxford Poverty and Human Development Initiative (OPHI) and is being used from the

49

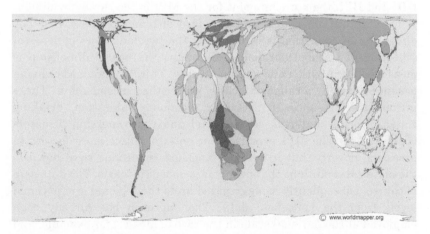

Figure 1.4.2   Human Poverty (size of country shows the proportion of the total world population living in poverty in that country).

Source: Worldmapper map number 174 © Copyright SASI Group (University of Sheffield)

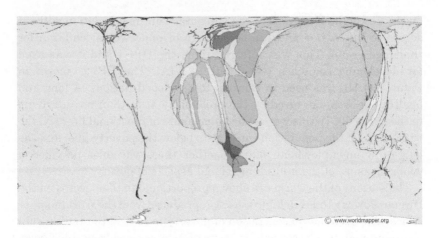

Figure 1.4.3 Girls not attending primary school (size of country shows the proportion of the total world female population not attending primary school in that country).

Source: Worldmapper map number 201 © Copyright SASI Group (University of Sheffield)

50

twentieth anniversary edition of the UNDP *Human Development Report* published in October 2010. The MPI assesses a range of critical factors, each held to be associated with the incidence of critical forms of deprivation at the household level, as listed in Table 1.4.2. Like the HDI and HPI, the starting point for the MPI is the three key dimensions of education, health and standard of living (Table 1.4.2). The dimension of education is reflected by the two indicators of years of schooling and school enrolment. Secondly, the health dimension is measured by nutrition and child mortality. Thirdly, standard of living is summarized by a range of factors, rather than income alone. These include the presence of electricity, adequate sanitation, drinking water, flooring material, cooking fuel and the ownership of assets (Table 1.4.2). The MPI promises not only to reflect more factors in assessing poverty, but it will also measure conditions right down to the material conditions that people face on a daily basis. The data can, of course, subsequently be aggregated up to the regional and national levels from the household data. The approach has already been employed at the national scale in the case of Mexico, for example, and promises to render a finer-grained multidimensional assessment of poverty.

Table 1.4.2 Definition and Measurement of the Multidimensional Poverty Index (MPI) at the Household level

Dimension	Indicator	Definition/measure of deprivation
Education:	Years of Schooling	Deprived if no member has completed 5 years of schooling
	School Enrolment	Deprived if any school-aged children are not attending school
Health:	Nutrition	Deprived if any adult or child is malnourished (on information available)
	Child Mortality	Deprived if any child has died in the family
Standard of Living:	Electricity	Deprived if the household has no electricity
	Sanitation	Deprived if the sanitation facility is not improved according to the MDG guidelines, or if improved but shared
	Water	Deprived if there is no access to clean drinking water according to MDG guidelines, or clean water is over 30 minutes' walk from the home
	Floor	Deprived if the floor is dirt, sand or dung
	Cooking Fuel	No details given
	Asset Ownership	No details given

Source: UNDP, 2010

51

KEY POINTS

- Many regard poverty reduction as the principal focus of development practice in the twenty-first century.
- Poverty may be defined in simple terms as a lack of income and the consequent lack of goods and services that can be obtained.
- It is generally agreed, however, that it is more fitting that poverty should be defined in multidimensional terms. This is because poverty involves non-economic factors, including health, education, housing, social conditions, quality of life, environment quality and wider freedoms.

- Income poverty can be defined by the poverty headcount, for example, the proportion of the population living on less than US$1.25 per day.
- The Human Poverty Index (HPI-1 and 2), a development of the United Nations' HDI, is an effective measure of a wider set of indicators reflecting poverty. In 2010 it was superseded by the Multidimensional Poverty Index (MPI) as a wider multidimensional assessment of poverty.

FURTHER READING

Howard White's (2008) essay on 'The measurement of poverty', in Desai and Potter's *Companion to Development Studies* (2008) provides a good overview of poverty concepts, measures of poverty and a brief survey of 'dollar a day' estimates of poverty for the regions making up the developing world. Good data are given year by year for regions of the developing world in the United Nations Development Programme's (UNDP) *Human Development Reports*, which can be downloaded from the UNDP website (www.undp.org).

1.5 THE MILLENNIUM DEVELOPMENT GOALS

TARGETING DEVELOPMENT

The Origins and Nature of the Millennium Development Goals

In Chapter 1.2 it was noted that what are referred to as the Millennium Development Goals (MDGs) can be regarded as representing a hands-on approach to monitoring global and regional development targets that have been promoted since 2000. The goals aim to map out what needs to be done in order to work towards a more equal world at the beginning of the twenty-first century. Thus, reflecting the enormous magnitude of the inequalities that characterize the contemporary world, the intention to do something about it exists in the form of an agreed international set of development targets – the Millennium Development Goals – to which the 192 United Nations member states and approximately 23 international organizations committed their support at the start of the Millennium.

In fact, the MDGs were formally adopted at the General Assembly of the United Nations held in New York on 18 September 2000, a meeting that was referred to as the United Nations Millennium Summit (Rigg, 2008). But the targets had first been enumerated by the Organization for Economic Cooperation and Development (OECD) in a document entitled *Shaping the Twenty-First Century* (OECD, 1996), and were strongly supported in the United Kingdom by the Department for International Development (DFID) as the International Development Targets (see, for example, the United Kingdom White Paper, DFID, 2000b).

The MDGs consist of eight overarching goals, each to be achieved by 2015:

- Eradicate extreme hunger and poverty
- Achieve universal primary education
- Promote gender equality and empower women
- Reduce child mortality
- Improve maternal health
- Combat HIV, malaria and other diseases
- Ensure environmental sustainability
- Develop a global partnership for development.

These eight specific goals are reflected in 18 associated targets (Rigg, 2008). In turn, the targets are linked to 48 detailed indicators although, as argued by Black and White (2004), not all of these are defined in very precise terms. Together they can be regarded as comprising a comprehensive agenda for global development in the twenty-first century.

The whole idea is that the MDGs should amount to realistic and achievable goals and targets. Reflecting their earlier origins, statistics measuring progress with the MDGs are frequently presented from 1990, although the MDGs proper relate to the period 2000–15. Thus, 2007–8 represented the midpoint toward the achievement of the MDGs, as originally defined.

54

Progress in Achieving the MDGs to 2015

The vital issue is, of course, how much exactly has been achieved so far and, on the present trends, which of the goals are likely to be achieved by the 2015 deadline? As Rigg (2008) concludes, the unequivocal answer has to be that while there has been good progress in respect of some of the goals in certain regions of the world, overall progress can only be described as 'patchy'. For example, progress has and will be made in respect of one of the major targets relating to the 'eradication' of poverty and hunger – that of reducing by half the proportion of people living on less than around US$1 a day (although this indicator has lately been increased to US$1.25 a day), as shown by the data in Table 1.4.1 in Chapter 1.4.

Overall, this measure of poverty has fallen since 1990 and, if the current rate remains on track, it is estimated that this global poverty indicator will fall to 12.5 per cent in 2005, less than half the level recorded in 1990. Table 1.4.1 shows the relevant data for 1990, 1999 and 2005, derived from the United Nations. As the table shows, by 2005 the proportion living on less than US$1.00 in the developing world as a whole had fallen to 25 per cent, from 42 per cent in 1990. But it is apparent that progress has been uneven when viewed by major world region (Table 1.4.1). While very substantial progress has been made in the case of Eastern Asia, Southern Asia, and South-East Asia, little progress has been recorded in the case of sub-Saharan Africa, where over fifty per cent of the total population still live on less than US$1.00 per day.

In much the same way, we can look at the likelihood that the MDG targets will be met in the various developing world regions by the year 2015. This has been assessed by the Millennium Project, which is supported by the United Nations Development Programme (United Nations, 2010a), and the results are shown in Table 1.5.1. The 16 targets that can be quantified have been assessed for the ten regions of the globe (see Table 1.5.1). Of the total of 160 cases thereby identified, in 16 the target has already been met or is very close to being met. In some 40 other cases, it is expected that the target will be met by 2015. However, in 55

Table 1.5.1 Progress with the Millennium Development Goals by Region by 2005

Region	No progress	Not expected	Expected	Met or close	Insufficient data
Sub-Saharan Africa	10	6	0	0	–
Southern Asia	2	12	2	0	–
South-east Asia	1	7	6	2	–
Eastern Asia	2	6	5	3	–
Latin America & the Caribbean	1	8	5	2	–
Western Asia	4	8	3	–	1
C.I.S. Europe	3	5	4	4	–
C.I.S. Asia	5	4	3	4	–
Oceania	6	5	3	–	2
North Africa	0	5	9	1	1
	34	**66**	**40**	**16**	**4**

Source: UNEP (2005a) The Millennium Development Project

respect of 34 targets, no progress has been made or deterioration and reversal have occurred. Finally, in as many as a further 66 cases, it is not expected that the MDG targets will have been met by 2015.

Thus in respect of the majority of targets viewed by continental division, that is some 100 out of 160, the outcome looks set to be negative by 2015 judging by present progress. Table 1.5.1 shows where the biggest numbers of missed targets are likely to be encountered – namely in sub-Saharan Africa, followed by Oceania, CIS Asia and Western Asia.

The situation pertaining to sub-Saharan Africa is by far and away the most worrying, with all 16 constituent boxes showing either no progress or that the target is not expected to be met by 2015. Overall, therefore, there clearly remains a great deal to be done. Rigg (2008) has posed the question as to whether the mechanisms are in place to achieve the MDGs, other than by exhortation and moral persuasion. For example, forms of global taxation, such as those involved in what is known as Tobin-style taxes (see Chapter 5.4) could, at a stroke, raise the annual monies needed to establish universal primary education rather than moving slowly toward the target over 15 years (Potter et al., 2008). This argument is covered in detail in Chapter 5.4.

Once more we reach the same general conclusion regarding the current nature and disposition of global development patterns as we did in Chapters 1.1 to 1.4. While progress is being made in certain regions, and in particular respects, there remains an enormous amount to do if gross inequalities are to be meaningfully reduced and development enhanced by the end of the first quarter of the twenty-first century.

KEY POINTS

- The MDGs are a set of agreed international development targets by means of which it is intended that the world can move toward a more equitable pattern of development by 2015.
- There are eight main MDGs and 18 associated targets which are in turn represented by 48 variables – for example, the percentage of the population living on US$1.25 or less a day as a measure of poverty.
- While some progress has been made, the overall situation with regard to achieving the MDGs is patchy at best.
- Little or no progress appears to be being made in respect of sub-Saharan Africa. On the other hand, considerable progress has been made in Eastern Asia, South-Eastern Asia and Southern Asia.

A collection of sixteen essays edited by Richard Black and Howard White under the title *Targeting Development: Critical Perspectives on the Millennium Goals* (2004) covers diverse aspects of the MDGs – from the 'new poverty agenda', halving world poverty, clean water and development, to the global challenge of HIV – and, thereby, offers a good starting point for the interested reader. The MDGs and progress in reaching the targets are covered in general texts, including Rob Potter et al.'s *Geographies of Development* (2008, Chapter 1). A good overview is provided in Jonathan Rigg's 'The Millennium Development Goals' as Chapter 1.7 in *The Companion to Development Studies* (2008). The United Nations Development Programme's website (www.undp. org) is an excellent up-to-date source, covering the goals and targets as well as progress at the national and continental levels.

Section 2
Theory and
Practice of
Development

INTRODUCTION

This second section of *Key Concepts in Development Geography* presents a critical assessment of the theoretical and applied explanations that have charted development practices 'for the better or the worse' throughout the Third World or global South. A critical perspective is believed to be the most useful approach, because the world's divisions do not always reflect wealth inequalities that have continued to persist despite over sixty years of 'development effort'. Equally troubling are the immense differences in development experiences that have resulted from the conventional theories and approaches that have been embraced by the 'development establishment', comprised of global development forums, major development banks, international financial institutions and governmental international aid agencies. As the chapters in this section will argue, these institutions' adherence to conventional, capitalist economic models is far too often 'top-down' and externally imposed or influenced. While radical, more people-centred alternative approaches are often proposed, they are only occasionally implemented. Yet we need to better understand the development challenges that Section 1 highlighted. So it behoves us to listen to the multitude of 'voices from below' that call for justice, gainful employment, social democracy, and health and education opportunities for the impoverished and powerless to be found living in the global South.

The main theories forwarded as conceptual guides to promote economic development and societal transformation in Third World countries are examined in Chapter 2.1. Tracing the temporal record from the 1940s onward, the earliest development concepts – like modernity and modernization – proposed that Western capitalist models of urban growth and regional economic expansion needed to replace the traditional and backward ways of rural, agrarian societies that had apparently been obstacles to Third World development in the past. Later, in the 1970s and 1980s, intellectual debates arose over the utility of more humanistic concepts such as postmodernism and post-structuralism as replacement explanations of how the world was becoming more diversified and differentiated. Despite this challenging 'cultural turn' in ideological thinking, Chapter 2.1 provides theoretical and geo-political reasons why modernity would continue its dominance as the most influential economic structural force in the global South and across the globalizing world that came into being from the 1980s onward.

The arguments provided in the chapters of Section 1 have already demonstrated that the modern era of development did not, in fact, bring about the development and societal transformations that the theories reviewed in Chapter 2.1 promised. Before continuing with further chapters that provide more detailed economic explanations of how this disappointing situation came about, however, a review of alternative, radical approaches is provided in Chapter 2.2. This enables the two chapters to provide a comparative global picture of conventional versus alternative models and ideologies of what might be construed as 'Third World development'. More specifically, Chapter 2.2 focuses attention on people's ideas and writings on radical and alternative approaches to development. Because many of these approaches represented Third World/global South 'voices from below', this review assesses the development potential of various alternative models of 'grassroots development' that were people-centred, humanitarian, socially just, and ethical as well as environmentally sensitive.

This Section's coverage then returns to the documentation of the temporal changes underway by offering a more detailed account of how the global political and economic systems of both the global North and global South were fundamentally transformed after the global economic downturn of the early 1980s. Focusing on economic changes, neoliberalism's ascendency – by which we mean the renewed faith in the efficiency of the free market – is first explained in Chapter 2.3. Then the all-encompassing widening scale and scope of globalizing forces during the post-1980s era of globalization are detailed. As an accompanying feature of neoliberal capitalism's dominance in geo-economic and geo-political affairs, the overview provided in Chapter 2.3 illuminates how the many changes brought about by globalization's influences range from positive to negative and from destructive to constructive in what Giddens (2003) has characterized as a globalizing 'runaway world'.

Chapter 2.4 then documents how, for many in the 'development establishment' such as development banks, international aid agencies, and international financial institutions, the outlined conventional capitalist practices and development solutions were always preferred – despite the counter-arguments of alternative, people-centred, 'development from below' approaches. The critical assessment of these development institutions' performances in Chapter 2.4 finds institutional rigidity in ideological persuasion and practical applications towards development projects and planning initiatives. Despite their charge to serve as the responsible agencies that would deliver international development to the global South, their self-serving agendas too often came first and foremost. Over fifty years of disappointment characterize the overall performances of these international development institutions and agencies. Perhaps only the United Nations and its associated development institutions stand apart from the rest, in terms of this institution's altruistic fairness and humanistic objectives.

In Chapter 2.5, the account then turns to the future. In this selective overview, the difficulties inherent in achieving sustainable development while at the same time planning a future that is also environmentally sustainable appear to be many, if not insurmountable. It seems that development options that seek to merge the multiplicity of goals for human societal transformation and development with the need to ensure a future environmental sustainability for all in the global South and North are still far from being realized.

63

2.1 MODERNITY, MODERNIZATION, POSTMODERNISM AND POST-STRUCTURALISM

In this chapter we provide an overview of the changing concepts that have directed 'development' in the Third World or global South (see Chapter 1.3). At the outset the chapter considers the multidisciplinary concept of modernity. Having done so, the account turns to the rise of postmodernism, postmodernity and post-structuralism as new intellectual, academic frameworks that respectively reject notions of 'modernism' and 'structuralism'. The chapter critiques these approaches and their utility in the contemporary context. In so doing, modernity in its current neoliberal guise is found to be an extremely resilient factor in the development process.

It can be argued that the wholesale acceptance of modernity as a 'development ideology' has made things worse in the Third World, bringing about greater inequality, vulnerability and social disruption. As Section 1 has demonstrated, the disadvantaged and powerless underclasses have not experienced much development at all. Conversely, the already privileged elite proponents in the Anglo-European West and their neoclassical capitalist allies in the Third World have prospered.

As noted in the Introduction to Section 1, modernity and modernization would both become the main conventional economic models favoured by the development establishment during the first major capitalist era in the second half of the twentieth century. Similarly, as Chapter 2.3 explains, between 1945 and 1980 modernity and robust economic growth were also at the heart of the Keynesian model of advanced capitalism which prevailed in the developed 'First World' of the United States, the reconstructed 'war-torn' economies of Europe and a rebuilt Japan. Keynesian capitalism favoured governmental intervention in many economic sectors, so that both social welfare safety nets and public subsidization programmes were common partners to private enterprise in the global North and global South.

During the post-1980 era of globalization, neoliberal capitalism and its championing of deregulation, the efficiency of the free market and the opening of new markets for trade and commerce would replace the Keynesian model as a development generator. Many pundits and believers in the financial power of free-market economics touted this 'neoliberal turn' as a new global economic cycle of unparalleled promise. Predictably, a global recession in 2007–2011 would bring the promised good times to a calamitous end. Contrary to the history of business-cycle dynamics, however, this recession would not presage the formation of a different capitalist solution to the financial and economic crisis. Instead, the world's systems of production and commerce appear to be continuing unchanged and unchallenged as a thinly-disguised, neoliberal rebirth (Murray and Overton, 2011). In short, modernity continues apace, and there is no 'after-modernity'.

65

Modernity and Modernism: European Philosophical Origins of the 'Modern Age of Development' in the Post-1945 Era

In the mid-eighteenth century, the ideological notion of modernity was conceived as a distinct opposite to 'traditionalism', and as a logical evolutionary replacement for 'backward' social traits. It was born on the back of optimism that the new urban industrial regime that was underway would be able to bring order and reason to the many social disorders of the time that appeared to be hindering progress and development. Enlightenment thinking (see Chapter 1.1) among European free-thinking 'men of letters' was a new framework of ideas and rational 'truths' about the relationships between humanity, society and nature. It sought to challenge existing traditional worldviews dominated by Christianity. Accordingly, modern traits, methods, institutions and means could be expected to deliver progress and change, as the existing resistant traditions were overcome, replaced and rendered ineffective.

Derived from the word modern to mean a sense of present times in contrast to ancient times, the modernism of the nineteenth and twentieth centuries was also to be viewed in contrast to earlier traditional customs. As an intellectual movement in the arts, literature, architecture and cultural fashions, modernism brought about a transformation of society modelled upon Western, European rational thought, character and practice. Modernity, on the other hand, though also derived from the word modern, is a distinct concept. This is because it focuses upon the transformation of social relations related to the emergence and domination of capitalism in its successive forms – from early urban industrialization, to advanced capitalism, and on to neoliberal and global capitalism. In addition modernity, as Western modernist thought, firmly placed Third World or global South 'traditional' societies as 'backward' if not also 'savage' and 'uncivilized'. For development and progress to take place, modernist changes similar to those in play in Europe and the West had to occur (Power, 2008).

Modernity, therefore, is distinguishable from modernism in terms of the new technologies and innovations that accompany capitalism's evolutionary transformations and scale changes of its interrelated political–economic systems. Modernity brings about new modes of transport, new sources of energy, new management and communication technologies, new media forms and the like. These, in turn, change social relations, power relations, institutional structures and supplant, or modify, previous 'ways and means'. To Giddens and Pierson modernity is:

66

> associated with (1) a certain set of attitudes towards the world, the idea of the world as open to transformation, by human intervention; (2) a complex of economic institutions, especially industrial production and a market economy; (3) a certain range of political institutions, including the nation-state and mass democracy. Largely as a result of these characteristics, modernity is vastly more dynamic than any previous type of social order. It is a society... which... lives in the future, rather than the past. (Giddens and Pierson, 1998: 94)

Early Modernity and Modernization Theories: their Multidisciplinary Pedigrees

Sociologists were among the first to advance conceptual notions concerning the dichotomy between traditional and modern societal orders.

The latter was expected to grow at the expense of the former as the external dynamics of modernization brought about societal change. This externally driven change comes about in stages of 'development' in which rationality, disenchantment with nature, social differentiation and specialization serve to distinguish modernizing societies from traditional. The traditional rural societies of Africa and Asia are expected inevitably to give way to the urban-industrial and modernized capitalist societies that Europe and North America have become. Unfortunately, the sociological jargon that was so familiarly used by the lauded sociological authorities to explain how such modernization should occur was so turgid in its formulations as to render many sociological explanations tautological, vague and unintelligible.

Psychological versions of modernization theory also partnered those formulated by sociologists, in which psychological motives and values lead 'modern men' to behave rationally and entrepreneurially. This followed Weber's connection between the Protestant ethic and the spirit of capitalism, claiming it as a European advantage and a demonstration of Western superiority and advancement. Such was the persuasiveness of this construct that, in the late 1960s, Harvard researcher Alex Inkeles undertook field research to search for the common values and attitudes among 6,000 'modern men' in six developing countries: Argentina, Chile, India, Israel, Pakistan and Nigeria (Inkeles, 1969).

67

It was, however, the economic constructs built upon modernization's 'top-down' tenets that had the most lasting influence during these early development decades of the 1950s, 1960s and 1970s. Central to this economic formulation was the work of W.W. Rostow and his influential book *The Stages of Economic Growth: A Non-communist Manifesto* published in the 1960s. As evidenced in the title, Rostow had interwoven two major concerns: one political and strategic, the other economic and developmental. Rostow was geo-politically concerned with the international and political contexts of the process of transition in Third World nation states. His model, accordingly, was constructed in large part to further the strategic influence of the United States. It was aimed at countering the USSR's expansionist superpower designs that the US feared would promote 'development' via communism and socialist regimes in post-colonial Africa, Asia and Latin America.

Rostow's model proposed that all societies would be able to pass through five stages: traditional society, preconditions for take-off, take-off, the road to maturity and the age of mass consumption. Crucial to his take-off and road to maturity stages were the infusion from out-side (presumably the USA or its Western allies) of two factors of modern industrial success: (1) the existence of already-functioning modern technology which can be made available by technology transfer from benevolent outsiders and public–private partners, and (2) the existence of international aid and technical assistance (including technical education, and consultants) provided by the governments of developed countries and their contracted professional/technical advisers.

Another contribution from economics, this by Hirschman in his 1958 volume, *The Strategy of Economic Development*, also promoted the take-off notion, but in his view this should lead to the encouragement of 'growth poles' to prompt regional development, not national or overall societal development. In one sense, this represented a rejection of the 'balanced growth' idealistic notions that had prevailed in the immediate post-1945 period. Geographers took up this idea and their contribution to this multidisciplinary mix was the mapping of so-called modernization surfaces, in which patterns of regional development, innovation diffusion, and metropolitan and regional nodes of development, or growth poles, could be spatially identified.

68

Postmodernism, Post-structuralism or Modernity Reconfigured? Geo-economic 'Development' in the Post-1980s era of Globalization

The shortcomings of modernization theories, as abstract and ahistorical depictions of developed and underdeveloped societies, appear to have been repeated in postmodernist 'deconstructions' and sociocultural critiques:

- **Postmodernism** was the earliest cultural and phenomenological construct advocated as the contemporary successor to modernism in art, literature and philosophy. It was also trumpeted as a philosophically-humanistic critique of cultural change, dissemination and difference, claiming it represented:

  a shift ... into the heteroglossia of inter-cultural change, as idioms, discourse across the arts and academy and across these and other popular or mass forms, are montaged, blended and blurred together. (Brooker, 1992: 20)

- **Postmodernity**, like its intellectual partner postmodernism, was defined as a 'postmodern condition' of society that came into being after 'modernity'. However, inconclusive debates surround when the transformation might have occurred. Some advocates suggested that this social transformation was a long-running status quo of constant change, rather than a temporal shift and evolution of society into a new technological phase. Questions concerning whether there was/is such an 'after-modernity' also further complicated things.
- **Post-structuralism**, which emerged in France in the 1960s as the latest variant of postmodernist anti-modernist thought, was a somewhat disparate philosophical movement of literary criticism. As such, it has been found to be phenomenological and nihilist in extreme, so that its value to the development discourse is highly problematic.

These three alternative humanistic interpretations of 'self', 'identity' and 'plurality of meaning' reject the objectivity and scientific rationality of modernism and structuralism. As philosophical constructs, they characterize the post-1980s globalization era in sociocultural contextual terms in which the 'systems of knowledge' that produce human and societal 'objects' also have to be examined to explain the 'object' under critical scrutiny more holistically. Specifically, 'agency' is privileged and postmodernism and post-structuralism, in particular, choose to ignore 'structural' societal complexities such as the political economic relations that determined the power relationships, production and commercial structures and class systems of capitalist and non-capitalist societies.

69

After the inevitable global recession of the early 1980s, modernity was reconfigured. As Chapter 2.3 explains, all sectors of advanced capitalism changed their scales of operation to international and global-to-local relationships. Rapid technological change brought more global exchanges and system dynamics, and helped global production–commercial networks, chains and management systems, and financial 'worlds' grow more and more powerful. Neoliberalism and deregulation became the unchallenged and unfettered practices of the next three decades until the calamitous recession of 2007–2011.

Secondly, an emerging geo-economic phase of global capitalism has come to the fore (Sparke, 2007). This era has been associated with geo-political realignments such as the collapse of the Soviet Union (leaving the US as the sole military 'superpower') and the rapid growth of several new 'emerging' economic powers such as the BRICs (Brazil, Russia, India and China). Fundamentally reconfiguring modernity, the diffusion and adoption of transformational new technologies during this newest phase of modernity has helped to re-conceptualize the societal and economic transitions that national and global social systems were, and are, undergoing.

Conclusions

There is considerable debate about whether postmodernity is in reality a 'game-changing' societal construct. Certainly, postmodernity has found academic authority in its linguistic presentations as a counter-narrative, or alternative discourse, in which the non-Western 'vernacular world' should be given equal attention to Western, Anglo-European modernity. However, in global geo-economic relations and particularly in development circles, as well as in the halls of its most powerful institutions – the World Bank, the IMF, World Trade Organization, World Economic Forum and the like – modernity in its neoliberal guise is unfettered, and unchanged as a top-down instrument of power and capitalist authority.

70

Following Giddens (1990) it would appear most prudent to build our examination of the 'transitionary phases of development' that have occurred 'for better or for worse' throughout the Developing world (since 1945), on the persistence of modernity and its evolving capitalist structures and institutions. Debates still abound about whether the post-1980s era is a distinct break from the continuity of modernity, thereby bringing in a postmodernist or post-structuralist era. Alternatively, is it a new reconfigured era of modernity, with this latest phase being characterized by new technological and data management innovations brought about by computing and information transfer system 'revolutions'? In the institutional spheres of the private and public sectors of national and global economies, this reconfigured modernity is still the dominant paradigm. On the other hand, postmodernist, post-structuralist critiques and discourse analyses remain more an academic (and polemic) exercise than a rigorous examination of 'development for the better or the worse'. Succinctly, there is no 'after-modernity' as yet.

Such after-modernity cultural deconstructions lead to an avoidance of social science tenets of critical assessment and rigorous analysis. They ignore the much more grounded empirical record, that capitalism still divides and conquers, still extracts surplus from labour, and accumulates at the expense of those still too powerless to negotiate democratically for social justice and basic human rights. Lest we forget, the originator of Keynesian economic thought, John Maynard Keynes, is credited by *The New Internationalist* (2003) with the comment: 'Capitalism is the extraordinary belief that the nastiest of men for the nastiest of motives will somehow work for the benefit of all'.

KEY POINTS

- 'Modernity' determined and directed the post-1945 'modern era of development'.
- From its inception, modernity was rooted in Western, Enlightenment notions of European superiority. This urban–industrial model of transformation was conceptually, philosophically and hypothetically expected to bring progress and change to the underdeveloped nations of the global South.
- Modernization theory was multidisciplinary in construction and ideology, but its most powerful influence was the promotion of Western, capitalist economic models and the diffusion of modern innovations and technologies to underdeveloped, client states.
- Just as Keynesianism prevailed as the dominant political, economic and industrial capitalist mantra during the post-1945 era, the ensuing era of globalization that followed the deep recession of the early 1980s continues to be dominated by neoliberal capitalism and its free-market ideological faiths.

71

FURTHER READING

The argument in favour of the view that 'modernity' continues to be the guiding geo-economic notion shaping the 'development futures' of most Third World or global South societies in the current era of globalization is forcefully presented by Anthony Giddens in *The Consequences of Modernity* (1990). Globalization and neoliberalism's many destructive dimensions that accompanied modernity are detailed in Dennis Conway and Nik Heynen's *Globalization's Contradictions: Geographies of Discipline, Destruction and Transformation* (2005). A parallel story on the geo-political transitions that eventually gave rise to an emerging global geo-economic order in contemporary times is detailed in Matthew Sparke's 'Geopolitical fears, geoeconomic hopes and the responsibilities of geography' (2007).

2.2 RADICAL APPROACHES TO DEVELOPMENT

Revolutionary and radical ideas concerning society were commonplace during the second half of the twentieth century; and the period was associated with societal upheavals, popular resistances, elite power-brokering, militarism, pacifism, colonial oppression and post-colonial independence movements. Writings that enflamed passions, ignited revolutionary (or radical) ardour and which cried out for social justice for all – not just for the wealthy and privileged – were as much at the heart of violent revolutionary action as they were central to the development of radical approaches to development.

This chapter, therefore, undertakes an historical journey through the last half of the twentieth century, and focuses attention on people's ideas and writings on 'radical' or 'alternative' approaches to development and social progress in the underdeveloped Third World/global South. Early on, radical critiques and 'anti-development' arguments were levelled at Westernization, imperialism, modernization and neocolonialism by Third World spokesmen. Following on from such critiques, the chapter details a representative set of critical, alternative models that their advocates felt could, or would, bring about development from below. This alternative approach culminates in a people-centred development model, which combines development ethics and sustainability in its advocacy. Thus it promotes 'capacity building' and 'community empowerment' as progressive means for the poor majority to achieve development.

'Cold War' Radical, Marxist Models of 'Non-capitalist Development'

Anti-imperialism certainly prompted much scholarly and 'activist' criticism. Some of the radical approaches that were offered as alternatives to the Western, Eurocentric, modernity-based models of the post-1945 'modern era of development' were idealistic, geo-political, formulations of 'non-capitalist development' that were written by Soviet scholars. For example, Soviet scholarly references were written in English by Solodovnikov and Bogoslovsky in 1975 and Andreyev in 1977 to help foment a 'non-capitalist' path to development by the New Jewel Movement in Grenada's 'Revolution' in 1979–83. Often, translations of Lenin's writings on 'Imperialism, the Highest Stage of Capitalism' (1963) and 'The Right of Nations to Self-Determination' (1972), as well as those of Karl Marx and Frederick Engels, were used as theoretical and ideological guidance by local revolutionaries and radicals. Some academically trained political leaders of newly independent countries wrote their own nationalistic manifestos advocating such socialist revolutionary models; see Tanzanian Julius Nyerere's *Ujamaa: Essays on Socialism* (1968), and Ghanaian Kwame Nkrumah's *Neocolonialism: the Last Stage of Imperialism* (1965).

Other radical authors penned socialist and Marxist critiques that became well-cited authoritative texts for decades. One such 'exemplar' is Brazilian-born Paulo Friere's *Pedagogy of the Oppressed* (2000, first published 1970), which grew to become an extremely influential text for educators interested in improvements in literacy in Third World territories. Another exemplar is Martinique-born Franz Fanon whose *The Wretched of the Earth* (1967), was a devastating critique of colonialism's damaging impacts on the psyche of colonized societies. Particularly perceptive was Fanon's personification of the imitative attitudes of the new generation(s) of Third World leaders, which would lead them to follow in the footsteps of their recently deposed colonial masters and to continue similar paths of servitude and diffidence to these 'outsiders' in their post-colonial relations.

73

Early Radical 'Anti-development' Critiques: *dependencia* and the 'development of underdevelopment'

In his influential 1957 anti-capitalist treatise *Political Economy of Growth*, Russian-American, Marxist-economist Paul Baran described the reasons for Latin America's underdevelopment as being a consequence of the forming of special partnerships between advanced nations and powerful elite classes in the continent's underdeveloped, or pre-capitalist countries. These special partnerships perpetuated the ability of advanced capitalist, core countries to maintain traditional systems of surplus extraction and ensured the periphery's domestic resources would be continuously available. By such means, they made economic development unlikely, since any surplus generated was appropriated by these client elites. This would then enable core countries to keep their own monopoly-power over cheap primary resources (Baran and Sweezy, 1966).

Notably, these alternative 'anti-capitalism' ideas on uneven exchange, surplus redistribution and expropriation would be developed further by a chorus of 'voices from below': Latin American political-economy scholars, collectively known as ECLA structuralists and later as *dependistas* or the Dependency School. They included Argentinian Raúl Prebisch, Brazilians Paul Singer and Celso Furtado and Chilean Osvaldo Sunkel, among their spokesmen. Although their neo-Marxist critiques differed in theoretical detail, all argued that Latin America's historical marginalization and resultant underdevelopment was perpetuated by such unequal commercial arrangements with core countries, particularly the United States, benefitting at the expense of Latin America.

74   German-American André Gunder Frank (1967, 1979) soon became the *dependistas* main advocate. Focusing upon the dependent character of peripheral Latin American economies, Frank coined the notion of the 'development of underdevelopment' to characterize the capitalist dynamics that developed core countries while at the same time causing greater levels of underdevelopment and dependency within Latin American countries. Frank's conceptual framework, therefore, explained the dualistic capitalist relations which had occurred, and which he felt would continue to occur between Latin American and core countries. In line with other anti-capitalism critiques, Frank (1969) argued that any change for the better would only be possible through revolutionary action which would install socialist ideals within the political systems of Latin America's dependent countries and usurp the client elites' special relationships.

Equally persuasive, and also in line with the *dependistas'* assessment of Latin American underdevelopment, Guyana's Walter Rodney depicted the historical underdevelopment of the African continent and its peoples as a consequence of capitalism, colonialism and imperialism in *How Europe Underdeveloped Africa* (1974). Another highly influential and passionate 'Third World voice', Egyptian-born Samir Amin, also expanded upon the notion of *dependencia* in his critical examinations of the dependent economic relations of Africa since European colonization, and found them destructive and disastrous consequences of that continent's peripheral capitalist condition. His writings, spanning the 1970s to the present, are too voluminous to summarize here but together they provide a comprehensive and persuasive case for the failure of the 'development project' all over Africa (Amin, 2007). Amin goes so far as to propose extreme measures to overcome the decades of failed 'Eurocentrism' and its modernization approaches, such as 'delinking' from Europe and starting afresh (Amin, 1990).

'Development from Below' as an Answer to 'Development from Above'

Western modernity's externally driven strategies to bring about economic, social, political and cultural changes in the underdeveloped client states of the Third World came to be characterized as development from above by its radical critics. They criticized its 'import-substitution industrialization' and its monolithic and uniform value systems, which lauded capitalist entrepreneurialism, urban living and intellectual modernity. Such externally directed economic development commonly perpetuated *dependencia* and reduced the effectiveness of internally directed initiatives. As a result, national authority and endogenous autonomy were inevitably compromised.

75

In contrast, development from below sought to replace such externally driven dependent and subordinate relations. It sought the creation of dynamic development impulses within less-developed areas, such as those regions less favourable to urban-industrial growth and 'growth pole' development, like rural peripheries and the more remote hinterlands. Thus, development from below was expected to increase equity rather than inequity across regions.

From its inception in the 1970s, development from below was an activist agenda with a progressive message on the need for radical change in policy formulation and implementation. Succinctly, it was maintained that economic '*growth* from above' needed to be supplanted by '*development* from below' for people's basic, human needs to be met, rather than the former's focus on the needs of elite minorities and the powerful classes. Policy emphases needed to be reoriented towards territorially organized basic-needs service provision. Rural and village development should be as much a focus as urban-located development. Labour-intensive activities and microeconomic small businesses and projects should be favoured over high-technology entrepreneurialism.

Such 'territorially-integrated development' should aim to provide the full employment and involvement of regional human, natural and institutional resources. It was argued that intermediate technologies, small- and medium-sized projects, locally designed and executed projects, should be integral parts of the mix of development strategies from below (Stohr and Taylor, 1981). For the next three decades, a mix of alternative approaches, most seeking similar objectives for their humanistic 'development paths', would be launched in academia or in policy circles.

People-centred Approaches

The notion of people-centred development explicitly blends societal and environmental sustainability in terms of its hoped-for futures. In its advocacy to promote 'capacity building' and 'community empowerment' as progressive means for the poor majority to achieve development, people-centred approaches have grown to be the contemporary successor to development from below alternatives (Eade, 1997). Saliently, civil society, NGOs and other grassroots philanthropic organizations are embracing this notion. So too is the United Nations Development Programme, and its Human Development Index (HDI) developed by Mahbub ul Haq et al., 1995 (see Chapter 1.1 and 1.2 for more on the HDI).

People-centred Development

People-centred approaches to development have an ethical position which partners that found in Denis Goulet's (1996) 'development ethics' (see Chapter 2.5), in which both wish to render the real-life economy of people more human and humane, as well as ecologically sustainable (Korten and Klauss, 1984; Korten, 1990). Both seek to keep hope alive in the face of the seeming impossibility of achieving human development for all, utilizing current paradigms. Both seek progressive change and a path forward that builds self-reliance, empowers men and women, and puts the 'first last' in terms of which people are the most deserving: principally, the poor (mostly rural) majority who have been left out of the 'development project' to date (Chambers, 1997). Both approaches challenge conventional economic thinking and seek humanistic solutions, in which development is conceived in terms of people's sovereignty. People's participatory involvement in controlling resources, thereby gives rise to individual, familial and communal empowerment. As noted in Chapter 1.1, Goulet (1971) also recognized three 'social freedoms' as crucial quality of life components of a people-centred development which follows ethical tenets: (i) life sustenance and the provision of basic needs, (ii) self-esteem acquired through self-respect and independence, or autonomy, and (iii) freedom for people to determine their own future.

Another Development

The above interdisciplinary approaches built upon a 1975 Report of the Dag Hammarskjöld Foundation entitled, *What Now? Another Development* (later reaffirmed by Paul Ekins in 1992), in which four basic humanistic principles of 'alternative development' were conceptualized as:

- Need-oriented – responding to both material and non-material human needs
- Endogenous – derived from locally-determined priorities
- Self-reliant – maximizing community strengths and resources
- Ecologically sound – promoting sustainable and equitable resource uses.

77

Another Development was to be geared to the satisfaction of people's needs, beginning with the basic needs of the poor – the world's majority. At the same time the approach should ensure the humanization of men and women, by the satisfaction of their needs for expression and freedom of speech, creativity, conviviality and by encouraging self-reliance, endogenous authority and participatory action. Another Development also advocated overcoming discrimination of any kind – whether social, sexual, ethnic or economic. In terms of policy implementation, the Dag Hammarskjöld Foundation's Reports to the United Nations offered an effective institutional 'voice' to challenge the establishment and questioned the top-down strategies that were not working to further the well-being of the majority (also see Chapter 2.4).

Real-life Economics

Ekins (1992) argued that, given the structural rigidity and persistence of the stark global problems presented by war, insecurity and militarism, the persistence of poverty, the denial of human rights and the occurrence of environmental degradation, a 'New World Order' was required. Decrying the roots of the current 'global problematique' – Western modernity, scientism and developmentalism, the nation state's political limits – Ekins sought a New World Order of 'democratic popular mobilization'. He believed this radical option would be better able to bring about peace, human dignity and ecological sustainability for all. Not inconsequentially, Real-life Economics became another alternative progressive idea on how development from below might be re-conceptualized in people-oriented terms (Ekins and Max-Neef, 1992).

Real-life economics was never offered as a complete alternative to conventional political-economic orthodoxy. The structural, geo-economic forces at work globally pose so many diverse problems that such a local level perspective can scarcely be viewed as an all-encompassing, equivalent (see the Introduction to Section 2 for an explanation of geo-economic relationships). Rather, the approach was an intellectual, theoretical alternative, and the basis for a new interpretation of people's 'day-to-day' economic strategies. In support, Ekins and Max-Neef (1992) marshalled a community of like-minded scholars to offer their alternative views on 'living economics' in which real-life economics, ethics, environmentalism and sustainable development should be considered inseparable dimensions in tomorrow's thinking about human life and livelihoods in the future. They warned that the market, the state and civil society – singly or in combination – are all potential creators or destroyers of wealth. They cautioned that monetary concerns are not the only motivations for economic choice, and livelihood behaviours do not have to be rational; rather, habits, intuition and bounded 'satisfying' rationality guide human decision making. Love, altruism, duty, respect, dignity and obligations are all meaningful influences equal to economic rationality and wealth accumulation.

Empowerment and Self-reliance

Bringing non-government organizations (NGOs) and civil society into the picture, John Friedmann (1992) viewed their roles in 'alternative development' as expressions of militancy and activism (see Chapter 5.2). Upholding universal human rights has to be the prime political objective, especially the rights of the disempowered poor majority of the global South. For Friedmann, the empowerment approach is fundamental to such an alternative approach, because it places emphasis on autonomy in the decision making of territorially organized communities. It thereby brings about local self-reliance (but not unrestricted power), direct (participatory) democracy in communal affairs, and experiential social learning. With people empowered by participatory democratic involvement at the local level, they will become engaged in the larger processes of representative governance and experience progressive alternative development.

Capacity Building

The central idea behind local institutional capacity building is about how 'outsiders' such as NGOs and private–public partners in development projects can help foster community authority and managerial expertise in the provision of social capital, social welfare and services, agricultural extension services, urban neighbourhood community projects and the like (Eades, 1997). With governmental involvement being an enabler, rather than an active participant or as leaders and managers, this people-centred strategy seeks to strengthen institutional and social capacity to support greater local control, accountability, transparency, initiative and self-reliance for urban and rural communities of the global South (Korten, 1987). A recent reflective assessment by Oxfam UK and Ireland summarizes the potential of this current 'development mantra' this way:

79

> The concept and practice of capacity building has to be tested against whether it can contribute to creating the synergy between different actors which can confront and challenge existing imbalances of power. (Eade, 1997: v)

Women's Role in People-centred Development

This chapter has not explicitly dealt with gender issues, and the essential part that women's roles and radical feminism's 'activism' played in the emergence of many of the radical alternatives to the predominant Western-directed, development from above that this account has detailed. Such issues are discussed in Chapter 4.1. Two points of note, however, concern the fundamental changes that eventually occurred in the recognition and incorporation of women's empowerment and the essential roles women need to play in further development and progressive change in the global South. Prior to the 1970s, the prevailing wisdom was that men were the unchallenged 'agents of change' – the entrepreneurial pioneers, modernity intellectuals, innovators and leaders.

It is beyond question that women *must* be included in today's people-centred development projects if such projects are to succeed. Furthermore, we now also know that 'outsiders' – whether men or women – cannot bring about meaningful change to the lives of 'insiders'. Rather, local community capacity building and the empowerment of people to determine their own futures are the measures of outsiders' successful participation and assistance in development from below oriented approaches.

People-centred development has emerged as a widely held alternative notion among those development thinkers and practitioners who are convinced that the neoclassical, economic models of capitalist development imposed upon the global South by the North have not worked. As an alternative development from below approach, people-centred development and its capacity-building possibilities certainly have the potential to bring about 'real-life development' for future generations. This is because it promises inclusiveness, democratic participation and peaceful consensus-building as means to a sustainable future for our *ecumene*: in other words, a 'sustainable development' we can live with.

80

KEY POINTS

- The dependency school of activists represented an early, and highly influential, 'voice from below' during early post-colonial times.
- Development from below represents a humanistic alternative to the failed top-down, development from above approaches that have consistently been promoted by Western capitalism's development establishment.
- People-centred development combines development ethics and sustainability in its advocacy to promote capacity building and community empowerment as progressive means for the poor to enjoy the full range of human rights to which they are entitled as global citizens.
- It is beyond question that women *must* be included in today's people-centred development projects if they are to succeed.

FURTHER READING

Chilcote's *Theories of Development and Underdevelopment* (1984) effectively situates the various approaches to the 'development of underdevelopment' – structuralism, *dependencia*, internal colonialism, neo-Marxism, even Trotskyism – as a full set of alternative theoretical perspectives on post-colonial core-periphery relations. Harold Brookfield's *Interdependent Development* (1975) provides comprehensive coverage of these 'voices from the Third World'. Walter Stohr and David Taylor's *Development from Above or Below?* (1981) is a lucid comparison between the development from above and development from below approaches. John Brohman's (1996) comprehensive re-think of *Popular Development* (1981) summarizes the wider critical field in exemplary fashion. Other essential readings are Fritz Schumacher's *Small is Beautiful* (1973), Paul Ekins and Manfred Max-Neef's *Real-Life Economics: Understanding Wealth Creation* (1992), and Wolfgang Sach's *The Development Dictionary* (1992).

2.3 NEOLIBERALISM AND GLOBALIZATION

This chapter documents the ascendency of neoliberalism as a new, neo-conservative economic model for the post-1980s era of globalization that would become the dominant ideology and 'new faith' of global capitalism (Cox, 1999): in short, capitalism's 'latest reincarnation' (Harvey 2005). First, neoliberalism's ideological pedigree is detailed and its ascendency explained. As the latest version of capitalism to dominate a new global geo-economic system (see Chapter 2.1), it was anything but coordinated and led purposefully by the world's economic giants, as earlier capitalist business cycles were. Rather, a 'new international economic (dis)order' emerged in which multiple players took part, and where crises and struggles periodically arose to make the system's growth and transformation volatile and unpredictable (Thrift, 1986; Conway and Heynen, 2005).

Globalization's emergence and deepening complexity is then detailed, in which multiple dimensions of global-to-local interaction and interrelationships come to the fore to partner, and in some cases dominate, political–economic forces. In many unforeseen ways, globalization's contradictory, destructive and productive forces play out across multiple scales of society: globally, nationally, regionally and locally. Also, the time–space compression of globalization's transitionary changes to many spheres of people's lives, makes this era's trends and processes particularly unpredictable.

Neoliberalism's Ascendency

Following the 1979–83 global recession, neoliberal capitalism replaced Keynesian models that had been the basis of post-World War II rebuilding and economic growth in advanced capitalist nations. Keynesian arguments could be considered 'socialist' or 'leftist' by persuasion because this post-World War II model favoured governmental safety nets to provide public services where the private sector could not visualize them as profitable sectors. In the UK, for example, this Keynesian managerial model lavishly provided public services for all, by way of universal national health coverage, affordable housing provision, public infrastructural development (railways, highways, waterways), comprehensive education subsidization (from elementary, through secondary to higher education and technical college, teacher training college and university attendance), free milk and subsidized school lunches, and benefits for the sick, poor and unemployed. In the US, a less comprehensive set of government interventions were practised, whereas in many of Europe's ex-colonial, newly independent nations, more comprehensive Keynesian models were widely adopted.

After two prosperous decades of capitalist growth and geo-political transformations of considerable significance – both in the advanced core countries and the Third World – it would be international events that brought the late-1970s economic crisis to a head, and helped bring on this post-World War II long-wave's recession. The 1970s witnessed 'an unusual bunching of unfortunate disturbances' in the West's financial and production sectors. There was the collapse of Keynesian stability, with the bankruptcy of New York City in 1973 being one indicator of this. There was the unravelling of the 1948 Bretton Woods currency agreement of fixed exchange-rates when, in response to the burgeoning trading of Euro-dollars, President Nixon took the US dollar off the gold standard in 1971 and major currencies became speculative commodities. In all major core countries, inflationary pressures, government overspending, high taxation rates, continued high military budgets, and general downturns in consumer confidence were the main features of this long wave's stagnation. The final 'nail in the coffin' was two OPEC-driven oil price hikes in 1974–75 and again in 1978–79, which effectively raised the price of a barrel of oil eightfold, dramatically raising energy costs and contributing to widespread indebtedness.

83

Neoliberalism as the New Ideological 'Faith'

With its weaknesses so glaringly exposed, Keynesian economics was pilloried as the cause of the deep recession and capitalist crisis that occurred in the late 1970s and early 1980s. In its place, neoliberal capitalism was trumpeted as a supply-side, free-market solution that would bring renewed levels of prosperity for electorates and revive national economies. Summarizing neoliberalism's ideological pedigree, Susan George insightfully observed that:

> Starting from a tiny embryo at the University of Chicago with the philosopher-economist Friedrick von Hayek and his students like Milton Friedman at its nucleus, the neoliberals and their funders have created a huge international network of foundations, institutes, research centers, publications, scholars, writers and public relations hacks to develop, package and push their ideas and doctrine relentlessly. ... So, from a small, unpopular sect with virtually no influence, neoliberalism has become the major world religion with its dogmatic doctrine, its priesthood, its law-giving institutions and perhaps most important of all, its hell for heathen and sinners who dare to contest the revealed truth. (1999: 2–3)

Though not originally thought to be a practical replacement for Keynesian economics, this 'Chicago School' neoliberal model nevertheless represented a neoconservative alternative that would address the inflationary problems that had emerged in the previous business cycle. It appealed to President Reagan and his Republican Party's calls for less governmental interference in American people's affairs and to business entrepreneurialism. With its privatization message also being embraced by Britain's Prime Minister, Margaret Thatcher, neoliberalism had two political champions with the 'gift of the gab' to convince their electorates and the wider world of neoliberalism's promise. As Susan George suggests, it not only became the new economic doctrine but also a faith in the 'market as God' that was so effectively promoted (Cox, 1999).

Neoliberal Restructuring Responses to the Late 1970s–Early 1980s Crisis

Three groups of major players who reacted to this looming economic crisis were national governments, banks and industrial corporations. All designed strategies that led to international solutions, or policies diversifying their economic plans to embrace international or global solutions. Faced with falling rates of profit, the global North's industrial corporations were forced to 'automate, emigrate or evaporate' (Thrift, 1983). Going international, newer automated production and commercial systems and networks would be developed. National industrial corporations streamlined their assembly-line operations to improve quality control. They embraced new technological and logistical methods of resource extraction and use, and looked beyond domestic opportunities both for resources and new markets. Consequently, transnational corpo-rations were able to take advantage of the deregulation of trade regimes and of the New International Division of Labour (NIDL) which provided lower labour costs in the Third World. They were, therefore, able to keep high-skilled employment at home in the West's core economies, which helped accumulate profits even further (Wright, 2002). Governments concerned with bloated budgets and declining revenues sought entrepre-neurial 'supply-side' solutions, and embraced free-marketeering, priva-tization and deregulation as their new policies. They replaced their managerial roles with entrepreneurialism, so that public subsidization of private sector initiatives became a bidding competition to attract cor-poration branch plants to their jurisdictions.

International finance also changed its character under neoliberal deregulation. Banks, no longer content to invest solely in domestic ven-tures, expanded their loan portfolios into international markets. International financial markets diversified and became an intercon-nected global system in which capital could be transferred instantly and freely, 24 hours a day. There was the growth of global accounting giants who served the interests of their corporate partners with the manage-ment of their portfolios, their capital transfers and the like, which effec-tively centralized global financial power. These oligarchic alliances accordingly promised security to international capital interests, but less accountability to nation states and governmental authority. 'Soft capital-ism' is Thrift's (2005) label for this deceptive and increasingly self-serving, global enterprise in which the international business and finance com-munities practised institutional and managerial knowledge-based, self-regulatory authority. In reality, their claims for caring and sharing, accountability and transparency were/are dubious covers for pursuing their shared interests in capital accumulation, profit and wealth crea-tion. Data management and manipulation, corporate-controlled 'science' and R&D, as well as fraudulent financial accounting practices, also find their way into this interconnected morass of academics and public–private sector assessment institutions, so that unethical practices and a disdain for accountability characterize these two partners' neoliberal, global worlds (Conway and Heynen, 2005).

85

Neoliberal capitalism's particular feat since its emergence in the 1980s has been to increase social divisions, widen the economic gap between the very rich and the very poor, and centralize authority for the manage-ment of corporate and financial capital. It has elevated 'soft capitalism' to a position of unassailable influence in global financial affairs, and given monopolistic/oligopolistic privileges to smaller and smaller groups of highly influential power brokers. As a consequence, it has encouraged insider-trading, corrupt practices of accounting, tax evasion and bribery of officialdom, avoidance of regulatory oversight, and the use of techno-logical fixes further hide the actual economic health of corporate enter-prises. Eventually, the 'Asian Meltdown' in 1997–98, in which several East Asian national economies suffered financial crises, would signal an end to the uncritical optimism that had prevailed since the late 1980s. Ten years later, a more severe global recession in 2007–2011 was brought on by a liquidity shortfall in the United States' banking system which resulted in the collapse of large financial institutions and major down-turns in global stock markets. Although neoliberalism's excesses had brought the world to this latest global economic cyclical crisis (Stiglitz, 2010), contrary to historical precedents, neoliberal capitalist orthodoxy appears to have survived almost intact as an entrenched ideological faith in the next phase of the new global geo-economic order (Sparke, 2007) that globalization is overseeing (as noted above, Chapter 2.1 introduced this geo-economic restructuring of global power relationships).

86

Contemporary Aspects of Globalization

The profound restructuring of national economies and international cor-porate capitalism that followed in the 1980s, and into and through the 1990s and 2000s, ushered in a global neoliberal capitalism phase that became known as the 'era of globalization'. Globalization's structural dimensions and complex global-to-local interactions and interrelation-ships, therefore, are the subject of this second part of the chapter. This is because they constitute a new phase of advanced capitalism, which we have characterized as neoliberalism, in which geographic, political, eco-nomic, technological, social, cultural and ecological dynamics have become much more diversified and have changed rapidly, while new hybrid relations are constantly appearing and new processes succeeding former out-of-date ones. Partnering advanced capitalism across the glo-bal South is its subordinate neoliberal model, peripheral capitalism, so that the era's core–periphery structural relations are interwoven, though extremely unequal in power and self-determination. Two terms which neatly characterize globalization are the notions that we now live in a 'hyperactive world' (Thrift, 2002) and a 'runaway world' (Giddens, 2003).

Globalization's dimensions

Twelve dimensions of trends in globalization can be identified that are changing the scale of influence on, and political economic power over, people's livelihoods and their interactions. The previous era's political economic systems and networks functioned largely at the level of the state or within state boundaries. This post-1980s era functions at the supranational and transnational levels, with global-to-local interactions occurring too. Though not in order of descending importance, they are:

- *Financial globalization* The 24-hours-a-day, 7-days-a-week world market for international financial transactions among world cities, moved capital (money) in quantities and at speeds never previously encountered. A complete deregulation of international financial markets occurred, which encouraged the growth of unscrupulous financial intermediaries to manage hedge funds, subprime mortgage-debt bundles and other kinds of 'fictitious capital' (Roberts, 1995). Though the ensuing investment practices brought spectacular gains to the privileged insiders and investor classes playing the markets, there was a general lack of global, or even national, accountability in such unruly trading practices.
- *Globalization of corporate power* Mega-mergers and oligopolies have increased transnational corporations' political power over nation states. The wealth of major global corporations now exceeds that of most nations. This extremely rapid capital accumulation is encouraging global investments, corruption, natural resources expropriation and 'predatory capitalism' (Annan, 2000).
- *Technological globalization* Combinations of information and communication technologies (including satellite links) are producing and transferring data and information across the cyber-connected world at unprecedented rates. Communications and IT technology innovations are unevenly shared globally, thereby causing a 'digital divide' between the 'haves' and the 'have nots'.
- *Political globalization* The diffusion of the political-economic ideology of neoliberalism, or laissez-faire free-trade economic agendas, has promoted deregulation, privatization, and the opening of protected national economies to create free markets. The role of nation state governments is to create and preserve institutional frameworks appropriate to the above practices.
- *Economic globalization* The development of new, flexible, integrated production and commercial systems is enabling transnational

87

corporations to utilize international sources of capital and labour. Globalization of the spheres of production, trade and commerce, and of associated transportation, accounting and data logistical systems, has greatly benefitted corporate capital accumulation. This geo-economic transformation is now worldwide in terms of its national origins, yet transnational in economic reach and penetration.

- *Ecological globalization* The growing, international activism by 'Green' parties, human rights groups and non-governmental agencies (NGOs) is collectively referred to as 'civil society'. As a people-centred institutional mix of NGOs, it seeks to resist the global forces contributing to the environment's degradation and reducing Earth's capacity to sustain people, animals and the biosphere.
- *Globalization of labour* There has been a dramatic increase of cross-border mobility of all classes of people from the dispossessed, impoverished, and desperate, low-skilled 'migrant workers' to the transnationally mobile, middle and upper classes and highly-skilled professional classes. This global circulation is answering opportunities provided by transnational corporations, emerging nations' business-world expansions and global capitalism's needs for 'the brightest and the best'.
- *Illegal globalization* The growth and spread of such international crimes as narcotics trade, arms smuggling, money laundering, human trafficking of children and women, illegal immigration, refugee smuggling and slavery, has accompanied globalization. Many in this illegal domain use global institutions and informal commercial networks to further the underworld's profit, influence, bribery and corruption.
- *Cultural globalizing* There has been a rapid diffusion and consumption of commodities globally, which is often characterized as a Western/modernizing, homogenizing spread and penetration of such commercial products as Coca-cola and rock-and-roll music. But, there are reversals of global acculturation flows, as reggae and soca music and rhythms from the Caribbean penetrate popular music culture in the US, Canada and the UK, for example.
- *Globalization of militarization, conflict and 'fear'* Post-Cold War rationales have continued by building upon post-9/11 tensions to heighten domestic, regional and global fears over 'homeland protection' and 'national security'. As a result, the dangers of global terrorism have been fomented such that the spectre of endless war has become imposed upon global social imaginations.
- *Globalization from below* Global, national and local resistance and human rights movements have emerged as activist opponents of

globalization's more destructive practices. Often their alternative anti-globalization messages were cast in anti-development discourse (see Chapter 2.2).

- *Geographical globalization* The re-ordering of world–national–local scales and 'livelihood' spaces has replaced national systems with overarching, interstate practices, cross-border transnational practices, and re-configured institutional organizations in an increasingly borderless world.

Continuing to characterize these various global dimensions is an accelerated internationalization of societal processes. At their heart is a neoliberal capitalist process that David Harvey (2005: 3) points out brings unbridled 'creative destruction' which not only challenges state sovereignty but also 'divisions of labor, social relations, welfare provisions, technological mixes, ways of life and thought, reproductive activities, attachments to land and habits of the heart'. Also causing crises and unpredictability in global monetary affairs is a frenetic international financial system which is insider-controlled and managed. It is deregulated to the point of being out of control, and influenced as much by new 'soft-capitalist' practices and their discourses (Thrift, 2005) as it is by 'hard capitalist' financial market signals and national economic growth assessments.

89

Most well known as a globalizing force, because of its unequivocal acceptance by more affluent youth worldwide and by those without landline phone services in the global South, is the 'cell phone/mobile revolution'. Together with the rapidly increasing use of microcomputers and new information technologies, these technological innovations are being more intensively undertaken in a manner Harvey (1990) has characterized as 'time–space compression'. A final point that differentiates this era from earlier capitalist phases is the increasing involvement (and interpretation) of *culture* as a factor of production and as a major force in bringing about hybridization and fusion in many current global practices, such as music, art, self-identification, food, commerce, and consumer markets worldwide (Shrestha and Conway, 2005).

The Future of Fair Globalization

In 2004, the World Commission on the Social Dimension of Globalization presented their report on Fair Globalization to the International

Labour Organization, in which they proposed a *fair* and *inclusive* globalization as a worldwide priority. Many domains of policy making and institutional organization were addressed, but the impacts of globalization on the life and work of people, on their families and on societies were specifically singled out. Concerns were raised about the impact of globalization on employment, working conditions and income inequalities. The Commission also felt that a 'fair globalization project' should include social protection issues beyond the world of work; importantly, security, culture and identity, inclusion and/or exclusion and the cohesiveness of families and communities should be safeguarded.

The World Commission's vision was that a better world was do-able but that it would take a major commitment for a sustainable future to be achieved. Notably, the strategies which were advocated built upon social democratic practices, not neoliberal tenets. Several themes underpinned the Commission's recommendations. The most important were: 'beginning at home', in local and national arenas and 'fair rules and equitable policies' in the governance of global markets. Important at the supranational scale was 'reinforcing the UN multilateral system' by improving the quality of global governance, and democratizing parallel governing institutions. At the local scale, 'buy-ins of multiple stakeholders' were recommended to increase accountability and citizenry participation. Finally, 'utilizing the value and power of dialogue' as an instrument for change was recommended at local, national, regional and global levels (ILO, 2004). They were all 'people-centred solutions' (see Chapter 2.2).

90

KEY POINTS

- Neoliberal capitalism would become the dominant ideology and 'new faith' of the post-1980s era of globalization, while excessively favouring the world's wealthy elites.
- An accelerated internationalization of societal, financial and economic processes is at the heart of neoliberalism's ascendency to geo-economic dominance and globalization's influences, practices and consequences.
- Globalization's often-contradictory, destructive and disruptive forces play out across multiple scales of society: globally, nationally, regionally and locally.

FURTHER READING

A more advanced account is provided in Dennis Conway and Nik Heynen's collection *Globalization's Contradictions: Geographies of Discipline, Destruction and Transformation* (2005), which charts neoliberalism's ascendency in Chapter 2, and comprehensively examines how the many dimensions of globalization have come about. The last two chapters of the book, entitled 'Globalization from below' and 'Towards "fair globalization"' are especially helpful.

91

2.4 THE DEVELOPMENT PROGRAMMES OF GLOBAL INSTITUTIONS

This chapter tells the story of academic, institutional and popular opposition to the development programmes and regulatory missions of many of the West's global capitalist institutions. Specifically, the Washington-based development banks, international financial regulatory institutions, and global business economic forums are the focus. In addition, global institutions which made the rules governing the post-1948 multilateral trading system known as The General Agreement on Tariffs and Trade (GATT) and its 1994 successor, the World Trade Organization (WTO), are also implicated in this top-down display of capitalism's power. So they too are critically assessed. Self-serving objectives were always part of aid and assistance efforts by the advanced nations of the global North. Many policies and programmes devised by global and governmental 'development institutions' had the profiteering of Western, core nations and transnational corporate interests very much in mind.

Overall it can be argued that the record is a disappointing one of tunnel vision, misguided philanthropy and, in later decades, destruction and disappointment, rather than progress and transformative changes for the better (see Chapter 2.3 for globalization's effects). Too often the development practices of many of the West's development and aid agencies – both global and national by remit – have been at odds with declared programme objectives that hypothetically promised client states development and/or modernity. Though alternative paths were advocated by a succession of UN commissions, human rights interest groups, and civil society, most institutional 'messages' to further human needs, rights and securities (health, food, welfare) have not been heeded. Instead, transnational corporations, transnational financial institutions, the wealthiest of stockholders, and national and transnational elites have been the beneficiaries. Meanwhile, the poor majority in the global South has been left out in the cold, or has even suffered directly from misguided policy directives.

Post-World War II Global Institutions: Opposites not Equals

International Financial Institutions

Anticipating their military victory in Europe, in 1944 the Allies signed the Bretton Woods Agreement to lay the foundation for a 'new international economic order' that would not suffer from the political economic crises that had brought about the Great Depression of the 1930s, the rise of Hitler's Nazi regime and World War II (Jacque, 2010). The Bretton Woods Agreement created two new international financial institutions (IFIs): the International Bank for Reconstruction and Development (IBRD), which would later become the World Bank, and the International Monetary Fund (IMF). Both had headquarters in Washington DC. Both initially, had quite specific mandates: the IBRD helping the redevelopment of war-torn economies; the IMF to assist with short-term bridging loans to help indebted nations overcome their balance of payments problems. Eventually, during the post-1980 era of globalization, these two IFIs in particular would assume wider, global roles to facilitate neoliberal solutions 'everywhere' (see Chapter 2.3). Often working in tandem, they directed development finance, enforced the privatization of publicly owned industry and negotiated reductions in tariff barriers. They brought about a complete set of structural adjustment programmes (SAPs) (detailed later in this chapter) to liberalize global trade and commerce on behalf of neoliberal capitalism and its corporate and client elites in the global North and South.

93

The United Nations

The United Nations was brought into existence in June 1945 with the signing of the UN Charter; one of its chief aims was the maintenance of peace, international security and respect for human rights. The rise to 'superpower' status of the Soviet Union, challenging the United States' post-1945 hegemony in global affairs, then thrust the world into geo-political struggles between 'East' and 'West' or, as ideological and militaristic propaganda would label it: 'communism versus capitalism'. With peace and security and General Assembly negotiations being the heart of its mandate, the United Nations was never able to become fully involved in the 'development project', in comparison to the World Bank and other international financial institutions (IFIs).

Non-Aligned Movement

Elsewhere, the Non-Aligned Movement of newly independent nations would come into being in 1955. This was championed by the likes of Egypt's Nasser, India's Nehru, Ghana's Nkrumah, Yugoslavia's Tito, and Indonesia's Sukarno at the Bandung Conference in Indonesia. A decade later in 1966, at the Tri-Continental Conference called in defence of the Vietnamese revolution and held in Havana, Cuba, Che Guevara would sound the call for armed struggle in the pursuit of national liberation 'against the great enemy of mankind: the United States of America' – that would usher in years of military strife, dictatorial excesses, political coups, and disastrous revolutions and counter-revolutions. In terms of contributing to the social, economic and geo-political development of global South constituents, however, this Non-Aligned Movement would never become a major influence in global affairs.

United Nations' Commissions: Advocates of Alternative Development Strategies

As noted in Chapter 2.2, the Dag Hammarskjöld Foundation devoted considerable attention to an alternative development path – the 'What Now' project – which culminated in the 1975 Report, *What Now? Another Development*, and the monograph *Another Development: Approaches and Strategies* (1977). Prepared as independent contributions to Special Sessions of the United Nations General Assembly, *What Now* proposed a set of humanistic principles as alternatives to the established order and for the reformation of international relations and the United Nations system. The *What Now* Report was envisaged as a 'tribute to the man, who more than any other, gave the United Nations the authority which the world needs more than ever': Dag Hammarskjöld, who was UN Secretary-General from 1953 to 1961.

Starting in the 1980s, a succession of United Nations commissions would produce several significant reports that would call for 'alternative' visions of how inequality, people's general welfare and environmental sustainability might be better addressed than in previous decades. Two Brandt Reports, *North–South, A Programme for Survival* (UNDP 1980) and *Common Crisis* (UNDP 1983), would be followed by the Brundtland Commission's *Our Common Future* as a 1987 statement of the UN World Commission on Environment and Development (UNWEP 1987). Rounding out these UN Commission global visions was the extremely successful 'Environmental Summit' held in Rio de Janeiro in 1992, and the resultant progressive *Agenda 21* which explicitly focused upon the means by which 'sustainable development' could, and should, be pursued globally (see Chapter 2.5).

As noted previously, the United Nations was never able to become fully involved in assisting its developing country members; one reason was its preoccupation with peace and security issues in the earlier decades. Human rights, basic needs, health, education and welfare, child welfare, family planning and such, were on the agendas of some of its constituted affiliates, such as the World Health Organization (WHO), the Food and Agriculture Organization (FAO), and specialist branches such as the United Nations Educational, Scientific and Cultural Organization (UNESCO). On the other hand, the development missions of its member organizations such as the United Nations Industrial Development Organization (UNIDO), and the United Nations Conference on Trade and Development (UNCTAD) were discussion forums, never implementation agencies.

Later, in the post-1980 era of globalization, this 'mission-avoidance' would be partially rectified with the UN's involvement in the formulation of the Millennium Development Goals (see Chapter 1.5), and with the greater financial role played by the United Nations Development Programme (UNDP) in providing development grant assistance. Of note, in this respect, was the publication of UNDP's *Human Development Report 1990* in which 'people-centred development' was trumpeted as the best development strategy for the future global economy (see Chapter 2.2). When the World Bank and IMF structural adjustment programmes (SAPs) were in ascendance, however, the UN was powerless to intervene or intercede, thereby demonstrating the imbalance in geo-political, global authority of these IFIs over that of the UN and its affiliate organizations.

95

Reactions to the World Bank and IMF 'Conditionalities' and Structural Adjustment Programmes

Aided by the disastrous crisis brought on by the 1979–83 recession, and the ensuing unstoppable growth of indebtedness that many developing countries experienced, the central 'claim' touted as the World Bank and IMF's rationale for structural adjustment programmes (SAPs) revolved around debt reduction. More specifically, the imposition of 'conditionalities' by these IFIs fundamentally changed many aspects of society among the indebted nations of the global South, hitting their poor majorities the hardest. The comprehensive package of SAPs included monetary discipline, trade liberalization, reduction and/or the removal of public subsidies, price reforms, currency devaluation, privatization of public enterprises, reductions in public spending, wage restraints and the institutional reform of public services and public–private partnerships.

50 Years is Enough! Criticisms 'From Below' of the World Bank and IMF

Concerning the destructive consequences of SAPs, a UNICEF publication, *Adjustment with a Human Face* (1987) was mildly critical and argued for more consideration of the poor's suffering. A year later Susan George (1988) more forcefully and perceptively likened the World Bank and IMF's SAPs to 'international low-intensity conflict' as a war being waged between the world's rich and poor, in which these two IFIs were the major 'enforcers'.

Not surprisingly then, around the fiftieth anniversary of the World Bank's existence, anti-globalization fervour increased and anti-establishment commentary called for resistance and action to prevent a continuation of such punitive structural adjustment regimes. Acclaiming *50 Years is Enough*, Kevin Danaher (1994) edited a collection that forcibly and convincingly demonstrated the disastrous impacts of these neoliberal 'reforms'. Muhammed Yunus, the Bangladeshi who created the Grameen Bank for Micro-credit, provided the Preface to this collection, and many luminaries contributed critiques of SAPs and how the World Bank and IMF operated. Additionally, it provided empirical evidence of countries 'drowning in debt', gave attention to unheard voices – particularly environmentalists, women and tribal peoples – and offered alternatives to the conservative paths these two IFIs had doggedly pursued. Saliently, since their inception in the mid-1940s, both institutions have retained their conservative, neoclassical economic thought and praxis. Additionally, this ideological dogmatism prevails to this day, despite lip-service paid to the humanistic broadening of the development agenda that appeared as special emphases from time to time (Potter et al., 2008).

The World Bank and Other International Aid Agencies: 'Lords of Poverty'?

The power, prestige and corruption of the 'international aid business' was comprehensively exposed in a critique authored by an 'institutional insider and whistleblower', Graham Hancock (1989). His indictment of the 'Development Set' epitomizes the irony of the situation wherein these aid professionals' affluence and prosperity relies upon the perpetuation of global poverty:

> Despite the fads, fancies, 'new techniques', 'new directions', and endless 'policy rethinks' that have characterised the development business over the last half-century, and despite the expenditure of hundreds and billions of dollars, there is little evidence to prove that the poor of the Third World have actually *benefitted*. Year in year out, however, there can be no doubt that aid pays the hefty salaries and underwrites the privileged lifestyles of the international civil servants, 'development experts', consultants and assorted freeloaders who staff the aid agencies themselves. (Hancock, 1989: xv)

97

The Washington Consensus: Assessed and Reconsidered

The political apparatus of Washington made up of Congress, the White House and senior members of the administration, and the technocratic Washington of the US Federal Reserve Board, economic agencies of the US government, and the attendant think-tanks and consultancies were more than coincidental geo-political partners to the World Bank and IMF in their neoliberal directives. With the US at its heart and the World Bank and IMF policies in 'lock-step' with the neoliberal agendas of other global capitalist institutions such as the World Trade Organization (WTO) and the World Economic Forum (WEF), throughout the 1990s this hegemonic capitalist group became known and feared or distrusted as the 'Washington Consensus'. To the world beyond Washington and in the global South in particular, these American-led global power brokers were seen as willing partners and promoters of the United States' geo-political, commercial and corporate interests, both at home and abroad.

Eventually, in the first decade of the twenty-first century, economists and critics of the Washington Consensus' self-serving agenda and of its many unfortunate consequences, would argue in favour of a new approach to global governance in a collection co-authored by Narcis Serra and Joseph Stiglitz entitled *The Washington Consensus Reconsidered* (Serra and Stiglitz 2008). The contributors to this 'Barcelona Development Agenda' encouraged consensus-building to forge future macroeconomic strategies that would achieve more equitable growth globally. They sought macro-structural policy shifts that would bring about sustainable development and environmental sustainability (see Chapter 2.5).

Grassroots Anti-globalization Movements, Targeting Global Institutions: the World Bank, IMF, WTO, WEF

Beginning in the late 1990s, there was an upsurge of grassroots movements, national and regional activism which came together as a global coalition of opposition – a 'globalization from below' – to counter the immensely powerful, yet selfish agendas of global capitalism's 'establishment' – the Washington Consensus (Brecher and Costello, 1998).

Unanticipated activism in the streets of Seattle in 1999 thoroughly derailed the comfortable consensus that the World Trade Organization (WTO) appeared to be enjoying until that moment. This 1999 'Battle of Seattle' signalled the growing strength of cooperative activism (Smith, 2001) and a convergence of popular views that was always strongly anti-establishment, anti-corporatist, anti-capitalist, anti-elitist, and anti-neoconservative. In succeeding years, further mass demonstrations against globalization, the WTO, the IMF and the Washington Consensus, took place in Genoa, New York and Washington DC, thereby keeping the momentum going.

There was also a growing progressive confluence around the common values of social democracy (as a replacement for economic democracy), environmental conservation and societal sustainability, global justice, equality, and worldwide solidarity. As a consensual and enduring 'globalization from below', this global grassroots uprising was not so much 'anti-development' as a positive advocacy of 'alternative globalization' (International Forum on Globalization, 2002), and of 'fair globalization'

98

(ILO, 2004). These themes of sustainable development among others are covered in more detail in Chapter 2.5.

The World Social Forum Challenge

Seen by some as the successor to the Non-Aligned Movement (introduced earlier), the World Social Forum (WSF) was conceived as an international forum against neoliberal policies, international financial institutions and corporate globalization, built around the slogan: 'Another World Is Possible'. The Forum sought 'a space' where alternatives to neoliberal capitalist development could be discussed, people's experiences exchanged, and alliances forged between social movements, unions of the working people, and 'civil society' NGOs and IGOs. The first WSF held in January 2001 in the city of Porto Alegre, Brazil was timed to coincide with the holding of the World Economic Forum (WEF) in Davos, Switzerland. It deliberately positioned itself as a counterweight to the 'global solutions' proposed by the World Economic Forum, which is an annual meeting of chief executives of the world's most influential transnational corporations and IFIs with client academics and political leaders (Fisher and Ponniah, 2003).

99

After two successful forums in Porto Alegre, WSF organizers then decided that from 2003 onwards, the annual global meeting would be accompanied by regional, continental, and/or thematic Forums across the globe. At the 2004 meeting in Mumbai, India there were, however, internal disagreements about how the WSF should continue its mission. Divergent views emerged in Mumbai with the West's global dominance being challenged by the Eastern hemisphere's rapidly emerging global economic successes. Henceforth, there would be hemisphere agendas instead of undifferentiated global programmes seeking social justice.

The Mumbai WSF also achieved one of its purposes, however, with the WEF being 'pressured' to embrace issues of inequality and poverty alleviation, as is evident in its 2004 *Global Governance Initiative* (WEF, 2004). The World Economic Forum would still be held in closely guarded, secure locations like Doha, Qatar to avoid disruption and pressure from activist opposition; but the WEF's privileged global elites would now have to pay more than lip service to global problems of poverty alleviation, disease eradication, and related social crises afflicting the world's poor majority.

Conclusions: No Alternative to Neoliberalism in Sight, As Yet?

The alternative theories of development, which stress humanistic objectives and people-centred approaches (see Chapter 2.2), often underpinned the academic and intellectual challenges outlined in this chapter. Here, the conventional, neoliberal economic theories and models favoured by powerful international financial institutions – such as the World Bank and the International Monetary Fund specifically, and by the Washington Consensus more broadly – have been found to be disappointing at best, and destructive and harmful more often than not.

Despite their adoption in UN circles, among civil society and in anti-globalization rhetoric and activism, neither academic nor humanitarian institutional arguments have significantly altered global institutional policies and practices, which continue to favour neoliberal capitalist solutions in their 'development portfolios' to this day. But despite such apparent ineffectiveness in the powers of persuasion by these social critics 'from below', the record of achievements by the Washington Consensus and neoliberal agencies pale into insignificance compared to the harmfulness and destructiveness of their economic programmes – programmes that have been offered in the name of 'development'.

The macroeconomic programmes offered by the Washington Consensus need to be reconsidered, as Serra and Stiglitz (2008) advocate. The World Social Forum has fairer solutions for the world's majority than global businesses' World Economic Forum. Fortunately, there are signs that the United Nations is no longer an irrelevant and weak global institution, when it comes to helping to develop and direct development programmes for the world's needy and helpless.

KEY POINTS

- The United Nations was never able directly to involve itself in the operationalization of development programmes in the global South, although humanitarian 'calls to arms' and support of global health, education and welfare programmes have been achieved more recently.

- Conventional neoliberal economic programmes of capitalist development, trade and commerce would become common practice from the 1980s onward – largely dictated 'from above' under the collective authority of the Washington Consensus.
- In the post-1980s era, international financial institutions imposed (punitive) neoliberal, structural adjustments programmes (SAPs) on indebted nations in the global South.
- The World Social Forum was established as a counter to the World Economic Forum and similar neoliberal institutions which promised 'economic development'.

FURTHER READING

Several of the authorities referenced in this chapter deserve reading for the detail they provide, both on the destructive excesses wrought by the 'Washington Consensus', by neoliberal structural adjustment policies, and by mismanaged, misdirected and oft-times corrupt development bank practices. Kevin Danaher's *50 Years is Enough* (1994), Graham Hancock's *Lords of Poverty* (1989), Susan George's *A Fate Worse than Debt* (1988) as well as her *The Debt Boomerang* (1992), collectively detail the IFI excesses on behalf of neoliberal capitalism and transnational corporate accumulation – particularly at the expense of the poor majority, but also harming 'all of us'. The World Social Forum also deserves attention, and William Fisher and Thomas Ponniah's work, *Another World is Possible* (2003) details that alternative global forum's activism and creativity.

101

2.5 SUSTAINABLE DEVELOPMENT AND ENVIRONMENTAL SUSTAINABILITY

Debates erupted as soon as the term 'sustainable development' was brought into common usage in 1987 by the United Nation's Brundtland Commission. The Brundtland Report, Our Common Future (UNWEP, 1987) coined what has become the most often-quoted definition of sustainable development as 'development that meets the needs of the present without compromising the ability of future generations to meet their own needs'. Some condemned it as an oxymoron, and seriously questioned the ambiguities over the implied conflation of societal processes and environmental, or ecological, processes. Others questioned the concept's futuristic, yet imprecise, tenor. Still others, though not the scientific community, rejected the doomsday predictions about future climate change.

One generalization difficult to refute, or ignore, is that the current environmental and development paths the world is on are not sustainable (Mawhinney, 2003; Monbiot, 2007). Indeed, contemporary globalization processes are making things worse (see Chapter 2.3). This is because these current paths are extensions of existing global patterns of environmental degradation, natural resource-exploitation and widespread impoverishment. Also, there is greater inequality of wealth, major decreases in international assistance and increases in foreign debt, among other 'plagues of globalization' (Aguilar and Cavada, 2002).

This chapter critically appraises the ambiguities concerning how 'sustainable development' has been conceptualized and holistically conceived. Particular notice is taken of the complications we face when merging concerns for the human development of societies and people's needs and wants, resources access, food security and empowerment for all with concerns over the direct and indirect impacts of these imperatives on global, regional and local environmental changes – be they degrading, destructive, or even benign. There is an ethical dimension to such sustainability assessments that requires spelling out (Goulet, 1996). Major development concerns remain, just as there are ecological concerns and long-term environmental consequences to seriously consider (Redclift, 1987). This is because our global ecumene is growing into a highly interconnected system in which non-inhabited and inhabited regions are climatically tele-connected and the environmental 'envelopes' of north and south, east and west hemispheres are changing in unpredictable ways (Monbiot, 2004; 2007).

Sustainable Development's Ambiguities

First and foremost in this deliberation on sustainable development's ambiguous nature, is the mismatch between the power and consequential political economic authority of neoliberal capitalism's free-market messages and the eco-development messages that sustainable development promotes. The latter's stewardship of global environmental conservation and preservation is completely at odds with the former's singular concerns for the short-term profitability of neoliberalism's apparent need to derive maximum benefits from unregulated resource-exploitation, energy-wasteful production methods, its market-driven objectives and the many deficiencies and inequalities it causes (see Chapter 2.3). Indeed, as long as neoliberalism remains as the global 'faith' guiding contemporary (and future) political economic decision making, then a sustainable development that is 'socially just and fair for all' is highly unlikely. Neoliberalism's myopic pursuit of unfettered economic development, 'at all costs', is contrary to most sustainability objectives that favour long-term sustenance and survival for the majority, with the ecumene being preserved for future generations too.

103

One of the most obvious ambiguities results from the inclusion or exclusion of people-centred development in the ecological concept of sustainability when it focuses upon how the productivity of the earth's biomass resources can be sustained, preserved and conserved. Similarly, social scientists may exclude considerations of ecological sustainability and natural resources conservation and preservation in their disciplinary emphases on social justice, social inequality, and human rights issues (Elliott, 2006). In short, disciplinary perspectives hinder our pursuit of answers to sustainability questions and concerns that are inherently interdisciplinary in nature. Wolfgang Sachs (1993) would argue that there can be no sustainability without development, and echoes the ecological economist Herman Daly's ideas on this necessary nexus, if sustainability is to be sought, assessed, people-directed, and attained (Daly, 1973; 1996).

A final ambiguity that results from the diversity in approaches to sustainability – as ecological environmentalism or human, people-centred development, or both interacting as a merged concept – comes about because of the persuasive, indirect 'soft-influences' that neoliberal thinking cultivates among contemporary policymakers. Sachs depicts this co-opted discourse as follows:

> Once, environmentalists called for new public virtues, now they call for better managerial strategies. Once, they advocated more democracy and local self-reliance, now they tend to support the global empowerment of governments, corporations and science. Once, they strove for cultural diversity, now they see little choice but to push for a worldwide rationalization of life styles … In recent years, a discourse on global ecology has developed that is largely devoid of any considerations of power relations, cultural authenticity and moral choice; instead, it rather promotes the aspirations of a rising eco-cracy to manage nature and regulate people worldwide. (1993, xv)

Development Ethics and a People-centred Global Agenda

According to Denis Goulet (1996), the originator of the new discipline of 'development ethics', his enlightened vision for a much fairer future derives from a convergence of socially just ideas and practices. Succinctly, civil society's engagement in development action needs to build upon ethical theory so that our thinking can move beyond critiques of mainstream ethical theory to the crafting of normative strategies to guide development practice. In Goulet's words, 'Development ethics has a dual mission: to render the economy more human and to keep hope alive in the face of the seemingly impossibility of achieving human development for all' (1996: ii). He further refines his view that 'the true indicator of development is not increased production or material wellbeing but qualitative human enrichment'. Borrowing from one of Marx's insights Goulet then acclaims that: 'The beginning of

authentic developmental human history comes indeed with the abolition of alienation. Development's true task is precisely this: to abolish
all alienation – economic, social, political and technological' (Goulet
1996: 19).

To David Korten, an advocate of people-centred development (see
Chapter 2.3), sustainable development is all about creating the following
progressive conditions in the global South:

> i) sustainable economies that equitably meet human needs without
> extracting resource inputs or expelling wastes in excess of the environ-
> ment's regenerative capacity, and ii) sustainable human institutions that
> assure both security and opportunity for social, intellectual, and spiritual
> growth. (1996: 1)

Poor countries deserve to be helped to become sustainable by the global North's governments and corporations. After all, it is the latter
which have long benefitted from the exporting of their ecological defi-
cits to the South through trade and consumption, and the wholesale
appropriation of their environmental resources and sinks to service the
North's over-consumption. Furthermore, contemporary levels of global
inequality are a fundamental cause of many environmental problems.
The wealthy have freely passed on the social and ecological costs of
their over consumption to the poor, so that the most marginal of populations in the global South (not forgetting the indigenous North) have
constantly suffered from environmental degradation and resource
depletion.

105

Today's and tomorrow's democratically-elected governments must
not rely upon neoliberal market solutions to bring about development
and growth. Rather, they must regain their responsible role in helping
chart a sustainable future for all their constituents. For governments
to achieve social justice and environmental sustainability, 'they must
intervene to set a framework that assures full costs are internalized,
competition is maintained, benefits are justly distributed, and necessary public goods are provided' (Korten, 1996: 4). Korten (1990) firmly
believes that civil society's role in the twenty-first century is to be vigi-
lant, to assure the accountability of both government and the private
sector to serve the public interest as well as themselves (see Chapter 5.2).
He concludes that civil society and people-centred activist networks
must provide leadership in advancing social and technological innovation processes so that social inequalities and injustices become 'things
of the past'.

Ecological Economists' Perspectives

Challenging the often-used conflation of development and growth as if they are the same process, a group of ecological economists have argued that sustainable development does not need to continue to pursue capitalist 'hard growth'. Rather, a 'soft growth' path should be followed in which environmental concerns and quality of life concerns could be incorporated. Hard growth (quantitative, physical) involves an increase in size and scale based on increasing the amount of natural resources exploited. This, in turn, intensifies pressure on the natural resource base by increasing the flow of matter and energy through the economy. Soft growth (qualitative, non-physical), conversely, is based on improvement, efficiency and reaching a fuller, better state. The first is severely constrained by natural limits; the second would be potentially sustainable (Daly, 1990). According to Herman Daly, 'development is qualitative improvement or unfolding of potentialities' (1991: 402).

Initially, ecological economists were advocates for a global 'steady-state economy' in which there would be no throughput hard growth. But, acknowledging that global South poverty needed to be addressed if sustainability was to be achieved the need for hard and soft growth in the South became obvious. To balance the global account, therefore, Goodland et al. (1992) proposed that this necessary economic growth for the poor would need to be offset by reducing hard growth that caters to the rich (who predominantly reside in the global North). A steady-state sustainable system could then be maintained at the global level by such economic and ecological trade-offs that carry the world 'beyond growth' (Daly, 1996).

106

Future Development and Environment Sustainability

The Need for a Secure Terrestrial Base for Life

The crisis the world faces as we have started the second decade of the twenty-first century is very much in evidence (Monbiot, 2007; Rogers et al., 2008). A secure terrestrial base that will support the world's projected 9.5 billion population (by the year 2050) can best be achieved through the effective and efficient management of our natural resource bases, while minimizing negative environmental impacts. People's basic needs such as breathing, eating, drinking, being sheltered, staying healthy, being literate and educated, and being safe and free to move, serve as the collective demands on the world's natural resources. They have to be preserved, while being utilized, consumed, depleted, and revitalized, among other resource transformations.

Consensus Building

Inevitably, conflicts have arisen and continue to arise from the conjunction of environment and resource crises, in which the noted inequalities of current and future resource endowments feature as global South and North 'divides' – born out of historical geo-political relations since colonialism. Past patterns that have rendered such inequalities and brought on intensely conflictual situations, have considerable inertia. Changing paths towards a more equitable, sustainable future for all, therefore, is bound to be conflict-ridden and conflict-driven. Rogers et al. accordingly arrive at the following set of questions that sum up the *compromises* the world needs to consider making to achieve a sustainable future for all:

- Will the currently wealthy countries and groups within them, be willing to reduce their consumption of the planet's resources and also be willing to reduce the environmental effects associated with the current use of resources?
- What political, social and economic mechanisms could be used to facilitate these compromises among the 'privileged' global North countries?
- Will these compromises have to be enforced by multilateral (UN) actions or can they arise from bi-lateral negotiations among the world's rich and poor nations?
- What is to be expected of the poor global South countries in their plans for sustainable futures? (Rogers et al., 2008: 380)

Little Policy-making Progress

To date, and despite UN summits, World Summits on Global Environmental Change, G-7 and G-20 meetings to build a global consensus on how to accomplish environmental sustainability, and devise solutions to achieve sustainable development, a reasoned consensus is yet to be formulated. Little progress has been made to reconcile the objectives of development and growth paths that are sustainable, with those of global environmental sustainability. Global mandatory compliance to regulate environmental excesses is still a long way off. Notably, the less powerful and disenfranchised and their 'sustainable development' are not being considered seriously by policymakers in the global North or South. The Millennium Goals (see Chapter 1.5), that sought to bring about less global inequality, more social justice and better livelihoods for the poor majority, have not been incorporated into contemporary 'environmentalist blueprints'. Therefore, the plight of the global South's poor majority does not feature prominently among the global goals of contemporary sustainable development.

KEY POINTS

- Sustainable development as a global objective is replete with ambiguities, because it has to reconcile two very different growth trajectories, short-term hard growth and long-term environmental sustainability.
- Neoliberalism's persistence as a dominant global economic faith prevents environmental sustainability from being pursued.
- Globalization's many destructive and unruly tendencies have contributed to the maintenance of unsustainable patterns of resource-use, ecosystem exploitation and human impoverishment.

FURTHER READING

Two complementary texts, Jennifer Elliott's *An Introduction to Sustainable Development* (2006) and Peter Rogers et al.'s *An Introduction to Sustainable Development* (2008), provide much more complete coverage of sustainable development's many challenges – in which the significance of place, difference and cultural diversity are given considerable emphasis. For example, concerns for sustainable urbanism and sustainable rural livelihoods in an increasingly diverse global South require dramatically different development solutions. George Monbiot's *Manifesto for a New World Order* (2004), and *Heat: How to Stop the Planet from Burning* (2007), are equally challenging 'blueprints' that contain detailed arguments around how our unsustainable ways must be stopped and how a sustainable future might be possible if the world acts sooner rather than later – or most pressingly, right now.

Section 3
Work, Employment and Development

Section 3

New
Environment
and
Development

INTRODUCTION

We are currently living in an era of accelerated globalization that is having unprecedented impacts upon the economic, social and political landscape of the global South. Given the increasing vulnerability of the world's 184 million unemployed and 550 million 'working poor', interest in the provision of 'decent work' in the global South is a priority for multilateral agencies and Non-Governmental Organizations (NGOs), but the extent to which globalization has enhanced employment opportunities for local workers is still widely contested. This section of the book provides a focused series of discussions that examine the impact of economic globalization on the employment, livelihoods and well-being of individuals and communities in the global South over time and space. Through a focus on the ways in which global processes are embedded in different livelihood trajectories, it explores how neoliberal transformations have shaped changes in agriculture, industry, services, technology, trade and aid over the last forty years. While there is much evidence to suggest that globalization is exacerbating inequalities and fragmenting societies through complex networks of inclusion and exclusion, it has also become increasingly clear that it also enables the development of new social spaces and modes of resistance that cut across traditional North–South divides.

Despite the diverse range of issues discussed in the forthcoming chapters, three interconnecting themes provide a framework for linking the concepts introduced in each chapter. First, in relation to the interdependence of poverty and global economic forces, neoliberal trade reforms have been closely associated with the extensive liberalization of the agricultural, industrial and service economies of the global South, a process that has widespread impacts on the livelihoods and everyday trajectories of local workers and communities. However, the outcomes of corporate dominance and the New International Division of Labour (NIDL) are contradictory and far from uniform. Against the tide of global capitalism, advances in information and communication technologies (ICTs) have increased the capacity for local social movements and civil society organizations to empower local communities through grassroots mobilization.

Secondly, the reality of the contemporary global economy is that the majority of its workforce is employed in casual, contractual and unregulated work in all spaces of the economy, escaping government regulations and social legislation. As a consequence of neoliberal strategies that undermine workers' rights, commentators have argued that much employment in the so-called formal global economy has become 'informalized' with insecure work becoming the norm in both the global North and South, a situation that weaves common bonds of vulnerability and deregulation between many workers in the present decade. Central to these debates is a growing body of research that examines the relationship between sustainable development, livelihoods, labour standards and social justice.

Thirdly, contemporary debates over the negative effects of globalization have also drawn attention to increasing proportions of female workers who are trapped in part-time, insecure, contractual or home-based work linked to global supply chains. An emerging body of work on the exploitative articulation of labour in the global South highlights structural gender discrimination in many spaces of the economy. Persistent gender inequality and discrimination are still major obstacles to livelihood security throughout the global South, and gender equity is a theme that runs throughout the discussions.

112

In order to address the diversity of concepts and approaches that have framed key debates on work and development in an era of globalization, this section is divided into five interrelated chapters. Chapter 3.1 on rural livelihoods and sustainable communities provides an introduction to past and present approaches to understanding rural development, agricultural change and sustainable livelihoods. This is followed in Chapter 3.2 by a detailed critique of the impact of industrialization and the New International Division of Labour on countries of the global South, with a particular focus on the growth of export-oriented manufacturing, the cheap labour economy and Multinational Corporations (MNCs). Chapter 3.3 then discusses the unprecedented growth of the informal sector in the global South as labour force growth outpaces employment opportunities, a trend that is predicted to continue over the next twenty-five years. In light of recent debates over decent work and risk, the chapter explores the ways in which new gendered perspectives have informed policy and practice in the contemporary informal sector. The impact of the ITC and digital revolution on shaping livelihood opportunities is the subject of Chapter 3.4, with particular attention given to debates surrounding the digital divide and the mobile phone revolution in Africa and Asia. The concluding chapter moves away from examining everyday local geographies by exploring macroeconomic transformations in trade and aid that have served to shape the global distribution of flows of commodities, capital and labour in an increasingly interdependent world. Through an example of fair trade, Chapter 3.5 concludes by highlighting the role of small-scale and grassroots movements in providing an alternative globalization from 'below' that could provide pathways to a more sustainable future for many communities in the global South.

3.1 RURAL LIVELIHOODS AND SUSTAINABLE COMMUNITIES

Rural Poverty, Vulnerability and Development

Despite recent figures from United Nations Habitat, which state that the global population is becoming increasingly urban, rural poverty and agriculture continue to remain at the heart of global development agendas, particularly as the proportion of the world's poorest people living in rural areas has continued to increase in many countries of the global South. In fact, levels of rural poverty continue to outstrip urban poverty, with higher proportions of the 'poorest of the poor' living in rural rather than urban areas. Recent figures suggest that three out of every four poor individuals are rural (World Bank, 2007) and 70 per cent of the 1.4 billion people living in extreme poverty reside in rural areas, a situation that is particularly marked in South Asia and sub-Saharan Africa (International Fund for Agricultural Development (IFAD), 2010).

Rural poverty is complex and multidimensional, and may be linked to a wide range of structural factors such as the unequal distribution of land ownership or tenure, urban bias of development policies, a neoliberal system that prioritizes export crops over domestic food production, global market fluctuations in primary commodity prices, political instability, and external shocks like natural hazards or long-term climate change. In recent years, increasing recognition has also been paid to the agency of households to respond to structural problems by employing a diverse range of livelihood and coping strategies to counteract poverty and risk, where risk is defined as the 'likelihood of being faced with decline in well-being' (Rigg, 2007: 233). A household's resilience to recover from crisis is also shaped by a range of social and cultural processes such as gender, local power relations and social capital (see Chapter 5.2).

Despite transitions in the emphasis placed on different conceptual and policy approaches to rural development, three main issues have endured though time. First, it is difficult to talk about rural livelihoods and poverty without thinking about the concept of sustainable development, which has framed environmental and development discourses since the 1980s. Issues relating to the sustainability of resources and eco-systems and the negative impacts of climate change on developing countries are likely to continue to dominate international policy agendas throughout the twenty-first century.

Secondly, and most importantly, the agricultural sector not only continues to be an important source of national income for many nations, but it plays an essential role in providing local livelihoods for a substantial proportion of the population in the global South, although the nature of these livelihood strategies may transform over time. A third and interrelated theme is the problem of engendering equity and social justice, particularly in relation to *gender*, which also continues to   115 undermine interventions to empower vulnerable and impoverished rural communities.

In order fully to understand the complexities of rural living, the chapter starts with a brief synopsis of the overarching rural development agendas that have framed livelihoods approaches over time, before moving on to discuss sustainable rural livelihood approaches and the gender gap in rural development.

Rural Development Agendas: Transformations and Transitions

The colonial experience of most countries in the developing world was focused on the production of raw materials and primary products for export, extracted through the use of slave and indentured labour in the plantation system (Potter et al., 2008). The overwhelming reliance of many ex-colonies on export commodities like sugar or cotton has largely resulted in instability, stagnation and domestic food shortages. Away from the plantations, many small-scale farmers engaged in subsistence farming methods in order to sustain livelihoods and to feed local communities. Although subsistence farming methods tended to be environmentally sustainable, they were regarded as traditional and backward in the post-independence era. In regions like the Caribbean, national attempts to overcome widespread rural poverty in the 1970s centred on integrated development and rural extension programmes (McAfee, 1991). Often led by partnerships between the state and multilateral institutions, these initiatives aimed to improve the agricultural production of small-scale farmers and encourage diversification into non-agricultural activities such as trading, small business and infrastructure (Pretty, 2002). Projects were often large-scale, top-down and sought to drive technological solutions to increasing agricultural production, which was identified as the main solution to rural famine and poverty.

The Green Revolution, which refers to the introduction of High Yield Variety (HYV) seeds selected to produce higher crop yields in wheat and maize, also spread across parts of the global South from the 1960s onwards (Williams et al., 2009). Although dramatic increases in yields occurred in some regions, such as the Punjab, success was highly dependent on the commercialization of agriculture, particularly the use of fertilizers and irrigation, which led to increasing inequalities within farming communities and dependence on Western expertise and products. Despite the importance attached to rural development by national governments, many newly independent nations were unable to diversify away from export-oriented crops or grow sufficient food for their local populations. In the immediate aftermath of the 1980s debt crisis, scholars and practitioners started to question the relevance of previous development policies for the majority of the rural and landless poor. In his ground-breaking book, *Putting the Last First*, Robert Chambers (1983) asked policymakers to rethink technological solutions to underdevelopment by putting people back in the heart of development policy and practice by adopting a 'livelihoods' perspective. As outlined below, livelihood approaches to poverty have continued to dominate development praxis, and they have made substantial contributions to understanding the everyday lives of communities in the global South (Rigg, 2007).

In the current era, the terms of trade for developing countries, which are increasingly influenced by neoliberal institutions like the World Trade Organization (WTO) and dominated by free-trade discourses, have led to price fluctuations, instability and falling revenues for many agricultural products, a situation that has severe implications for small-scale farmers. Although primary production is still a major source of export earnings for many countries in Africa and Asia, changes in the global economy have led to a 'deagrarianization' of the countryside as farming has become increasingly commercialized and dominated by powerful global agri-business and MNCs (see Chapter 3.2). Rural workers are increasingly dependent on seasonal contracts or insecure work in the rural informal sector (Chapter 3.3), a situation that is seen by many as untenable. The World Bank's solution to smallholder poverty lies in what it calls the new agriculture, a set of approaches that advocate the rise of large-scale corporate agri-businesses, aided by the state (World Bank, 2007; McMichael, 2009). The problems associated with the increasing power of the global food industry and the exploitation of low-paid female workers in what Robinson (2004) calls 'the new plantations' in high value products like flowers, have been well documented (Oxfam 2004; Hale and Opondo, 2005; McMichael, 2009). As a consequence, fair trade initiatives that offer farmers a fair price, security and better working conditions, have achieved increasing support from consumers and retailers in the global North (Raynolds et al., 2007; Le Mare, 2008). Other pro-poor solutions 117 include a re-engagement with land reform and redistribution, and there has been a recent increase in grassroots support for reform in countries like Brazil and Mexico (Jacobs, 2009) in order to build more secure livelihoods for rural communities. The redistribution of land to the poor is one of the most effective ways of securing more sustainable livelihoods for rural communities.

Sustainable Rural Livelihoods: Challenges and Interventions

Although the concept of 'sustainable development' remains highly contested, one of the most enduring definitions stems from the Brundtland Commission's notion of intergenerational equality and their definition of sustainability as 'development that meets the needs of the present without compromising those of future generations' (World Commission on Environment and Development, 1987; Whitehead, 2007). Drawing on the African experience, Amanor and Moyo (2008: 3) suggest that there are two contrasting paradigms of sustainable development that prevail today. The first is rooted in neoliberal thinking and views unsustainable development as a result of chronic poverty and inappropriate technology. Focusing on technological, educational and market-based solutions to mobilizing rural communities to manage their natural resources more effectively, this approach sees sustainable development as a product of effective linkages between government, civil society and industry (see Chapter 5.2), and has resonance with the findings of Agenda 21 and the 1992 UNCED meeting in Rio de Janeiro. Another equally powerful paradigm argues that sustainability must be grounded in political and socio-economic frameworks that emphasize social justice and power relations (Redclift, 1987; Smith et al., 2007). For many scholars, unsustainable development is the product of an inequitable global capitalist system that produced widespread structural inequalities at a range of spatial scales. From this perspective, sustainable development requires a redistribution of the world's resources and widespread social change at both global and local scales (Redclift, 2008).

118

The mainstreaming of livelihood perspectives in development theory and practice in the 1990s was paramount in bringing together new understandings of sustainable development and poverty through a focus on people's own interpretations and priorities. As was argued earlier, interest in the livelihoods of the rural poor can largely be attributed to the work of Robert Chambers and a groundbreaking paper that proposed that a livelihood consisted of the *capabilities*, material and social *assets* and *activities* needed to make a living (Chambers and Conway, 1992). Chambers identified the importance of *intangible* ways of accessing assets (such as social networks) as well as those that were more *tangible* and easily measured (land or property ownership). Livelihood perspectives also aimed to put people back in the centre of the development process, recognizing their agency over decision making and seeing them as actors not victims. Moreover, a sustainable livelihood was one that could combat risk and shocks and stresses without undermining the livelihood opportunities of the next generation. These approaches were also grounded in the development of participatory research methods, such as Rural Rapid Appraisal (RRA) and Participatory Rural Appraisal (PRA), which were devised to understand rural poverty and vulnerability at the local scale.

Livelihood approaches symbolized an elemental shift in development thinking from top-down, macro-development policies that viewed the rural poor as victims of structural constraints, to a more grassroots and empowering approach that emphasized the agency of households over their lives – a factor that Chambers (1997) would continue to stress in his later works. Although there have been many versions of the livelihoods framework, a key component has been to identify access to, and use of, a range of physical, natural, human, social and financial assets by individuals, households and communities. These assets are commonly associated with different types of capital: human, natural, physical, social and financial (see Table 3.1.1) – an approach that has been adopted by the Department for International

Table 3.1.1 Sustainable Rural Livelihoods Framework

Natural Capital	Land and environmental resources
	Private and communal property rights in land, pastures, forests and water
Physical Capital	Property and goods
Note: some asset frameworks have a separate category for infrastructure	Transport
	Machines and tools
	Domestic animals stocks
	Food
	Energy
	Communications (including ICTs and mobile phone access)
	Infrastructure e.g. access to water and sanitation
Human Capital	Labour provided by members of household and community comprising of different genders, generation and age, health and ability
	Education, qualifications and skills
Social Capital	Social resources such as networks, memberships of groups and support mechanisms
	Trust and reciprocity
	Diasporic networks – migration
	Cultural Capital (shared cultural or religious values; language and other markers of cultural identity)
Financial Capital	Income
	Savings (including jewellery)
	Access to credit
	Remittances
	Pensions

Source: adapted from Carney (1998)

119

Development's widely used Sustainable Livelihoods Framework (SLA) (Carney, 1998; Department for International Development (DFID), 1999; Ellis, 2000). The importance attached to social capital as a key asset for poor families will be discussed in more depth in Chapter 5.2. In addition, a household's rights in acquiring assets will also be influenced by a range of public and private sector structures and institutional policies, processes and freedoms, such as the ability to participate in community decision making or political mobilization. Multilateral agencies such as the World Bank embraced livelihoods perspectives in the 1990s, and they formed an integral part of their Participatory Poverty Appraisals (PPAs). Rural Livelihood approaches have also been modified for use in urban environments (Rakodi, 2002).

Despite its practical merits in targeting areas for combating poverty, the sustainable livelihoods approach has been criticized for failing to recognize the social and cultural bases for living, such as the role played by self-esteem, identity and aspiration in people's attitudes to making a living. Other shortcomings include an overemphasis on materiality and the propensity to perceive livelihoods as fixed and static, rather than fluid and shifting over time (Rigg, 2007). Many scholars now prefer to talk about livelihood 'transitions' while others propose that livelihoods should be seen in 'relational' terms, focusing more on the power relationships and negotiations between household members and different communities (Leach et al., 1999). As Rigg (2006) asserts, the reality of rural livelihoods today may be somewhat different from the traditional conceptions of rural living that have dominated academic and policy discourses over the last fifty years. While approaches may never be able fully to capture unpredictable events, he argues that seeing livelihoods as 'pathways' allows for a more dynamic understanding of the way they change over time (Whitehead, 2002). Indeed, rural communities in many parts of the global South have been increasingly separated from the land and traditional agricultural occupations as a result of neoliberal global forces and the blurring of rural–urban activities. Contemporary rural households are likely to engage in 'livelihood multiplicity', a diverse range of occupations and migration strategies in order to ensure survival and well-being (Wright, 2003). However, despite the gains made by participatory and livelihoods perspectives in poverty alleviation, the stark reality remains that many rural women still have very low levels of assets which makes them highly vulnerable to risk and uncertainty.

Bridging the Gender Divide in Rural Communities

One of the enduring obstacles for rural development projects in the global South has been the lack of recognition of the essential role played by women in contributing to agricultural production, livelihoods and resource management – a situation that Ester Boserup first identified back in 1970 (Boserup, 1970; Momsen, 2004; Jacobs, 2008). Although women in sub-Saharan Africa produce and market approximately three-quarters of domestic food (Robinson, 2004), women consistently have less access to the resources and opportunities they need to be more productive (see Chapter 4.1). A recent report by the FAO (Food and Agriculture Organization, 2010) states that women comprise 43 per cent of agricultural labour in the global South, ranging from 20 per cent in Latin America to 50 per cent in East Asia and sub-Saharan Africa. Yet women operate smaller farms, on average one-half to two-thirds the size of male farms, keep less livestock, and endure a greater workload that includes a higher burden of less productive activities such as fetching water and firewood. Women may lack access to resources due to the following factors:

121

- Less access to education, information, credit and finance
- Less likely to purchase fertilizers, new seeds and equipment
- More likely to be in insecure, part-time and low-paid jobs in the informal sector
- Receive lower wages for the same work as men
- Lack legal rights to land ownership and inheritance.

The report also states that if women had the same resources as men they could increase their yields by 20–30 per cent, raising agricultural production by 2.5 to 4 per cent in the global South and reducing the world's hungry population by 12–17 per cent. Initiatives to help address the gender gap include micro-credit, more equitable land rights and legal inheritance, and policies that mainstream social justice and gender equity. For example, land reform programmes have been increasingly undermined by structural gender discrimination in the enforcement of women's land rights, including the failure legally to recognize women as 'household heads' or as landowners, a situation that has further disadvantaged female smallholders (Jacobs, 2009). Research has also focused on the gendering of intra-household assets and the effect on intergenerational poverty (Kabeer, 1994; Chant, 2007a). Solutions to widespread rural poverty are not easy, but it is clear that the current gender gap in women's access to rural assets is undermining many efforts to engender sustainable livelihoods throughout the global South.

KEY POINTS

- Since the 1990s, livelihoods perspectives have played a crucial role in re-focusing development initiatives on local people and the diverse ways in which they make a living.
- An important way of understanding livelihoods has been to identify the variety of assets, and returns on them, held at the household, community and supra-community levels. These assets are often associated with five different types of capital: natural, physical, human, social and financial.
- Widespread gender discrimination in many rural communities is a major obstacle to poverty alleviation, agricultural production and ecosystem management. Closing the gender gap will require the mainstreaming of policies that are gender sensitive and empowering for rural women.
- Contemporary debates over global food security, environmental degradation and climate change will continue to benefit from rural poverty approaches that aim to understand the role of social justice, equity and livelihoods transitions in building sustainable communities at the local level.

122

FURTHER READING

Section 3, on rural development, in Desai and Potter's *Companion to Development Studies* (2008) provides a good introduction to many of the concepts explored in this chapter. Robert Chambers' book *Whose Reality Counts?* (1997) explores the conceptual and practical applications of participatory development, while Jonathan Rigg offers a critical discussion of rural poverty and livelihood transitions in the twenty-first century in *An Everyday Geography of the Global South* (2007). Further explorations into the gendering of rural livelihoods are provided by Nalia Kabeer's text *Reversed Realities* (1994) and the FAO's, *The State of Food and Agriculture Report* (2010), which provides a comprehensive review of the gender gap in rural development (available to download from www.fao.org/publications).

3.2 INDUSTRIALIZATION AND THE NEW INTERNATIONAL DIVISION OF LABOUR

Globalization and Industrialization in the Global South

In the last forty years, global work and employment patterns have undergone a multidimensional restructuring as a result of internationalization. Although it can be argued that world labour markets have been interconnected since the 1500s, the current form of economic globalization has involved a more rapid and intensive interplay between economic, political and social processes. As multinational corporations (MNCs) have looked across international borders to recruit cheaper and more submissive labour forces in a world that is hungry for work, there has been a significant reshaping of local labour markets in the global South. Consequently, academics and policymakers alike have argued that this New International Division of Labour (NIDL) has given rise to 'unprecedented market expansion and widespread disruption' (Mittleman, 1995: 273). However, the nature of this disruption and its impact on development is far from uniform as the intricacies of this spatial division of labour are complex and contradictory.

In an attempt to unravel the key processes that shape these outcomes, this chapter explores three key issues that have dominated academic and policy discourses on the NIDL and development. First, it examines the transitions in industrialization strategies employed by countries in the global South since the 1950s, and explores the factors behind the rise of global export-oriented production. Second, through a focus on gender, the chapter discusses whether the NIDL offers new opportunities for workers in the global South or rather exacerbates uneven spatial development and poverty. Finally, the chapter critically explores the responses of international agencies and businesses to alleviate the negative impacts of the global division of labour.

The World Market for Labour: Trends and Transitions since the Twentieth Century

Increasingly seen as contributing to uneven development and social polarization between people and places, economic globalization has evolved as a result of the internationalization of trade, production and consumption through a global shift in manufacturing since the 1950s (Dicken, 2007). During the aftermath of World War II, advanced industrial nations focused their production on the American-derived Fordist factory system, which was based on the standardized production of assembly goods and a rigid division of labour. At the same time, many countries in the global South were attempting to decrease their reliance on imported goods by adopting strategies of industrialization. This trend was closely associated with the policy of import-substitution, which aimed to increase self-sufficiency and reduce dependence on expensive imports. Key industrial sectors for development included food, drink, clothing, tobacco and textiles, with resource-rich nations also developing heavy industries in oil and steel. Import substitution was enthusiastically adopted but, despite some successes in large nations like India, increasing competition, combined with shortages in capital, technology and infrastructure, made import substitution difficult.

In the 1960s a number of developing nations abandoned import-substitution to embark upon export-oriented policies of light industrialization by means of making available fiscal incentives to attract foreign direct investment (FDI). The policy of 'industrialization by invitation', which was advocated by the Caribbean-born economist Sir Arthur Lewis, involved the establishment of branch plants by overseas firms in order to take advantage of cheaper labour costs. Also referred to as 'enclave industrialization', the approach is closely associated with the establishment of Free Trade Zones (FTZs) and Export Processing Zones (EPZs) and specialist industrial estates where trade is unrestricted and duty free. Within the EPZ, the host nation provides buildings and services, together with a package of incentives which usually includes freedom from local taxes and labour regulations. Flexible specialization, cheaper transportation and advances in global technology allowed corporations to be more responsive to market demands by adopting a just-in-time (JIT) system that allowed greater fragmentation of the production process and the employment of cheaper, semi-skilled labour outside of European and North American labour markets.

In the 1900s, the EPZs increased at unprecedented rates across Latin America, the Caribbean and Asia, as global brands like Disney and Nike sought to reduce labour costs and expand their market share. Partly fuelled by a retail revolution in the US, and advocated by the World Bank and IMF as a solution to the debt crisis of the 1980s (see Chapter 2.3), many countries in the global South had little choice but to open their borders to free trade, FDI and 'world market factories'. This promotion of export-oriented manufacturing in the global South, combined with technological advances and the demand for cheaper, unregulated labour by firms, provided the impetus for what became known as the New International Division of Labour (NIDL).

Labelled as 'footloose' (Safa, 1981), due to their ability to move around the globe in search of cheap, non-militant labour and tax incentives, vast numbers of global businesses relocated parts of their production process to developing countries; by 2003 there were 3,000 EPZs worldwide. Problems of structural unemployment and domestic recession resulted in increasing competition between Southern governments in order to attract FDI and export firms. Starting with Mexico, India, the Caribbean and Malaysia, firms were quick to expand into lower-waged nations like Vietnam, Indonesia, the Philippines and, more recently, China. Originally focusing on primary and low technology products such as minerals, oil and textiles, the NIDL saw a rapid transition to medium- and high-technology industries such as electronics, pharmaceuticals and data-processing in the 1990s. For example, primary products accounted for 45 per cent of Mexico's total exports to the US in 1998 but by 2008, medium–high technology products and services made up 60 per cent of its US$234b exports (Sturgeon and Gereffi, 2009).

125

In an attempt better to understand the inter-organizational networks that link households, businesses and states together in the global economy, Gereffi's (1994) work on global commodity chains provided the rationale for global institutions like the International Labour Organization (ILO) to explore the socio-economic impacts of the NIDL on workers in the global South. In particular, concern has focused on the flexible subcontraction chains that employ small-scale and home-based workers, often working informally in sweatshop conditions (see Chapter 3.3). Research also suggests that many of the world's 218 million child labourers and 27 million modern-day slaves are linked to profitable global supply chains in plantations, textiles and minerals. Underpinned by neoliberal strategies of free trade, privatization and deregulation, it has been argued that the success of the NIDL is attributable to a vast reserve army of cheap, willing and unregulated labour. A specific requirement by MNCs for a 'cheap, passive and nimble-fingered workforce' has also led to a feminization of the labour force in EPZs and global supply chains (Chant and McIlwaine, 1995; Standing, 1999). In the late 1990s it was estimated that around 80 per cent of global export workers were female, with employers having a preference for unmarried women under 25 years of age.

The latest phase in what many commentators now call the 'global division of labour' (Huws, 2007) has been the unprecedented drive towards outsourcing via global value chains in high technology goods and services. Labelled as the 'second global shift', the rapid growth of data-processing firms, information technology and financial services has characterized the latest phase of offshore development, particularly in countries with highly skilled workers such as India and South Africa (see Chapter 3.4). In 2008, the world's hundred largest MNCs together accounted for around four per cent of global GDP. Despite their importance, however, there has been a tendency to see corporate capital as the only significant agent in the global economy. In order to highlight the importance of local social processes, such as gender and class, many economic geographers prefer to use the term Global Production Networks (GPNs). This approach also emphasizes the existence of a wide range of non-corporate actors, such as NGOs and civil society organizations, community groups and trade unions that shape the everyday trajectories of individual workers in the global economy.

126

New Opportunities or 'Immiserizing' Growth? The Impact of the NIDL on Workers in the Global South

One of the main arguments in support of the NIDL as a tool for development is that it allows a much-needed reallocation of jobs, infrastructural upgrading, knowledge transfer and foreign currency from North to South. On the positive side, EPZs and global supply chains have created employment opportunities in the South, particularly for women. There is also evidence to suggest that offshore production has contributed to technological advances, some localized economic growth and the development of niche industries in the rapidly developing economies of Asia. Rigg (2007) notes that export-oriented production strategies have been more successful in Asia than in Latin America due to differences in national governance, local state involvement and worker militancy. Despite widespread concerns over working conditions, the NIDL has provided some women with new work opportunities that have enabled them to earn higher wages, return to education, and gain some social mobility. As Freeman (2000) asserts, the offshore data-processing industries of the Caribbean provide young women with an alternative to arduous agricultural work and the chance to save towards small business development. However, it is often only more educated and skilled female workers that have been able to take advantage of the new opportunities, and research suggests that such work can increase the 'triple burden' on such women in undertaking paid labour, reproductive responsibilities and community care (see Chapters 4.1 and 4.3).

According to the ILO (2010), 'vulnerable employment' is characterized by inadequate earnings, low productivity and a lack of social protection. Despite the fact that there were 3,500 EPZs employing 66 million workers worldwide in 2008 (ILO, 2010), the NIDL has only provided a fraction of the jobs needed to tackle a global vulnerable employment rate of 1.6 billion workers. Profits from export industries are also largely accumulated outside the host nation with little trickle-down in terms of wealth and development in the local economy. New jobs are often deskilled, hazardous, insecure and highly competitive, with coercive management structures and poor worker rights in many regions (Mackinnon and Cumbers, 2007). In the 1990s, the 'Maquiladora' (factory) plants along the US and Mexican border were synonymous with environmental pollution, poverty and exploitation (Potter and Lloyd-Evans, 1998). The negative consequences of economic globalization, and in particular the social and environmental costs associated with the NIDL, have increasingly been highlighted by Non-Governmental and Civil Society Organizations (Oxfam, 2004). The last decade has also been witness to huge public discontent with global capitalism as media coverage of sweatshop labour, child workers, and modern-day slavery, has led international institutions to question whether the global expansion of labour markets has shaped development outcomes for the better.

127

Table 3.2.1 Job Losses in Export Manufacturing Industries since 2008

Country	Industrial Sector	Job Losses (around 80% female)
India	Clothing and Textiles	700,000
Philippines	Export Processing Zones	20,000
Sri Lanka	Garments	30,000
Cambodia	Garments	30,000
Nicaragua	Export Processing Zones	16,000

Source: Oxfam, 2009: 5

These debates have drawn particular attention to the exploitative articulation of female labour in the global South (Afshar and Barrientos, 1999), with women more likely to be engaged in low-paid, insecure and exploitative work in both the formal and informal economies (Carr and Chen, 2004). In particular, the emergence of a largely female, impoverished and unregulated workforce linked to insecure home-based or home working in global supply chains has prompted organizations like Oxfam (2009) to identify women workers as the 'development engine' behind global capital accumulation. Kaplinsky's (2000) argument that greater economic activity has in reality led only to 'immizerising growth' for the majority of workers is particularly salient in the current economic climate. In a recent report, Oxfam argues that the 2008 global financial crisis is having a devastating impact on women working in export manufacturing as they are the first to be laid off by employers, often with pay outstanding (see Table 3.2.1). As supply chains are squeezed by falling demand, the World Bank predicts that 22 million women will lose their jobs in 33 countries in the global South over the next few years, about half of them in sub-Saharan Africa.

128

Rights, Responsibilities and Social Protection

As argued, the benefits of globalization which were promised to much of the global South, namely formal job creation through FDI and export-oriented production, have in reality led only to a rise in insecure and low-paid contractual work. In response, notions of global civil society (see Chapter 5.2) and corporate citizenship have intertwined to engender a new geo-political force of 'contested globalization' that places social justice at the heart of the agenda (Sadler, 2004). The focus of anti-globalization movements on multinational corporations, due in part to a backlash against widely advertised worker exploitation in campaigns such as Oxfam's 'Make Trade Fair' advocacy and 'Let's Clean up Fashion', have provoked governments and the business community to re-address workers' rights through Corporate Social Responsibility (CSR). Despite scepticism over the real impact of CSR, there is a move towards new alliances between local, grassroots movements and more top-down programmes on international labour standards driven by the ILO, to promote global economic democracy, gender equity and the introduction of a 'living wage' for workers. For example, a grassroots workers' organization 'Homenet' has been working with the UK's 'Ethical Trading Initiative' and the 'Clean Clothes Campaign' to explore possibilities for protecting homeworkers linked to the global fashion industry. Improving workers' rights, including their right to unionize, is seen by many agencies as the fundamental goal of social protection (Kabeer, 2008b). Although there are voluntary international codes of conduct for MNCs, such as the United Nation's 'Global Compact', many NGOs argue for compulsory regulation for businesses   129 that govern wages, working conditions and rights (see Chapter 3.5). The overarching goal of such a policy approach should be to mainstream *gender sensitive* and *participatory programmes* that take into account the diversity of roles and responsibilities of workers in different spaces of the global economy.

'Footloose Capital' in a Hungry World

A global neoliberal consensus driven since the early 1990s, which rewards capital relative to labour, has empowered multinational corporations over workers, leading to a global cheap labour economy. As this chapter has highlighted, the NIDL has simultaneously marginalized and pauperized many vulnerable workers while providing opportunities for others. In her analysis, Huws (2007) uses the metaphor 'defragmenting' to describe the contemporary global division of labour, whereby units of human skill and knowledge are broken down into increasingly interchangeable units and then combined and reconfigured across countries. While the NIDL exacerbated uneven spatial development between the North and South in the 1990s, it is increasingly argued that the contemporary division of labour has started to cut across these traditional divides. Part-time, unregulated and low-paid jobs also characterize sectors of advanced economies while due to the importance of the emerging BRICS (Brazil, Russia, India, China and South Africa) and the resulting multi-polarity taking place in international development, South–South investment in export industries has increased. Furthermore, rates of internationalization and FDI are slowing down, resulting in widespread factory closures, redundancies and unemployment, which will serve to reconfigure labour markets once more. As the gendered implications of the global recession are only just becoming apparent, it looks as though the devastating impact of the retrenchment of global export production on livelihoods and workers' rights looks set to frame development agendas over the next decade.

KEY POINTS

130

- Global work and employment patterns have undergone a multidimensional restructuring as a result of the internationalization of economic production. As a result, many workers in the global South have become increasingly linked to the 'footloose' global networks of MNCs.
- The promotion of export-oriented manufacturing in the global South, combined with technological advances and the demand for cheaper, unregulated labour by firms, provided the impetus for what became known as the New International Division of Labour (NIDL) and, more recently, has been labelled by some commentators as the 'Global Division of Labour'.
- One of the key characteristics of the NIDL has been the widespread feminization of the labour force in export factories and home-based or outputting work in global supply chains.
- In seeking to understand the impact of the global division of labour on poorer nations in the South, it is important to remember that the outcomes of economic globalization are geographically uneven and embedded in local social processes. While export industries have provided jobs and new employment opportunities for some workers, they have exacerbated the vulnerability and exploitation of others through the deregulation of labour standards.

- The outcomes of the NIDL are also highly gendered, and there is consensus that it is low-skilled female workers embedded in global supply chains working for meagre piece rates with no rights, that have gained the least from economic globalization.
- International agencies and NGOs are placing increasing pressure on MNCs to be more socially responsible and work towards the universal goal of providing social protection and decent work.

FURTHER READING

Good introductions on the impacts of the NIDL on the global South are provided by Williams et al. (2009) *Geographies of Developing Areas* (Chapter 4) and Mackinnon and Cumbers' *An Introduction to Economic Geography, Globalization, Uneven Development and Place* (2007). A more theoretical analysis of the gendering of export-oriented production is given by Afshar and Barrientos in *Women, Globalization and Fragmentation in the Developing World* (1999), while more recent research can be found in Oxfam's 2004 report, *Trading away our rights: women working in global supply chains* (download available from www.oxfam.org.uk) and Naila Kabeer's (2008a) essay in the IPC's *Poverty in Focus*, Issue 13, on 'Gender Equality'. Ruth Pearson's (2007) article in *Third World Quarterly* provides critical reflection on gender and CSR.

3.3 DECENT WORK, RISK AND THE INFORMAL SECTOR

Globalization, Decent Work and the Informal Sector

The 'informal sector' refers to a heterogeneous group of activities and employment relationships that share one common characteristic – the lack of legal recognition, regulation or protection. The sector encompasses a diverse range of activities from street trading and micro-enterprise to home working, service provision and domestic labour. In the last ten years, the informal sector has experienced unprecedented growth as labour force expansion has outpaced employment opportunities in many nations. As explored in Chapter 3.2, the reality of the contemporary global economy is that a majority of the workforce in the global South are employed in high risk, casual, home-based or own-account work in the informal economy, escaping government regulations and social legislation. Recent estimates by the International Labour Organization (ILO) suggest that the informal sector accounts for one half to three-quarters of non-agricultural employment in most countries of the global South: 51 per cent in Latin America and the Caribbean, 65 per cent in Asia, and 72 per cent in sub-Saharan Africa. When informal employment in agriculture is added, the proportion increases substantially in all regions, increasing the figure from 83 per cent to 93 per cent in India alone.

There are now well-established links between the informal sector, poverty and vulnerability worldwide (Chant, 2008; Kabeer, 2008a). Indeed, poverty and inequality, however defined, are inextricably linked to the availability of secure and decent work. The ILO defines 'decent work' as employment opportunities that are accompanied by 'rights, protection and voice'. Given the increasing vulnerability of the world's 184 million unemployed and 550 million 'working poor', particular attention has focused on the increasing numbers of informal female workers who are trapped in part-time, insecure, home-based or outputting work linked to global supply chains (see Chapter 3.2).

Thomas (2002) argues that globalization has increased informal employment in three main ways: through top-down processes such as the removal of labour market protection and increases in part-time, casual work; through jobless growth as a result of new technologies; and via bottom-up informality, which results from increased numbers of workers seeking informal jobs. As a result the livelihood strategies of many households across the global South are increasingly characterized by risk and insecurity (see Chapter 3.1). Given recent transformations in global labour markets which have restricted well-paid, regulated and secure work, there is evidence that working conditions and labour relations once found in the informal sector have expanded into much of the formal economy worldwide, a trend that has given rise to a reconceptualization of the informal sector over the last decade (Kabeer, 2008b).

133

Reconceptualizing the Informal Sector in the Global South

It was in the light of growing underemployment and the lack of 'modern jobs' that theoretical debates began to focus on the dualistic structure of Third World economies after the Second World War. In the 1950s, it was argued by economists such as Arthur Lewis that Third World cities could be characterized by a dualist structure comprising two separate economies: a 'traditional', 'backward' and 'unproductive' economic sector and an 'advanced', 'modern' and productive sector. Dualist interpretations provided the framework for the informal–formal sector dichotomy in the 1970s and advocates regarded the traditional economic sector as the major barrier to development, one that would be eradicated once prosperity had been increased by industrial modernization.

A breakthrough in the negative interpretation of this traditional sector stemmed from a series of research 'missions' by the ILO in the 1970s. The mission to Kenya changed the focus from unemployment to a more positive interest in the 'working poor' and Keith Hart coined the sector 'informal' in 1973 in order to highlight it as a haven for creative entrepreneurs. While dualist perspectives have been criticized for failing to recognize the ways in which the economic sectors are inextricably linked, the premise that economies can be broken down into two or more segments has endured. From the 1980s onwards, the idea of an informal–formal continuum along which all economic activities take place has gained support.

Given its heterogeneous character, it is very difficult accurately to define what constitutes the informal sector in any nation. One way of understanding the huge body of literature on definitions is to differentiate between traditional approaches which have focused on the 'enterprise' and more recent interpretations that focus on the individual 'worker' (Lloyd-Evans, 2008a).

Traditional Enterprise Perspectives – Size, Legality and Mode of Production

In the 1970s, traditional definitions of the informal sector focused on the nature of the business. From an enterprise perspective, definitions of informal activities have focused on three main factors: enterprise size, legality and the mode of production, although there is considerable overlap between them:

- **Size** – many enterprise definitions started with the premise that informal operations are 'micro' or small-scale consisting of less than five workers, although size alone is a limited characteristic given the abundance of small-scale formal businesses and the recent surge in larger informal enterprises.
- **Legality** – it is the unregistered and untaxed element of the informal sector that has been at the centre of most past and present definitions. Informal enterprises tend to exist outside the regulatory state apparatus and they are rarely registered, licensed, taxed or subject to statutory labour force regulations or social protection laws. De Soto's controversial book, *The Other Path* (1989), viewed the Peruvian informal sector as a response by the poor to the bureaucratic power of the state and its excessive regulatory framework. He argues that the informal sector consisted of 'plucky micro-entrepreneurs' who choose to operate informally to avoid the costs of formal registration and legislation. Non-regulation by the

State represents the fundamental difference between formal and informal activities for many researchers and policymakers today, including the ILO.

- **Mode of Production** – stemming from the structuralist school of thought, radical commentators like Moser identified the mode of production as the decisive factor in identifying informality. The sector was seen to employ a non-capital-intensive mode of production, exploited by capitalism and the formal sector through the transfer of economic surplus. Based on the Marxist concept of 'petty commodity production', and the 'theory of unequal exchange', the informal sector is seen to be a *reserve army of labour* willing to work at subsistence levels. Anyone observing women and children working in the home-based enterprises in global supply chains would argue that there is still much truth in this assertion.

Drawing on these approaches, the ILO adopted a simplified long-standing definition of the informal sector in 1993 that referred to employment and production that takes place in small, unregistered enterprises. While enterprise-based definitions were widely used by governments and international agencies to the end of the twentieth century, they were criticized for being gender-blind (Scott, 1994) and failing to capture recent trends in the global economy. New perspectives have sought to extend the definitional focus from enterprises that are not legally regulated to employment relationships or workers that are not legally regulated or protected, and they emphasize the blurring of boundaries between the informal and formal sectors.

135

Informal Relationships: Worker-centred Definitions, Gender and Hierarchies of Risk

In seeking to include the entire spectrum of informality, new perspectives centre upon the employment relationship or social relations of labour rather than merely the enterprise. The revised definition focuses both on enterprises that are not legally regulated and on employment relationships that are not legally regulated or protected in either the informal or formal economy. Here the informal sector is seen to be highly segmented according to location of work, production system and employment status, and to be composed of groups of skilled entrepreneurs, own-account workers, industrial outworkers and home-based producers, unpaid family labour and a wide range of casual and waged employees who have no formal contracts, benefits or social protection. In 2002, a group of researchers and activists, including the global research policy network, Women in Informal Employment: Globalizing and Organizing (WIEGO), worked with the ILO to broaden definitions of the informal sector to incorporate informal waged employment and homework that had been previously excluded. The ILO now prefer to use the term 'informal economy' instead of 'informal sector' in recognition of the need to include waged workers as well as own-account or self-employed workers (Chant and Pedwell, 2008). Using this definition, the ILO estimate that between 60 to 70 per cent of informal workers are self-employed or 'own account' with the remaining 30 to 40 per cent comprised of informal waged workers in both informal and formal businesses.

This worker-centred perspective has allowed a reappraisal of the composition and causes of informal employment, and has reasserted the role played by gender in shaping the structure and agency of informal workers within a hierarchy of poverty and risk. Although the informal economy is not a female-dominated sector overall, over 60 per cent of female workers in the global South work within its boundaries. Chen et al. (2006) have attempted to provide a more gender-sensitive model by illustrating the multi-segmented structure of the informal labour force with particular attention paid to the location of the working poor through a graphic depiction of an 'iceberg' divided into six segments. At the bottom of the triangle is the least visible and lowest waged segment comprising female homeworkers and low-paid own-account workers, with the higher earning self-employed operators and employers at the top. The iceberg also highlights a marked gender gap in earnings and status, with women overrepresented in the lowest half of the segment and with men predominantly at the top. Home-based workers and street vendors are two of the largest sub-groups of informal workers, accounting for 10–25 per cent of non-agricultural employment in the global South. In 2005, UNIFEM found that women are more likely than men to work as own-account workers, domestic workers and unpaid labourers in family business. Although gender differentiation can arise from structural disadvantages such as lower levels of education and skill, inequitable access to productive and financial assets, and household responsibilities (see Chapter 4.1), women often choose self-employment as a positive way of balancing their reproductive and market roles over the lifecycle (Chant and Pedwell, 2008).

136

Towards an Integrated Approach to the Informal Economy: Risk, Gender and Labour Relations

In an attempt to capture the informal sector's gendered and socio-spatial diversity previously discussed, it can be useful to employ an integrated approach (Lloyd-Evans, 2008a) which broadly classifies informal workers into four tiers according to their motivations for working informally, their labour relations, gender and risk, with the added premise that there will be changes over the life-course (see Figure 3.3.1):

- subsistence workers
- small-scale entrepreneurs and traders
- petty capitalists
- criminal operators.

First, there is the existence of *high-risk subsistence workers* who tend to be found in the lowest paid and most insecure jobs in the informal sector and in unregulated components of the formal sector. The prime motive of production is subsistence, rather than profit, and the sub-sector may include homeworkers (both employed and own-account), domestic labourers, low profit or dependent street vendors, irregular waged labourers, and unpaid family and child labour. Work is often arduous, low paid, insecure and risky, and includes occupations like sweet-drink sellers, garbage pickers and piece-rate producers. Some workers will have no choice in entering this type of work as they may lack the education, skills or resources required to access better jobs. Another unifying characteristic is the extent to which this type of work is gendered, as a majority of workers in this group will be female.

137

The second tier comprises a heterogeneous group of *small-scale entrepreneurs, petty-commodity entrepreneurs, petty-commodity traders, own-account workers and traders,* who primarily engage in the informal sector as a livelihood strategy but one that can offer additional benefits in terms of independence, flexibility, and risk aversion. Small-scale entrepreneurs may choose to work in this sector in order to meet family responsibilities or utilize a creative talent. Typical workers in this category are street traders, artisans, informal commercial importers, food sellers and some home-based producers where the unit of organization is family or kinship based, with some control over the means of production. Unequal access to micro-credit, training and infrastructure opportunities can

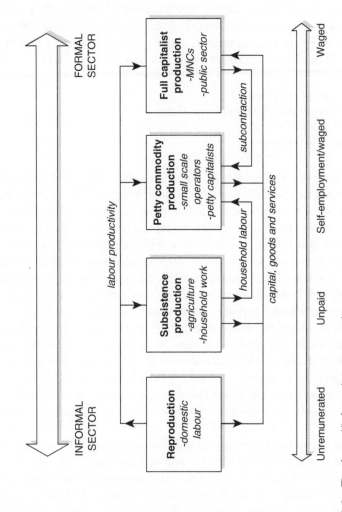

Figure 3.3.1 The formal/informal sector continuum

limit the growth potential of female-maintained businesses but women's engagement in both the subsistence and entrepreneurial tiers is highly fluid, with workers moving between the two according to processes of gender subordination, life stage and generation.

A third tier is a haven for the *most successful entrepreneurs*, who are also likely to be employers of insecure waged labour. The main occupants of this sector could be termed 'petty capitalists', as their main aim for establishing an informal business is the extraction of profits, which may be greater than in the formal sector. The avoidance both of taxes and of compliance with employment legislation such as minimum wages, hours and conditions, attracts many successful entrepreneurs to the informal sector. Many petty capitalists will employ casual waged labour, including children, in unregulated conditions to produce goods at low cost for both internal and global markets. As discussed in Chapter 3.2, the global supply chains of many multinational retailers can often be traced back to informal businesses in the global South. Such elements of the informal sector are well organized, dynamic and profitable, and now include recycling, Information Technology (IT), and media enterprises, as well as more traditional industries such as food and textiles.

139

One of the most hotly debated topics related to this part of the informal economy has been the increasing incidence of child labour in the global South (see Chapter 4.2). Increased awareness has escalated the issue of child labour as a priority for global institutions concerned with human rights, social justice and civil society in the twenty-first century. The ILO estimates that 218 million children aged 5–17 can be classified as child labourers with the 5–14 age group constituting 166 million. Child labour takes many forms, from paid work in factories and other forms of waged labour like street trading, to bonded domestic labour and prostitution. Although a fundamental reason why children work is poverty, child labour is also seen to be a consequence of neoliberalism and unequal trade resulting from economic globalization. However, many commentators argue that the concept of child labour is misunderstood and grounded in Western notions of childhood that have resulted in misguided policy initiatives to ban child labour (see Chapter 4.2).

The inclusion of a fourth tier is controversial, as many commentators argue that there is a distinct difference between the informal and illegal sectors of the economy. In his original classification, Keith Hart distinguished between legitimate informal enterprises, and illegitimate service and transfer activities such as smuggling, prostitution and petty theft. In the twenty-first century, it is difficult to ignore the growing incidence of *criminal operators* engaged in drug smuggling, theft, extortion, forced labour, human smuggling and prostitution, who are also likely to invest in the informal sector. Recent concern over the rapid growth of the human trafficking industry, which the UN estimates is worth £16 billion globally, fuels a supply of forced – mainly female – labour to the sex trade and industrial sweatshops (Shelley, 2007). Hence, there are tenuous boundaries between the exploitation of women and children in informal outworking businesses and global trafficking. Indeed, the failure of governments and agencies to protect the world's most vulnerable workers has opened up new spaces of exploitation that make it difficult to disconnect the informal sector from criminal networks in forced and trafficked labour.

Assisting Informal Workers in Old and New Spaces of the Informal Economy

140

New worker-oriented and gendered definitions of the informal sector, which encompass unregulated waged, home-based and even forced or trafficked labour, have reawakened an interest in the informal economy from a decent work and social justice perspective. Research suggests that poverty and vulnerability for many workers, particularly women, are more likely to be defined by the nature of their employment relationships rather than whether their work is situated in the informal or formal sectors of the economy per se. While traditional policies aimed at supporting the informal sector have focused on supporting entrepreneurs through the provision of micro-credit, training and small business development, recent policy analysis focuses on two interlinked objectives: the development of an appropriate regulatory framework which focuses on social protection for informal workers and a series of complementary development policies that include access to services, assets and entitlements in order to reduce intergenerational poverty. As will be discussed in Chapter 3.4, new technologies and the Internet can play a key role in mobilizing support for exploited workers in the global economy.

- The informal sector, or informal economy as it is more recently known, is an important provider of livelihoods for many workers in the global South, and it accounts for over 50 per cent of non-agricultural employment in many countries of the global South.
- The sector refers to a heterogeneous group of activities and relationships that lack legal recognition, regulation and social protection.
- Definitions of the informal economy are highly contested but conceptual approaches towards the informal sector have evolved from a focus on the *enterprise* to more recent *worker-focused* perspectives that encompass unregulated and vulnerable workers in the global economy.
- Recent perspectives, which suggest that there are multiple gendered divisions cutting across traditional informal–formal sector divides, have argued that women are often concentrated in the lower echelons of the economy. Research has also highlighted the importance of agency and generation in understanding women's informal work.
- Policies to support the informal sector include micro-credit and small business development, the ILO's decent work agenda and initiatives by Non-Governmental Organizations and Civil Society to engender social protection (see Chapter 5.2).

141

A good starting point is Sylvia Chant's essay, 'The informal sector and employment' (2008), in Desai and Potter's *Companion to Development Studies*, which provides an overview of recent trends and policy initiatives. A more in-depth analysis of past and present concepts of the informal sector is provided by Lloyd-Evans' article, 'Geographies of the contemporary informal sector: gender, employment and social protection' (2008) in *Geography Compass*. An extensive collection of recent academic articles and policy research on the gendering of the informal economy, including work by Martha Chen, can be downloaded from WIEGO: *Women in Informal Employment: Globalizing and Organizing* (www.wiego.org).

3.4 THE DIGITAL ECONOMY AND NEW SPACES OF WORK

New Digital Economies, Cities and the Global South

Recent transformations in the dispersal of information and communication technologies (ICTs) in the global South are closely tied to wider processes of globalization, urbanization and power. According to recent projections, 61 per cent of the world's population will be living in cities by 2030, with cities in the South growing four to five times faster than in the developed world. As economic, social and political life in the twenty-first century will become increasingly digitized, cities will continue to act as sites of capital accumulation and centres of diffusion for knowledge, technology and information (Lloyd-Evans and Potter, 2009). A key element of the global ICT business has been the development of linkages between the world's cities and their importance as nodes for flows of information, services, and finance (Sassen, 2002). Transformations in the international commodification of digital products and services (Scholte, 2000) have shaped flows of information and knowledge around the world, connecting some people and disconnecting others (Castells, 2001).

Although the revolution in ICT has undoubtedly facilitated faster and stronger networks between people and places, the outcomes of this revolution are geographically uneven (Perrons, 2004). By providing a critical discussion of the impact of the digital revolution in creating new spaces of work and livelihood opportunities for communities in the global South, the chapter explores the profound impact of ICT transitions in addressing the development goals of the twenty-first century. As previous chapters in this section have focused on the ways in which shifts in the agricultural and industrial sectors of the economy have impacted upon livelihoods, this chapter starts with a focus on the new service economy and the processes of digitization that have created new spaces of work in the global South.

Global Services and Off-shoring: New Spaces of Work

From the late 1990s onwards, advances in ICT technologies enabled MNCs to outsource substantial components of their businesses in order to take advantage of cheaper labour and tax incentives. Originally centred on the provision of data-processing and back-office services such as credit card billing, sales and reservations, payroll accounting, and claims processing, offshore industries created routine, automated and labour intensive jobs in politically stable, English-speaking regions like the Caribbean. Typical examples of this work include health services and insurance in the Caribbean, shipping and legal services in the Philippines, telephone call centres in India, and pharmaceutical research and development in China. In the latest wave of development, firms like Amazon have invested in software development in South Africa and France was reported to have outsourced US$35 million of call-centre and transcription work to subcontractors in Morocco and Tunisia. The global division of labour in IT industries is also changing, with hardware being produced in Malaysia and Taiwan, software enterprises developing in India and China, and back-office services relocating to Brazil and South Africa. The rise of the Asian computer gaming industry is creating new innovative work opportunities for local youth, including the trading of 'in-game currencies' (potions or armour) to wealthy global consumers in multiplayer games like 'World of Warcraft' (Heeks, 2008).

143

Back-office and data-processing industries often have a preference for young, female labour as a result of the gender stereotyping of routine tasks as 'women's work', discussed in Chapter 3.2. In the 1990s, 90 per cent of Jamaica's data-processing labour force was female. The extent to which data-processing firms have provided new opportunities for women in the global South has been a topic of intense discussion within academic and scholarly circles (Perrons, 2004; Pearson, 2007). While some commentators have identified offshore industries as sites of capital exploitation due to a long-hours and low-pay culture, others have argued that high tech industries can provide social mobility for women as they offer better employment prospects than agriculture or the informal sector. As previously discussed in this section, Freeman's (2000) work highlights the popularity of high tech occupations for women in the Caribbean and indentifies these industries as sites of agency for some young women. More recently, there is evidence of a changing gender division of labour within the off-shoring industries due to the latest wave of high value ICT and media industries that employ highly skilled workers, many of whom are male.

One of the most widely publicised and controversial strategies has been the movement of call centres from the global North to countries such as India and South Africa. Although development gains have been seen in terms of jobs, income, economic diversification and foreign capital creation, the wider external benefits to countries may be limited. Although the development of India's IT sector has added a significant amount to growth and export revenues in the country, much of the development has been in fortified enclaves like Bangalore's Information Technology Park (Graham, 2002). Poorer communities are unlikely to gain directly from enclave developments as the majority of service industries, like call centres, are foreign owned and employ educated and middle-class urban workers. Indirect benefits may arise from increases in the demand for unskilled domestic and manual labour to service executive households and businesses, although the exploitative relations of employment that link poor workers to the global service economy can hardly be termed 'development'. The low cost service economy often employs migrants, women and other vulnerable workers in insecure and exploitative conditions (see Chapter 3.3). However, there have been other recent transformations in ICT, often termed the 'digital revolution', which may bring more direct benefits to marginalized and disenfranchised communities in the global South.

ICTs and the Global South: The Digital Divide

Back in the 1990s, Friedman talked about a 'techno-apartheid' that divided the world into 'fast' and 'slow' worlds. Although ICT was predicted to be a 'magic bullet' for development, traditional projects were often expensive, inappropriate and reliant on non-existent infrastructure such as electricity and telephone landlines. While earlier patterns of global ICT penetration could partly be explained by the traditional 'core–periphery' model of development, as the geography of telecommunications networks tended to be linked to the location of offshore capital and urban elites, recent evidence suggests that digitization is destabilizing these traditional geographical polarities (Moriset and Malecki, 2009). The 'digital revolution' in ICT, which refers to the introduction of new digital media platforms like the Internet, Wireless technologies and 3G mobile phones, provided a major turning point in the application of ICT for development purposes. Much of the contemporary work exploring the impact of ICT in the global South has focused on the inequalities of ICT diffusion which has produced a 'digital divide' between the global North and South, and within countries and cities. The rapid spread of digitized information and communication technologies has the potential to engender widespread changes in labour mobility, social networking, production and knowledge transfer, although the intersection of socio-economic status, age, gender, generation and geography tends to increase the gap between the information 'have mores' and those who 'have less'. One of the most important characteristics of the global digital divide has been the capacity of different media platforms in connecting poor, isolated communities.

145

Internet Access in the Global South

Much of the literature on the digital divide has focused on the continued existence of a N–S divergence in Internet access. Although the Internet has been an important tool in mobilizing new social movements and enabling communities to campaign on social justice and human rights issues, its overall impact has been limited in some regions. Until recently, the reliance on Personal Computers (PCs) and fixed telephone lines for accessing the Internet has restricted access in the poorer countries of the world. Country averages for fixed line telephone services have reached 60 per cent in Europe, but only 30 per cent in the global South and 10 per cent in the world's 'least wired' region – Africa. Although two billion people now have access to the Internet worldwide, only 21 per cent of people in the global South are online. Regional figures mask internal disparities within nations as South America's Internet access ranges from 80 per cent in Argentina to under 30 per cent in Bolivia and Peru. Although Internet penetration in Africa has dramatically increased since 2006, only 9.6 per cent of Africans were online in 2010. Of these, less than 1 per cent had fixed line Internet access compared to 40 per cent in Europe, the Americas and Oceania. Solutions to solving the digital divide for PC and Internet users have included:

- Community access points, such as rural 'telecentres' or street kiosks, which help poor communities access banking and financial services, telemedicine and education
- Technical innovations in developing more robust and environmentally appropriate hardware, including low cost and low power consumption laptops
- Projects like the 'One Laptop One Child' programme, which aims to supply schools with cheap PCs that run on Open Source Software (OSS)
- Cooperatively owned IT enterprises, such as the Kudumbashree project in Kerala, India, that helps disadvantaged women offer IT services to the public sector. The project aims to empower women through job creation and saving schemes (www.kudumbashree.org).

146 Structural barriers to Internet projects have included the high cost of hardware/software, a lack of infrastructure and local expertise, the dominance of English-speaking language and content, and issues relating to governance and censorship. Despite advances in the diffusion of Internet networks across many parts of the global South, mobile phones rather than PCs are more likely to bring about greater social change.

The Mobile Phone 'Revolution'

The explosive growth in the mobile phone industry in the global South, driven by new affordable and accessible technologies, is leading an ICT revolution among the poorer communities of the world. In 2010, 73 per cent of all new mobile subscribers came from the global South, and mobile penetration rates for Africa were predicted to reach 41 per cent by the end of the year (compared to the global rate of 76 per cent). Furthermore, mobile connections in the 48 Least Developed Countries have risen by 28 per cent in the previous decade. Advances in wireless technologies have opened up a realm of new possibilities for connecting remote rural communities to a range of local education, health, employment and financial services. Mobile phones dominate the African ICT network, and as 65 per cent of Africans now live within reach of a wireless voice network, mobiles are the single largest platform for delivering government services in isolated rural villages. Mobile technologies can also help communities build social capital and tackle issues related to social exclusion (Overa, 2006); additionally, businesses like Facebook are developing strategies to provide zero-cost access to some of Africa's poorest nations. Other initiatives include the use of mobile phone games by NGOs to raise awareness of HIV and AIDs among African youth (see Chapter 4.3).

Significant attention has also been focused on the potential for mobile phones to address the financial needs of people who are currently unbanked or financially excluded. As mobile phones are part of everyday lives, they have the potential to become a low-cost delivery channel for financial information, electronic transfers and micro-credit. Mobile banking is rapidly expanding in sub-Saharan Africa and South Asia, and its capacity for accessing remittances and low value 'person to person' transactions has huge implications for livelihoods (Cracknell, 2004; Overa, 2006). However, the financial needs of the rural poor are diverse and issues relating to trust, risk and cultural norms often 147 prevent uptake. While there is evidence to suggest that mobiles are reaching into some of the poorest communities, factors such as cost, electricity and wireless coverage still present barriers for many disadvantaged communities and households (Norris, 2001). As mobile phones are often used as a communal rather than a personal resource, further research and investment is needed to develop low-cost, shared access models and what some commentators term 'Blackberrys for development'.

ICTs and Development

New technologies have proved to be useful tools in enabling poor households to collect electronic remittances and access government services, create new virtual communities for political mobilization, build social capital, and engage in grassroots democratization. Labelled by policy practitioners as 'ICT4D', some of the most innovative uses of ICT in the South occur in social development.

Examples of ICT-based development programmes include:

- The Grameen Bank's funding of mobile phone exchanges, operated by rural women in rural Bangladesh, although evidence suggests that the poorest households are still unable to use these services.
- Wireless-enabled mobile phones in Senegal that help farmers obtain market prices for fruit and vegetables.
- Indian online public sector services, including rural employment schemes that foster self-governance through transparency. However, illiteracy is a still a major barrier in realizing the potential for such schemes.

In order to further global development agendas, ICTs will need to be adapted to suit local pockets, operate in a wide range of environmental conditions, support multiple language translation and develop more locally suitable content. NGOs are playing a major role in promoting the use of mobile phones in their social development projects and in building partnerships with global IT corporations to deliver low-cost initiatives (see Chapter 5.2), although state support remains essential for delivering infrastructure and addressing issues of regulation and governance.

148

The openness of global digital infrastructure means that countries in the global South may finally have the capacity to access and adapt ICT to suit their own agendas (Boas et al., 2005). Despite the so-called mobile revolution taking place within low-income communities, however, the digital divide still exists on a range of spatial and social scales. Although it is not yet possible to predict the precise outcome brought about by digital ICT, the largest gaps in the global South tend to be between young, affluent, urban men and older, poor, rural women. The ultimate challenge will be to find ways of diffusing new technologies throughout disadvantaged rural communities, empowering them to drive local development agendas and reducing information poverty.

KEY POINTS

- The new information economy has provided new labour market opportunities in the global South, but the impacts on poorer communities in the global South have been widely contested.

- Society wide transformations have been made in ICT in the last few years but the social diffusion of ICT networks has produced a digital divide between the global North and South, and within countries.
- Increasing attention has been paid to the impact of the ICT 'revolution' on development, but the outcomes are still unclear as wide disparities exist in the diffusion of the Internet and other digital platforms as a result of the intersection between socio-economic status, age, gender and geography.
- The current mobile phone revolution is transforming the IT landscape in the global South and it has the potential to empower disadvantaged communities by facilitating better access to local services, democratization and social networks.
- ICTs may well have the capacity to drive local development agendas but new innovative approaches are required to mainstream access in the world's poorest communities.

FURTHER READING

Diane Perron's book, *Globalization and Social Change: People and Places in a Divided World* (2004), provides a detailed discussion of the impact of the new ICT economy on communities in the global South, while Pippa Norris offers a more detailed analysis of poverty and the digital divide in *Digital Divide: Civic Engagement, Information Poverty and the Internet* (2001). A special issue of the journal *Studies in Comparative International Development* (2005, 40, Summer) examines the impact of the digital divide on development in the global South and recent case studies on a range of ICT and development-related issues, including mobile phones and telecentres, can be found by accessing the online *Development Informatics Working Group Papers*, edited by Richard Heeks, at the Institute for Development Policy and Management, University of Manchester (download available from www.sed.manchester. ac.uk/idpm/research/publications/wp/di/).

3.5 GLOBAL TRADE, AID AND REGULATION

Global Trade and Aid in an Interdependent World

In 1980, the Independent Commission on International Development Issues (1980) published its famous report *North-South: A Programme for Survival,* which emphasized the interdependency of the world economic and political system and advocated a set of global solutions to the problems facing many countries at the time. Famous for the iconic map that divided the 'rich North' from the 'poorer South', the Commission fundamentally believed in a substantial redistribution of resources from North to South, mainly via trade, aid and more effective global governance (Potter and Lloyd-Evans, 2009). This chapter discusses the extent to which these visions have been addressed over time, first through a brief discussion of international development aid and, secondly, through an analysis of recent transformations in global trade.

International Development Aid

International development assistance still plays a key role in global interventions concerned with growth, poverty and inequality. Foreign aid from official sources to developing countries amounted to around US$103 billion in 2006 and over $2.3 trillion over the past fifty years (Easterly and Pfutze, 2008). Official Development Aid (ODA) is at the centre of foreign aid, and is largely provided by country members of the Development Assistance Committee (DAC), although NGOs like Oxfam also contribute around US$6 billion per annum (Burnell, 2008). Aid can be given in several forms: commodities, food, loans, finance, technical cooperation, debt relief (see Potter et al., 2008) or emergency aid. While there is a general consensus that emergency or disaster aid is necessary in an unstable and interconnected world, development aid has long been criticized as a neocolonial tool that increases the dependency of poorer nations on the West for three main reasons.

First, development assistance has often been 'tied' to economic or political objectives that serve the interests of donor countries. The practice of conditionality, whereby aid or loans come with a set of specific actions like trade liberalization, has often been employed by multilateral agencies like the World Bank and IMF (Cho, 1995). Secondly, scholars, agencies and governments increasingly question the effectiveness of the 'aid business' in tackling the fundamental causes of poverty and inequality. Enduring problems include a lack of transparency, corruption, the ineffective channelling of resources through tied aid, the misappropriation of aid for military spending, and fragmentation of the aid effort across small bureaucratic agencies worldwide. Increasingly, development experts have argued that official aid agencies are not set up to work with poor communities and they argue that a grassroots approach to administering aid is urgently overdue (Mitlin and Satterthwaite, 2007).

Thirdly, the geography of ODA is constantly changing according to prevailing global economic and geo-political agendas. While the dawn of the twenty-first century brought a new lease of life for international aid, driven by the Millennium Development Goals (MDGs) and pledges by some European governments to double aid efforts in the poorest nations of the world, the 2008 global financial crisis has changed the playing field once again. In a recent move by the UK government to realign aid spending with national security interests, the UK will focus upon efforts to improve world security in war-torn countries like Afghanistan, Somalia and Yemen, while other nations like Burundi, Cambodia, Liberia and Iraq will see their aid budgets severely reduced. The conditional and insecure nature of international aid has led many neoliberal proponents to argue that 'freer' trade, rather than aid, has greater potential to eradicate poverty and reduce global inequalities in the twenty-first century.

151

Global Trade, Aid and Development: the Key Debates

In the last half century, the world has witnessed a significant shift in attitudes towards international trade and economic development by moving towards a reduction in tariffs and restrictions on trade

(Greenaway and Milner, 2008), but it is increasingly argued that rules governing world trade are rigged in favour of the world's richer nations. Although there is a substantial body of literature that critiques the most effective ways to manage and regulate international trade (Stiglitz and Charlton, 2005), debates over the relationship between trade and development have tended to focus on three main issues: the role of the World Trade Organization (WTO) in regulating global trade; the extent to which trade liberalization acts as a driver or barrier to development in the global South; and the free trade versus fair trade approaches to tackling global inequalities.

Global Governance: the World Trade Organization (WTO)

The immediate aftermath of World War II saw the introduction of the General Agreement on Tariffs and Trade (GATT), which was a multi-lateral forum created to reconstruct the world economy via free trade and economic growth in 1947. GATT was founded on four main principles (Gwynne, 2008: 201): non-discrimination, reciprocity, transparency, and fairness; it was replaced in 1994, however, by the World Trade Organization (WTO) following the Uruguay Round of trade negotiations which highlighted the need for a more democratic and stronger institution with similar legal powers to the United Nations. The central goals of the WTO are to improve access to, and security of, international markets for its member states. In 2008 the WTO had 153 member countries, two-thirds of which were from the global South; however, critics like Oxfam argue that their interests are still marginalized due to their dependency on trade in primary products and the alignment of the WTO with the interest of corporate capital (Narlikar, 2005).

In its defence, the WTO argues that it helps countries in the global South by safeguarding their interests through policies on anti-dumping, technical assistance and trading support. For example, the WTO's *Agreement on Trade-related Aspects of Intellectual Property Rights (TRIPS)* has focused on increasing access to generic HIV drugs in sub-Saharan Africa. The WTO also argues that the *Doha Development Agenda (DDA),* launched in 2001, places development firmly at the centre of the international trade agenda. The DDA requires countries of the global South to undertake further steps towards trade liberalization, which the WTO argues will help them achieve greater economic development. However, negotiations have broken down since 2008 due to disagreements over agricultural imports and subsidies. Led by India and Brazil, many poorer nations have campaigned to get rich countries like the US to remove farm subsidies and import tariffs that penalize developing countries. The protectionist agricultural policies adopted by the European Union (EU), for example, can lead to the stockpiling of food surpluses and the subsequent dumping of products in the global South, a process that destabilizes local food markets and prices. The increasing resistance by India, Argentina, Brazil and China against unequal trade liberalization strategies in the North could finally be signalling a shift in the traditional power base of the WTO.

Trade Liberalization and Development

Trade liberalization is the broad term given to the removal of trade tariffs and restrictions deemed necessary if countries are to follow the principles of free trade (Murray, 2006). Tariffs are the taxes paid on the value of imported goods at the point of entry into the importing country, and they are seen as a major barrier to global free trade. Non-tariff trade barriers can include quota limits on the quantities of items that may be imported, such as cars or electrical items. Neoliberal supporters argue that free trade has the capacity to promote economic growth and eliminate poverty in every country; as a result trade liberalization policies have been heavily promoted in the global South by a range of multilateral institutions, including the IMF and the World Bank. Trade reforms, such as tariff reductions, the elimination of quota restrictions, relaxation of import licensing or the removal of protectionist strategies, have been routinely applied in countries undergoing Structural Adjustment Policies. In the 1990s, a surge of regional trade agreements and Free Trade Associations including the European Union, North American Free Trade Association (NAFTA), Association of Southeast Asian Nations (ASEAN), and the Common Market of the South (MERCOSUR), were also introduced to promote free trade between regions. The creation of the North American Free Trade Association (NAFTA) in 1994, a free trade zone comprising the US, Canada and Mexico, was welcomed by American businesses searching for cheap, unregulated labour but criticized for reducing wages and labour standards in Mexico.

Trade liberalization may have served to increase foreign exchange earnings and levels of Foreign Direct Investment (FDI) in export-oriented

153

industries across Asia, Africa, Latin America and the Caribbean (see Chapter 3.3), but it has also increased unemployment, reduced real wages and removed domestic food subsidies. Contrary to Brandt's vision, the version of trade liberalization adopted by the WTO has largely accrued benefits to MNCs and the richer countries of the global North. A recent report from War on Want (2009) provides detailed evidence on the significant job losses experienced by the majority of the countries in the global South following thirty years of free market enterprise and trade liberalization. By directing the rules of international trade towards the needs of more powerful nations, many NGOs argue that both the 'rules' and the 'playing field' are inherently unfair for countries in the global South – a belief that has fuelled anti-globalization protests over the last decade.

Empowering Producers in the Global South: 'Fair Trade not Aid'

The free trade ideology promotes the import and export of goods without any barriers, but the extent to which international trade is actually 'free' or unfettered is a highly contentious topic. In reality, higher income countries are often reluctant to open up their markets to imports or reduce subsidies on products where low-income countries have an advantage (Stiglitz and Charlton, 2005). Recently, the European Union has been negotiating Economic Partnerships Agreements (EPAs) with 76 former colonies in Africa, the Caribbean and the Pacific (ACPs) in order to promote greater market access to new and existing markets in the global South. In the past, the EU has been strongly criticized for maintaining preferential historical agreements with ACP countries, a situation that led to the long and bitter 'banana wars' between Europe and the US over the export of non-ACP bananas to Europe. EPAs will allow the EU to maintain preferential trading agreements but they will require Southern nations to reciprocate by fully opening their markets to EU exports. Critics like Action Aid argue that EPAs will continue to exacerbate poverty in poorer countries as they will be forced to open up their markets to floods of cheap manufactured imports, subsidized agricultural products and further economic domination by global business.

Research on global commodity chains in products like coffee (Bacon, 2005) has highlighted the exploitation of small farmers by large MNCs, who frequently undercut prices in a 'race to the bottom' (see Chapter 3.1).

Small-scale family farms produce over 70 per cent of the world's coffee in 85 countries across Latin America, Asia and Africa and falling coffee prices have destabilized rural livelihoods, prompting many NGOs to advocate 'fair trade' as a more sustainable alternative. Fair trade, which developed as part of the 1960s movement for 'trade not aid', is defined as a trading partnership based on dialogue, transparency and respect, that seeks: greater equity in international trade; guarantees producers a 'fair' price for their products above world market price and stable supply relationships; access to credit; and a social premium for community development projects. In return grower co-operatives must be democratically organized, use the social premium for the benefit of its members, and commit to improving environmental conditions (Raynolds et al., 2007).

The popularity of fair trade food products like coffee, bananas and chocolate has grown markedly since the 1990s, and in 1997 attempts to standardize the movement internationally were undertaken by the Fairtrade Labelling Organization (FLO). In 2006, FLO was working with 6,569 Fair Trade Certified Producer Organizations and over 1.4 million farmers and workers in Africa, Asia and Latin America. Although many commentators argue that fair trade should be viewed as a resistance to the hegemony of an unequal global trading system, others state that as fair trade products only account for a small percentage of global trade, they fail significantly to challenge structural inequalities. There are also concerns that the recent mainstreaming of fair trade products by super-markets signifies a 'selling out' by fair trade organizations to corporate business as they may lose sight of their political principles and commit-ments to challenging unfair global relationships (Goodman, 2004). Despite much scepticism over the corporate exploitation of the fair trade label, the movement has continued to gain popularity in the UK and is seen by many as a better alternative to free trade and aid.

KEY POINTS

- Trade and aid are important tools for redistributing wealth between the global North and South, but they have been criticized for exacer-bating poverty and dependent development.
- Overseas development aid is decreasing in real terms, and there are concerns over the ineffectiveness of aid flows since the 1970s due to issues relating to conditionality, misappropriation and fragmentation.

- Free trade is seen by many multilateral agencies as the most effective way of addressing poverty in the global South but critics argue that trade liberalization has reduced employment and decent work in the global South.
- The WTO has governed world trade since 1995, and its overriding objective is to keep global trade flowing freely and securely by removing obstacles and barriers, but it has been criticized for rigging the terms of international trade in favour of richer nations and corporate business.
- The Fair Trade movement connects small-scale producers in the South with consumers in the North, in order to address the inequalities of the global system. Despite its popularity, there is concern that fair trade will fail to challenge neoliberal trade relations in order to achieve sustainable development in the long term.

FURTHER READING

Sound introductions to trade and aid can be found in Desai and Potter's *Companion to Development Studies* (2008), particularly Burnell's chapter on 'Foreign aid in a changing world' (Chapter 10.1) and Gwynne's discussion of 'Free trade and fair trade' in Chapter 4.4. A more detailed critique of the local impacts of economic globalization and free trade on the global South is provided by Chapter 4 in Warwick Murray's excellent text on *Geographies of Globalization* (2006), while detailed evidence on the impact of trade liberalization on employment is presented in War on Want's (2009) report, *Trading Away Our Jobs: How free trade threatens employment around the world* (download available from http://www.waronwant.org/campaigns/trade-justice/more/inform/ 16486-trading-away-our-jobs. Accessed 29.05.11). Further information on the relationship between fair trade and development can be found in Stiglitz and Charlton's, *Fair Trade for All: How Trade Can Promote Development* (2005).

Section 4
People, Culture and Development

INTRODUCTION

This section of the book focuses on people's everyday lives in the global South and helps to contextualize many of the theoretical and empirical issues discussed in the previous chapters. Drawing on grounded research from a range of contexts, we explore how people's lives are entwined with processes of development, culture and inequality from the micro- to the macro-levels. Placing people's everyday lives at the centre brings questions of poverty, inequality and difference sharply into focus. Such an approach clearly reveals the multidimensional nature of poverty and the ways this is linked to axes of social difference and inequality, including gender, age, disability and ill health, sexuality, race and ethnicity among other factors. The concept of intersectionality, which emerged from feminists' engagement with questions of difference, is particularly useful in exploring the ways that a range of markers of social difference intersect and interact throughout the lifecourse (Hopkins and Pain, 2007). Each of the chapters in this section takes a different dimension of social difference as its starting point: gender, childhood and youth, disability and ill health, sexualities, and ageing. However, it is important to acknowledge that people's experiences related to a particular marker of social difference (e.g. gender) intersect with other social inequalities and differences (e.g. age, disability and/or sexuality) and these interactions shape their ability to avoid poverty and participate in development processes.

Starting from people's everyday lives in the global South also enables us to recognize the ways that people exercise 'agency' and actively participate in, and contribute to 'development'. This approach, underpinned by the influential work of Amartya Sen (1999), Robert Chambers (1997) and others, helps to shift the discussion away from colonial and modernization development paradigms that view people as 'victims' and 'objects' of development towards perspectives that recognize people as 'social actors' who have dignity and who exercise at least some degree of agency and 'independence of action' (Rigg, 2007: 10). Women, men and children in rural and urban environments constantly adapt to their circumstances, manage vulnerabilities and diversify their livelihood strategies to break the cycle of poverty (Chambers, 1997).

Increasingly, international development discourses are moving away from welfare approaches that focus on 'needs', to rights-based approaches that recognize the entitlements of different social groups to express their views about matters affecting them and actively participate in decision-making processes – from the micro-level of the household to the macro-level of international policy arenas. Although many challenges remain in achieving meaningful participation in practice, each of the chapters in this section provides an overview of changing approaches to women, children, youth, disabled people, sexual minorities and older people within international development and human rights discourses in recent decades.

Starting from the micro-scale and people's everyday lives also enables us to explore questions of 'the body', or rather 'bodies' (reflecting the diversity of embodied experiences). Development policymakers and practitioners, to date, have been reluctant to engage explicitly with embodied experiences, such as disability, chronic illness, sexuality and ageing. However, a growing body of work by geographers and other social theorists has explored the cultural politics of bodies and places and the interconnections between these. We live our lives and experience places through our bodies, which are 'read' and positioned in different ways by broader sociocultural, economic and political processes. As Nast and Pile (1998: 4) argue: '(b)odies and places are woven together through intricate webs of social and spatial relations that are made by, and make, embodied subjects'. This section seeks to provide insight into the connections between embodied social identities and development, such as the marginalization of disabled people and sexual minorities in a range of cultural contexts.

These overarching themes are explored throughout the five chapters in this section. Chapter 4.1 discusses changing approaches to gender within development policy and planning over time and provides insights into key concepts used to analyse gendered power relations. These include social reproduction, the gendered division of labour and intra- and inter-household relations. Such analyses of power relations are also helpful in understanding the socio-economic position of children and youth, which forms the focus of Chapter 4.2. Although children and youth receive a great deal of attention within international development goals, they are often constructed as 'passive' and their contributions to their families and societies are overlooked. Chapter 4.2 discusses children's rights and global constructions of childhood and youth and provides an overview of recent policy and research about the paid and unpaid work, and education and transitions to adulthood that young people are engaged in.

Health concerns also form a key element of recent development agendas, but universalizing biomedical approaches often exclude disabled people and fail to acknowledge the structural inequalities that restrict access to healthcare. Chapter 4.3 provides an overview of policy approaches to disability and ill health, exploring disability politics, rights discourses, and cultural approaches to health and illness in relation to HIV and AIDS in Africa. Questions of the 'body' and the dominance of biomedical discourses also form the focus of the following chapter. Chapter 4.4 discusses the links between sexualities, poverty and marginalization and reveals how violations of sexual rights and poor sexual and reproductive health are central development concerns.

The importance of understanding the relational nature of people's lives is also demonstrated in the final chapter. Chapter 4.5 provides insight into life-course perspectives that analyse the situation of older people according to generational relations and life transitions over time. The challenges of population ageing in countries in the global South are explored, alongside policy responses.

161

Although it is beyond the scope of this section to explore some dimensions of social difference (such as race, ethnicity and religion) in any detail, we hope that when read together, the different chapters provide a helpful overview of key concepts, debates and development discourses, helping to place people's lives – in all their complexity – at the heart of cultural and development processes in the global South.

4.1 GENDER, HOUSEHOLDS AND DEVELOPMENT

Shifts in Thinking about Gender in Development Policy and Planning

By the 1970s, disenchantment with modernist approaches to development led to the emergence of a range of radical approaches to development, as noted in Chapter 2.2. This included the recognition that women's views, interests and experiences were an essential part of the development process that could no longer be ignored. Thinking about the links between gender and development has shifted over time. The first approach, Women in Development (WID) was largely inspired by Ester Boserup's (1970) critique of the ways that women had been left out of economic development and her calls for women's contributions to development to be recognized. In this approach, specific projects were developed, focusing primarily on what were considered 'women's issues' in inequalities in the labour market and often resulting in women-only income-generation projects. Many of the projects providing access to credit were unsuccessful and, in many ways, the approach reinforced the modernist development ideology that saw development only in terms of economic growth (see Chapter 1.1 and Chapter 2.1).

Growing criticism of the failure of WID to challenge international structures of inequality and to recognize women's work in both the public and the private domains led to the second approach, Women and Development (WAD). WAD drew on the radical ideas of dependency theory, which focused on the unequal relationship of 'dependency' between the 'developed' and 'underdeveloped' worlds within the global capitalist system (see Chapter 2.2). WAD analysed the ways that development shaped inequalities in women's paid and unpaid work within exploitative global capitalist relations of production. Both WID and WAD approaches, however, were criticised for tending to treat all women as a single homogeneous group – regardless of differences of social class, race, ethnicity, age, religion, disability and so on – and for focusing only on women's roles. Feminists increasingly highlighted the inadequacies of WID and WAD in analysing gender relations (the socially constructed form of relations between men and women) and how development may influence these.

From the 1980s, a greater focus on gender relations led to the third approach, Gender and Development (GAD). Informed by socialist feminist perspectives, this approach saw gender as socially, rather than biologically, constructed. As Momsen (2004: 2) explains, gender refers to 'the socially acquired notions of masculinity and femininity by which women and men are identified' and varies in different cultural contexts. GAD aimed to analyse the gendered division of labour within the public and the private spheres and transform unequal power relations between men and women. GAD viewed women (and men) as active agents rather than as passive recipients of 'development' and attempted to understand holistically the social, cultural, economic and political structures and institutions that perpetuate gender inequality (Young, 1997). Since the Fourth World UN Conference for Women in Beijing in 1995, the GAD approach has had a major influence on the agendas of mainstream development institutions such as the World Bank. Promoting gender equality and empowering women is now a key development priority, reflected in one of the eight overarching Millennium Development Goals (see Chapter 1.5).

163

Despite the relative success of GAD in mainstreaming gender issues within development, feminists in the global South and others have argued that the radical feminist goals of the original movement have become diluted and the approach has not adequately challenged dominant modernist and neoliberal ideologies. Further criticisms include a lack of attention to difference and diversity among women and to men's roles and identities. Feminist geographers have highlighted the importance of place and space in influencing gender relations and ideologies, emphasizing the need to contextualize local practices within specific socio-economic, political and cultural contexts.

The UN Vienna Conference on Human Rights in 1993 and the international ratification of a growing number of UN human rights treaties, including the Convention on the Elimination of Discrimination against Women (CEDAW), has resulted in greater recognition of women's human rights and the violence perpetrated against women, especially in situations of armed conflict. 'Rights-based approaches' have been used as the basis for campaigning on women's reproductive and sexual rights, and their rights to freedom from rape and other forms of gender-based violence and conflict. Criticisms of rights-based approaches include the fact that the focus tends to be on anti-discrimination measures rather than on promoting gender equality and that achieving women's human rights is difficult to translate into practice at the local level.

While the GAD approach tries to ensure that women's and men's views and interests are integral to the design and implementation of development interventions, commentators have argued that greater attention needs to be focused on involving men in tackling gender inequalities and deconstructing stereotypical representations of men and masculinities. These arguments relate to wider global concerns about a perceived 'crisis of masculinities' due to conventional male patriarchal authority being undermined in a range of contexts. Factors influencing this include the rapid increase in women's participation in the labour market, male unemployment and the increasingly informal, flexible and low paid nature of employment opportunities globally (both dimensions are often termed the 'feminization of labour'; see Chapter 3.2); growing numbers of households headed by women; increasing gender-based violence against women and girls; and trends towards lower educational attainment for boys and young men.

Masculinities approaches acknowledge that development has often failed to take account of men's roles and identities as gendered individuals, that not all men enjoy a patriarchal position of privilege, and that specific groups of men may be particularly marginalized by 'development'. This has led to greater efforts to 'engender' the development process by analysing both men's and women's differential positions, interests and participation (McIlwaine and Datta, 2003). However, a renewed focus on men's rights has been met by apprehension from some feminists who are concerned that a shift away from women's specific needs and rights, while they still generally occupy a lower socio-economic status than men in many societies, could lead to further exclusion of women from the development process.

Social Reproduction and the Gendered Division of Labour

Women, gender and development approaches have revealed the importance of analysing women's roles in social reproduction and the gendered division of labour that exists within households. Social reproductive work refers to activities that are carried out to maintain and care for families (Momsen, 2004). In most countries, these activities are performed predominantly by women and girls. Although notions of 'femininity' vary in different cultures and are historically and geographically contingent, in many societies, domestic and care work are often regarded as part of women's and girls' 'natural' roles as nurturers and homemakers. Time use surveys from many different countries have shown that women tend to work more hours than men and, as their involvement in paid work increases, men often do not increase their share of the unpaid housework and childcare (Momsen, 2004). Women living in rural areas in the majority world often have a higher work burden than those living in urban areas, due to reduced access to household services such as running water, electricity and gas for cooking. Gender and development proponents have argued that women undertake triple work roles within the family and community:

165

- **Productive work** – that brings in a cash income, including work in the formal or informal sector, agricultural labour for cash crops, the sale of produce or other goods.
- **Reproductive work** – care and maintenance of the household, childcare, food preparation, care of the sick, health, education and socialization of children, subsistence agriculture for food consumption.
- **Community management** – maintaining kinship ties, social networks with neighbours, carrying out religious, ceremonial and social obligations in the community, including participation in development initiatives.

Women are often seen as responsible for maintaining good relations with kin, neighbours and others in the community through their participation in social activities, events and development initiatives. The identification of this role through gender analysis was important in terms of valuing women's (and men's) time contributions to development projects and advocating for payments to compensate participants for their loss of time for productive and reproductive work. Furthermore, research from a range of urban and rural contexts has shown that women often rely on these social support networks as a key survival strategy when they face financial pressures.

Research has revealed the importance of analysing the interaction between the productive and reproductive spheres, since women often combine work which brings in a cash income with childcare and domestic duties. In rural households in sub-Saharan Africa, for example, women often combine their reproductive roles in producing food for the household and caring for their children, with their productive roles in selling any surplus in markets, producing cash crops and working as an unpaid family labourer on male household members' land (which are often cash crop fields). Despite estimates that around 70 per cent of Africa's food is produced by women, development interventions have tended to assume that farmers are male and have targeted agricultural extension services towards men.

Intra- and Inter-Household Relations

Although the terms 'family' and 'household' are often used interchangeably, it is important to understand the differences between these concepts in order to analyse gender and generational relations in particular cultural contexts. Varley (2008) suggests that households can be defined as 'task-oriented residence units', characterized by the following features: co-residence; economic cooperation; reproductive activities and socialization of children. 'Families' on the other hand are 'kinship units that need not be localized' and, indeed, family members may reside in different places at some distance from each other while still retaining kinship ties and responsibilities across space. Feminists sought to open up the hidden, private space of the household and expose the assumptions that underpinned classical economic models of the 'unitary household'. Such models assumed that households were monogamous nuclear family units headed by a male breadwinner. The 'unitary household' model tended to assume that households were characterized by cohesion, harmony and shared group preferences, and that income was pooled between men and women to meet the consumption needs of the family.

These models, however, took no account of women's triple work roles and failed to recognize the complexity of intra- and inter-household relations between kin and community members. Research in the global

South has shown that many of these assumptions about 'unitary households' are not borne out by the evidence. In many countries in Africa and Asia, a significant proportion of households are characterized by extended family structures rather than nuclear families, although nuclear family and women-headed households are becoming more common, in response to rapid processes of urbanization and economic change. Rather than being static residential units, many households in the global South are characterized by fluid structures and change over time, as family members move to live with other relatives and migrate for work, studies and care over the life-course. Households are usually linked in to extensive social networks and reciprocal flows of resources and assets between rural and urban areas, with household members regularly giving and receiving material, practical and emotional support to and from extended family members, neighbours and friends, and fulfilling kinship and communal responsibilities and inheritance practices.

Rather than being characterized by altruism and harmony, intra-household relations and decision-making processes are frequently characterized by unequal power relations and conflicting interests. Patterns of income earning, resource allocation and expenditure within households vary significantly according to gender and other sociocultural differences, which affects the well-being of children and other family members. In many countries around the world, research has shown that women generally spend a higher proportion of their income on family consumption and invest more in children's education and health, resulting in lower malnutrition rates and higher school enrolment rates, particularly for girls; while men tend to spend more of their income on personal expenses. Furthermore, in rural and urban areas in sub-Saharan Africa, Western notions of a male breadwinner with overall control of resource allocation are inappropriate; men's and women's incomes are not usually pooled and they have separate budgets, investments and different responsibilities for household expenditure. While men are responsible for housing the family, women are largely responsible for food production, cooking materials and children's clothes. Children's education and medical costs are usually a joint expenditure.

Women-headed households are often assumed to be poorer due to higher numbers of dependents (children and elderly or disabled relatives they care for), lower incomes and time pressures due to women's productive and reproductive roles. However, Momsen (2002) and Chant (2007a) have argued that the notion of woman-headed households in the global South as 'the poor of the poor' is a myth. They suggest that

167

targeting development interventions exclusively to female-headed households is highly problematic for a number of reasons, including the differential positions of women living in de jure and de facto female-headed households. De jure woman-headed households (where women are legally regarded as the head of the household due to the death of a male partner/relative, divorce or separation) are likely to be underrepresented in official statistics due to the fact that surveys rely on self-reporting and women may face social stigma if they are legally recognized as being divorced, separated, never married or widowed. De facto women-headed households (where a husband/male relative is absent for extended periods of time or is not considered to fulfil the role of male breadwinner due to disability or unemployment) may in practice receive remittances from migrant husbands or other relatives. The emphasis on household headship also ignores the financial, productive and reproductive resources that other co-resident family members, including children, contribute to households. Furthermore, gender discrimination in resource allocation and/or gender violence within male-headed households may be just as, if not more, detrimental to women and children than living in a poor female-headed household.

168   Amartya Sen's (1987; 1999) model of household resource allocation as characterized by 'co-operative conflict' rather than by 'altruism' and 'cohesion' is useful in understanding the complexity of intra- and inter-household relations. Sen argues that gender divisions within the household mean that men and women do not have the same entitlements and cannot negotiate resource allocation on an equal basis, due to differing perceptions of self-interest, self-worth and contributions to the household that are defined by cultural norms and traditional inequalities. Women with low social and economic status generally occupy a weak bargaining position in household allocations and entitlements, but are able to achieve a higher status through their involvement in paid work outside the household. Women who earn an income are regarded as making a greater contribution to the household and thus occupy a better fall-back position should negotiations break down. Drawing on these ideas, Naila Kabeer (1994) has pointed out that inequality is not confined to the household, but is reproduced across a range of institutions, including the state, the market, the community and family/kinship. Kabeer's social relations framework (in which the goal of development is human well-being) seeks to analyse gender inequalities in the distribution of resources, responsibilities and power, and to develop 'gender aware' policy and planning.

- The links between unequal gender relations and development have been increasingly recognized within development policy and planning.
- Promoting gender equality and empowering women is a key development priority and is one of the eight MDGs (see also Chapter 1.5).
- Women often have triple work roles within the family and community, comprised of productive, social reproductive and community managing roles.
- Social reproductive work within the household, such as domestic tasks, care of children and older or disabled relatives, subsistence agriculture and so on, is usually carried out by women and is often undervalued in both society and development policy and planning.
- Households are often characterized by unequal power relations and conflicting interests that result in women's and children's limited involvement in decision-making processes and inequalities in access to resources.
- Household members' access to resources is also influenced by wider social relations in rural and urban areas, alongside communal expectations and responsibilities that are institutionalized at a range of spatial scales.

169

Momsen's second edition of *Gender and Development* (2004) and Varley's essay, 'Gender, families and households', in Desai and Potter's second edition of *The Companion to Development Studies* (2008) provide helpful introductions to gender, households and development in the global South. Part 2 of Visvanathan et al.'s *The Women, Gender and Development Reader* (1997), focuses on 'Households and Families'. Chapters 5 and 10 of Kabeer's *Reversed Realities: Gender Hierarchies in Development Thought* (1994) provide in-depth discussion of gender and household economics and the social relations approach. McIlwaine and Datta's article, 'From feminising to engendering development' (2003) in *Gender, Place and Culture* provides a good overview of changing approaches to gender within development policy and planning, while Cornwall et al.'s *Feminisms in Development: Contradictions, Contestations and Challenges* (2007) contains feminist analyses of a range of contemporary development issues and concerns.

4.2 CHILDREN, YOUTH AND DEVELOPMENT

Children's Rights and Global Constructions of Childhood and Youth

Children occupy a prominent position in human rights and development discourses and anti-poverty targets are often measured explicitly in indicators of child mortality, health and education by the UN, World Bank and other development agencies. The UN Convention on the Rights of the Child (UNCRC, 2012), introduced in 1989 and rapidly ratified by all countries except the US and Somalia, provides a framework of universally applicable standards for safeguarding children's rights, while many of the MDG targets refer to children's health, education and welfare (see Chapter 1.5). However, despite the rhetoric of 'putting children first', there is evidence that child poverty and violence towards children appear to be increasing globally – often at a faster rate than poverty among adults (Edwards, 1996). Meanwhile, older children and youths are often regarded as a 'threat' to the social order due to high levels of youth unemployment and their potential engagement in 'risky' behaviour, violence and political unrest.

Such understandings have led to the marginalization of children and youth from 'adult' decision-making processes, from the micro-level of the household to macro-development planning at regional, national and international levels. Parallels have been drawn between the 'invisibility' of children and youth in development policy and planning and the situation of women forty years ago, when their contribution to development was largely ignored. Since the 1970s, scholars across the social sciences have critiqued development policy, planning and research that have constructed children as passive 'human becomings', failed to listen to their views or recognize their contributions to society. Childhood researchers have demonstrated children's competencies to express their views and participate in decision-making processes, argued that the perspectives and life worlds of children and youth are worthy of study in their own right, and have sought to deconstruct global and local discourses of childhood and youth.

The UN Convention provides a universal framework of rights to provision, protection and participation in the 'best interests of the child'. While the global focus on children's rights and, in particular, recognition of children's rights to express their views in all matters affecting them (Article 12) has been welcomed, researchers have revealed how the Convention conflicts with sociocultural understandings of childhood and the lived realities of children and youth in the global South. The rights discourse promotes a universal model of childhood, based on Western ideals, that has become globalized through international development and human rights discourses and national policies (Boyden, 1997). Western ideals of childhood are often based on notions of children's innocence, vulnerability and needs for education and socialization in preparation for their future adult lives. From this perspective, children need to be 'protected' from 'adult' responsibilities, exploitation and harm; they should be cared for predominantly by parents within the family home, and spend most of their time in full-time education, recreation and play.

Such ideals of childhood bear little resemblance to the lives of children and youth in the global South, where many children are expected to contribute to the household economy from an early age, where the living arrangements of children are characterized by a diversity of household forms and where there is limited public social protection to prevent child poverty. Children who do not conform to these understandings of childhood are constructed as 'Other' and are perceived as the focus for rescue, rehabilitation and intervention (Wells, 2009). The UN has identified some categories of children as particularly vulnerable, including 'street and working children', 'children affected by armed conflict', 'trafficked children', 'disabled children', and 'orphans and children made vulnerable by HIV/AIDS'. While recognition of the needs of children is important in enabling them to access support, researchers have also revealed the dangers in constructing particular groups of children and youth as 'different' and 'at risk' when measured against a single, universal model of childhood. Researchers call for greater recognition of the plurality and diversity of global childhoods that are historically and geographically contingent, showing how age intersects with other social identities such as class, gender, disability, race, ethnicity and urban–rural differences.

171

The UNCRC is based on an individualized notion of the child, rather than recognizing the communal value systems of many societies in the global South and the ways that children's lives are embedded in relationships with their families and communities. Boyden (1997) argues that the influence of Western discourses of psychology, social work and law on global and national social policy has resulted in an emphasis on individual remedial solutions and less attention being paid to the social structural inequalities that disadvantage people. Furthermore, the Convention is based on Western notions of the nuclear family that emphasize biological parents' primary responsibility to meet the child's needs, constructing non-nuclear families as deviant, despite the fact that these often constitute the majority of family forms in the global South (Stephens, 1995). Similarly, while the Convention addresses child military service, which mostly affects boys, it fails to mention child marriage, which mostly affects girls.

The UNCRC age-based definition of the 'child' as any person below 18 years of age is also problematic and overlaps with the commonly accepted UN definition of 'youth' as young people aged 15–24 (United Nations, 2007). The concept of 'youth' is often associated with Western understandings of an in-between phase between childhood and adulthood that is marked by young people's socially expected transitions to becoming an 'independent', 'responsible' and 'productive' adult, such as the completion of education, entry into the labour market, moving out of the parental home, marriage and establishing their own families. In many societies in the global South, young people's transitions to adulthood may be viewed as a series of gradual stages marked by life-course events – such as initiation rites, marriage or childbirth – rather than being defined according to age or entry into the labour market. The involvement of children and youth in 'unchildlike' activities (Aitken, 2001) deemed to be morally or physically harmful and usually associated with adulthood, such as hazardous work, violence, armed conflict or prostitution, poses a fundamental challenge to global notions of childhood.

The UNCRC definition of the 'child' may also conflict with national laws and policies that allow young people to engage in consensual sexual relations, marry or work, for example, at age 15 or 16. Furthermore, age is often used as the criterion for particular categories of children to receive assistance and support as specified by international donors, development agencies and immigration policies; this often results in gaps in service provision and protection for youth aged 18 or over who

172

may be equally as in need of assistance as those aged 17 years or under. 'Unaccompanied' young people who have been orphaned, displaced or who are seeking asylum outside their country of origin often face difficulties in providing proof of age and demonstrating their entitlements to assistance when they lack birth registration or identity documents, or parents/adult relatives who can advocate on their behalf.

Children, Youth and Work

The involvement of children and youth in work from a young age represents a key feature of many childhoods in the global South that conflicts with universal models. From the 1990s onwards, global concern about children's involvement in employment that harms their health, development and reduces their access to education has led to concerted international efforts to eliminate child labour, led by the International Labour Organization (ILO). The overall proportion of children involved in child labour globally has declined over the last decade, with an estimated 215 million children involved in child labour (ILO, 2010b). However, these global figures mask considerable differences between regions, genders and ages. The largest number of child labourers live in Asia and the Pacific; however, sub-Saharan Africa has the highest levels of child labour as a percentage of the child population, with over a quarter of children (25.3 per cent; 65 million) involved in child labour, compared to 13 per cent (113.6 million) in Asia-Pacific and 10 per cent (14 million) in Latin America and the Caribbean. While the number of children (aged 5–14) working declined in all other regions from 2004–2008, it increased sharply in sub-Saharan Africa. Reasons cited for the high levels of child labour in sub-Saharan Africa include historical and cultural influences, the impacts of structural adjustment, economic restructuring and rapid growth of the informal sector in the poorest world region, the large youthful population and the effects of HIV- and AIDS-related adult ill health and mortality (Bass, 2004).

Despite high profile anti-sweat shop campaigns and consumer boycotts of global fashion brands due to child labour concerns in recent years, the majority of child labourers globally continue to be unpaid family labourers working in agriculture (60 per cent of working children aged 5–17 in the world work in agriculture, 25.6 per cent in the service sector, 7 per cent in industry, 7.5 per cent not defined: ILO, 2010b). Boys are more likely to work in agriculture, mining, construction and as hawkers in the informal

173

sector, while girls are more likely to work in service and manufacturing industries, including domestic work, commercial sex work, assisting women in market trading and home-based activities such as the preparation of cooked food, home beer brewing, stitching, packing or other production work (Bhat, 2010). The likelihood of children's involvement in child labour and hazardous work increases with age. Young people aged 15–17 years involved in both child labour and hazardous work increased by 20 per cent from 2004–2008, with twice as many boys of this age involved in this work than girls (ILO, 2010b).

While the international focus on tackling child labour has been broadly welcomed, many researchers and NGOs have emphasized how children's work is interconnected with poverty and argued that interventions to 'rescue' children from work are unlikely to address the structural factors that draw children into child labour. Indeed, such efforts may result in children working in more hazardous illicit occupations that put them at greater risk. The type of work that children are involved in, the hours they work, labour relations, and the setting, remuneration, degree of hazard among other factors are key to assessing the extent to which work can be regarded as harmful for children (Ansell, 2005).

174 In many societies globally, sociocultural norms and levels of poverty mean that most children are expected to engage in paid and unpaid work from an early age as part of the household economy. Such responsibilities are usually valued as part of children's informal education and socialization in the family and community. Children often engage in both productive and social reproductive activities according to a gendered division of labour and age hierarchies. Although gender relations vary in different contexts, girls in many patriarchal cultures are expected to undertake domestic chores located in and around the home, such as fetching water and fuel, washing clothes, cooking, cleaning, caring for younger siblings, sick or elderly relatives; while boys have greater responsibilities for activities conducted outside the home, such as running errands, herding livestock, working in the informal sector (Nieuwenhuys, 1994). Older siblings often have greater responsibilities than younger siblings, and the extent and range of tasks that children are involved in usually increases with age, linked to perceptions of young people's physical strength and competencies to perform particular tasks (Evans, 2010). The tasks performed by girls and boys tend to be the low-status activities usually undertaken by women, such as household chores, load bearing and subsistence agriculture, while girls rarely do men's activities in any society (Bradley, 1993).

Despite the significant contributions that children make to their families, the ILO definition of 'children in employment' excludes work undertaken in the child's own household, rendering children's – especially girls' – unpaid work contributions within the family invisible. Girls' greater workload of domestic responsibilities may reduce their spatial mobility and mean that they have less time available for schooling, private study and outdoor play compared to boys, which can disrupt their school attendance, result in poor educational outcomes and reduce potential opportunities for informal learning, peer socialization and participation in the community. International child welfare concerns, however, are focused on the exploitation of children's labour in more visible forms of productive work and the gendered- and age-related impacts of children's social reproductive work within the family are rarely considered within development policy and planning.

Researchers and NGOs have also refuted assumptions that children who work in the global South have little access to education and few opportunities for play. Children often seek opportunities for play, recreation and social activities with their peers while they undertake paid and unpaid tasks within the family, at school, on the street and in other environments. Many children combine paid and unpaid work with their schooling and, in many cases, need to earn money since their families are unable to pay for educational expenses. Researchers and NGOs have proposed that supporting children's rights to earn an income, recognizing their unpaid social reproductive work and enabling them to develop sustainable livelihoods may be more helpful than denying children's right to work (Ansell, 2005). As Jennings et al. (2006) comment about children's work in supermarkets in Tijuana, Mexico, paid work may be associated with positive benefits for children, such as demonstrating personal agency and contributing to their family's economic needs. Similarly, involvement in unpaid domestic and care work within the family may provide opportunities for young people to develop life skills, take responsibility and demonstrate their competencies; and it may build resilience and strengthen family relationships, rather than necessarily leading to negative outcomes, depending on the extent and nature of their care work (Evans, 2010).

175

Education and Transitions to Adulthood

Education represents a central element in global constructions of a 'good childhood' and achieving universal primary education and eliminating gender disparities at all levels of education by 2015 are key MDG targets. Primary education in the global South tends to be affected by a range of structural constraints that result in poor quality education and low educational enrolment, attendance, completion and attainment rates. An estimated 93 million children of primary school age are out of school and only 60 per cent of children of secondary school age attend secondary school globally, with less than 30 per cent of children in sub-Saharan Africa attending secondary school (UNICEF, 2007). Factors influencing the quality of education include a lack of teaching materials and resources, large class sizes, poor school facilities and infrastructure, low wages, limited skills and training opportunities for teachers leading to high levels of absenteeism and poor teaching quality. Many countries in the global South were forced to cut government spending on education and introduce 'user fees' as part of Structural Adjustment Programmes from the 1980s, which often led to declining primary school enrolment and retention rates – and, in sub-Saharan Africa, a reversal of the progress made in previous decades. Recognition of the negative impacts of school fees on poor families in low income countries led to growing calls to eliminate user fees for basic services and the establishment of UNICEF and the World Bank's Education for All Fast Track Initiative (2002) and School Fee Abolition Initiative (2005). The abolition of primary school fees in several low income countries, mainly in sub-Saharan Africa, has led to rapid increases in primary school enrolment rates in recent years (Dean Nielsen, 2009).

Despite the policy priority accorded to universal primary education, however, poverty remains a major barrier in many countries in the global South. Even when school fees have been abolished, many parents still struggle to meet educational expenses for school uniforms, books, paper, pens, examination fees and parental contributions for school building maintenance. In households facing extreme financial pressure, children may never enrol in school or may drop out of school due to the family's inability to meet schooling expenses.

Other barriers to education include the opportunity costs of children attending school, due to the demands for their labour at home, as well as the poor quality of education, use of corporal punishment and gender discrimination. A range of factors create 'girl-unfriendly learning environments', including gender biases in the curriculum and teaching materials, inadequate and insanitary toilet facilities, sexual harassment and humiliation of girls by male peers and teachers, expulsion due to pregnancy and lack of childcare facilities to enable young mothers to complete their education (Heward and Bunwaree, 1999). These factors, combined with gender discriminatory attitudes which disadvantage girls, particularly in contexts of poverty where parents are forced to choose which of their children should continue their education, result in significant differences between girls' and boys' enrolment, attendance and attainment rates in rural and urban areas in several countries in the global South. Although gender gaps in primary education have closed in the regions of East Asia/Pacific, Latin America/Caribbean and Eastern/Southern Africa in recent years, girls of secondary school age are more likely to be out of school than boys, and girls are less likely to complete secondary and tertiary education (UNICEF, 2007). This is regarded as particularly detrimental to long-term development goals, since girls' completion of secondary education is perceived to have long-term benefits in terms of delaying the age at which young women first give birth, enhancing their bargaining power within households, and increasing women's economic, social and political participation (UNICEF, 2006).

Within the contemporary knowledge-based global economy, achieving a high level of education and financial autonomy are regarded as increasingly important goals for many young people in the global South. However, researchers have questioned the relevance of formal education when secondary education is beyond the means of most families; and even if young people manage to obtain secondary level qualifications, this is not necessarily sufficient to secure formal sector employment and may not enhance their livelihood outcomes (Ansell, 2004). Global processes such as economic decline and restricted labour markets, urbanization, food insecurity, armed conflict, and the HIV and AIDS epidemic mean that young people may be increasingly involved in activities, roles and responsibilities that are usually associated with 'adulthood'. In rural Bolivia, for example, structural constraints affecting the quality of education, household work demands and climatic conditions restricted educational choices and led to poor perceptions of schooling among children and parents (Punch, 2004). Formal education was viewed simply as a means to the acquisition of basic literacy and numeracy, and young people make early and rapid transitions from primary school into work between the ages of 12–14 years. In communities affected by HIV and AIDS in Eastern and Southern Africa, some young people – particularly girls – take on caring roles for family members living with HIV, orphaned children or elderly grandparents (Evans and Becker, 2009). Their transitions to independent adulthood, such as completing education, migrating for work opportunities or achieving the financial means to marry and support their own families may be delayed because of their caring responsibilities (Evans, 2011). These examples reveal the complexity and interdependent nature of youth transitions in the global South.

KEY POINTS

- Children and young people have often been marginalized within development processes, despite the prominence of children's rights discourses and indicators of child health, education and welfare within global development targets.
- Age intersects with other social identities, such as gender, race, ethnicity, disability, rural and urban differences and wider global processes to produce diverse childhoods and complex pathways to adulthood.
- International concern about child labour has focused on more visible forms of children's paid work and neglected the gendered- and age-related impacts of children's social reproductive work within the family.
- 'Education for All' policies, initiatives and MDG targets have helped to increase primary school enrolment rates and reduce gender disparities in many low income countries, but poverty, structural constraints affecting the quality of education and gender discrimination continue to restrict young people's (especially girls') access to education and educational outcomes at all levels.

FURTHER READING

Ansell's *Children, Youth and Development* (2005) and Wells' *Childhood in a Global Perspective* (2009) provide detailed discussions of global constructions of childhood and youth in relation to development, including children's rights, work, education, youth transitions and participation. Bourdillon's (2004) article in *Progress in Development Studies* gives a good introduction to children's participation in development, while Aitken's (2001) article in *Area* reflects on the historically and geographically contingent nature of childhood and youth. Panelli et al.'s edited collection, *Global Perspectives on Rural Childhood and Youth* (2007), provides helpful discussions of young people's lives in rural environments. Lloyd-Evans' chapter on 'Child labour' (2008b) in Desai and Potter's *The Companion to Development Studies* provides a good overview of definitions and debates regarding working children. Katz's *Growing Up Global: Economic Restructuring and Children's Everyday Lives* (2004) , provides a rich ethnographic account of children's everyday lives in Sudan and New York linked to wider global processes, while Evans' *Geography Compass* article (2010) provides a useful review of research on children's caring roles in Africa.

179

4.3 HEALTH, DISABILITY AND DEVELOPMENT

Health, Disability and Development

Health is a central concern of development policy and planning. Many of the Millennium Development Goals (see Chapter 1.5) identify global health targets that aim to combat hunger and under-nourishment, child- and maternal mortality, and the spread of HIV, malaria and other infectious diseases. The focus on these global health concerns and increases in donor aid in recent years, such as the Global Fund to Fight AIDS, Tuberculosis and Malaria, have been broadly welcomed. International development discourses tend, however, to adopt a universalizing approach that constructs disease and ill health as global problems to be eradicated, and prioritizes large-scale biomedical interventions to improve individuals' health. This has resulted in a lack of focus on the structural inequalities that restrict access to healthcare and lead to social exclusion.

The role of the state in meeting the healthcare needs of the population in many countries in the global South has been undermined by processes of globalization. Neoliberal ideologies underpinning globalization shift structural decision-making power away from the state and into global economic institutions, such as the World Bank and International Monetary Fund (Evans, 2002). Although the neoliberal agenda has been implemented in different ways in the global South (Mohan et al., 2000), the conditionality associated with SAPs resulted in cuts in government expenditure in health, education, housing and public sector development, such as sewage disposal in many heavily-indebted countries in the 1980s. SAPs also introduced user fees, which reduced access to healthcare for poor people and opened up greater opportunities for private providers of medical care and drugs.

The deterioration in staffing, infrastructure and the availability of drugs and equipment in basic healthcare in many low income countries, which resulted from reduced government expenditure, led to declines in child immunization programmes, and the re-emergence of manageable diseases such as typhoid, TB and hepatitis, increased child- and maternal-mortality rates, and high numbers of AIDS-related deaths (McIntyre, 2007).

In recent years, recognition of the potentially devastating effects of healthcare payments on poor households, combined with poverty reduction debt-relief initiatives, has led to the removal of some or all user fees at public health centres in several countries, including South Africa, Uganda and Zambia (McIntyre, 2007). Indeed, abolishing user fees at the point of service delivery leads to increased uptake of, and adherence to, antiretroviral treatment for HIV (World Health Organization (WHO), 2008). Challenges in improving healthcare systems within this macroeconomic policy environment, however, continue to restrict access to healthcare for the poorest people and result in significant health inequalities, particularly for women and children living in remote rural locations.

The dominance of constructions of health and disability as global problems to be eradicated or prevented within development discourses has also resulted in the neglect of disabled people's experiences. Yeo and Moore (2003) argue that disabled people have been largely excluded from participating in development processes and research, despite the fact that they are disproportionately represented among the poorest people. Although reliable statistical data on the incidence of disability/ impairment is not widely available and defining disability is problematic, an estimated 10 per cent of the world population is disabled (United Nations, 2011a). The United Nations Development Programme estimates that 80 per cent of persons with disabilities live in developing countries, which often have the least resources to meet their needs (United Nations, 2011a).

181

The high rates of impairment and preventable illness in the global South are largely caused by malnutrition, poverty, lack of access to sanitation, safe drinking water, healthcare and other services, hazardous work, landmines and armed conflict (Yeo and Moore, 2003; McEwan and Butler, 2007). Being poor also increases the likelihood of an individual experiencing ill health and becoming disabled (Yeo and Moore, 2003). Childhood impairment is often caused by preventable injuries in homes and neighbourhoods that are related to poor living conditions and accidents among working children (McEwan and Butler, 2007). Many disabled children are denied access to education, due largely to the fact that education systems in the global South lack the resources and skills to meet adequately the needs of disabled students. This in turn leads to high levels of illiteracy, reduced skills and employment opportunities for disabled people in adulthood (Yeo and Moore, 2003). Disabled women and girls often experience multiple disadvantages, on the basis of their gender and disability, and are particularly vulnerable to abuse, chronic poverty and exclusion (United Nations, 2011a).

Poverty and disability are, therefore, mutually reinforcing concepts and contribute to increased vulnerability and exclusion (Department for International Development, 2000a). In recent years, development agencies have increasingly acknowledged that poverty alleviation strategies are unlikely to succeed unless disabled people's rights and needs are taken into account. Improving health systems, infrastructure, and the prevention and treatment of diseases is critically important in the global South. Improving people's health and well-being, however, also requires efforts to tackle poverty and the sociocultural, political and economic inequalities that people with chronic illnesses and impairments experience.

182

Disability Politics and Rights Discourses

Acknowledgement of the links between poverty, ill health and disability within development policy and practice has been accompanied by growing recognition of the 'right to health' as a key socio-economic human right (Evans, 2002) and of disabled people's rights to non-discrimination and full participation in society (McEwan and Butler, 2007). Since the 1970s, disability activists in the global North have rejected medical, rehabilitative models of disability, arguing that these are based on assumptions that disabled people suffer primarily from physical and/or mental abnormalities that medicine can, and should treat, cure, or at least prevent (Oliver, 1990; Morris, 1991). Within the dominant 'medical model' approach, disability is perceived as an 'individual misfortune' or 'tragedy'. The disability movement in the global North (led by mainly UK-based activists and allies) instead developed a 'social model' of disability to focus attention on the sociocultural, economic, political and spatial barriers to participation that disabled people experience. An individual's 'impairment' was seen as separate from the social, attitudinal and environmental dimensions of 'disability' that exclude disabled people. The 'social model' thus focuses on changing society to facilitate the participation and inclusion of disabled people, rather than on efforts to 'rehabilitate' individuals and overcome biological constraints of the body.

These understandings of disability have been crucial to improving accessibility, achieving equality of opportunity and securing disabled people's rights within the public sphere in the global North. The appropriateness of applying Western-centric social models of disability in the global South has, however, been questioned (McEwan and Butler, 2007). The wider macroeconomic context, resource constraints and limited availability of technical solutions to make environments more accessible constrain the implementation of social model approaches to disability in many low income countries. Furthermore, the chronic poverty, limited income earning options, and restricted access to health and education that many disabled people experience all mean that access to basic services may represent a higher priority for disabled people, governments and policymakers, rather than issues of accessibility or assistive technology. Social model approaches have also been criticized for failing to acknowledge the materiality of the body and the effects of pain, chronic ill health and impairment on people's everyday lives.

183

Debates about the need to reconcile both medical and social models of disability in the 1980s led to the establishment of 'community-based rehabilitation' approaches to supporting disabled people in the global South. Such approaches aimed to provide rehabilitation through medical intervention and care, as well as promoting the social inclusion and participation of disabled people within their communities. Community-based rehabilitation projects have been criticized, however, for being ill-conceived and lacking sensitivity to local cultures and practices, including overlooking the existing care and support that many families and communities provide for disabled people (McEwan and Butler, 2007). Community-based rehabilitation can be seen as reinforcing medical/charitable models of disability that were introduced in the colonial era, perpetuating ideas that disabled people are dependent and need to be supported by charitable fundraising and donations (McEwan and Butler, 2007). Community-based rehabilitation projects have sought to shift towards a more community-development approach in recent years and increasingly aim to empower disabled people and facilitate their participation in the development process.

Organizations led by disabled people in the global South have played an important role in collective advocacy and lobbying for the representation of disabled people in all stages of the development process at the national and international levels. For example, the National Union of Disabled People of Uganda (NUDIPU) lobbied for the inclusion of disabled people at all levels of political administration (Mwenda et al., 2009). As a result, disabled people have achieved a higher level of political representation in Uganda than in any other country (McEwan and Butler, 2007). International non-governmental organizations (NGOs), coalitions and networks of disabled people, such as Disabled People's International (established in 1981), have helped to strengthen national disabled people's organizations and facilitate collective advocacy for disabled people's rights at the global level.

Growing recognition of disabled people's human rights led to the introduction of the UN Standard Rules on the Equalization of Opportunities for Persons with Disabilities in 1994, which aimed to facilitate participation and equality for 'persons with disabilities'. The rules were not legally enforceable, however, leading to calls for a specific convention that focused on the rights of disabled people. The UN Convention on the Rights of Persons with Disabilities (which entered into force in 2008) is broadly informed by the social model of disability. Disability and impairment are not explicitly defined, but 'persons with disabilities' include: 'those who have long-term physical, mental, intellectual or sensory impairments which in interaction with various barriers may hinder their full and effective participation in society on an equal basis with others' (United Nations, 2010b). Key tenets of the Convention are disabled people's rights to participation and inclusion, non-discrimination and accessibility (see www. un.org/disabilities). While the emphasis is on mainstreaming disability into all development activities, such as Poverty Reduction Strategy Papers and the MDGs, it is recognized that disability specific measures may be necessary to 'accelerate or achieve de facto equality of persons with disabilities' (United Nations, 2010b). The UN Secretariat for the Convention acknowledges that the MDGs will not be achieved if persons with disabilities are not included. Yet there is no specific mention of persons with disabilities in the MDGs, or in the policies or guidance in meeting the targets.

Sociocultural Understandings of Disability, Health and Illness

Holistic development approaches that aim to enhance human capacities and well-being have been influenced by disability politics and social theories of the body, health and disability that developed from the 1970s onwards. Geographers and other social scientists have revealed how understandings of bodies, health and illness vary according to the economic, geo-political, sociocultural and spatial context (Longhurst, 2005). Although social research on disability and illness has been largely dominated by urban, Anglophone and Western-centric concerns to date, the need to investigate the interconnections between sociocultural representations of health, illness and disability and development processes at both a local and global scale has been increasingly recognized (Power, 2001; Somma and Bodiang, 2004; McEwan and Butler, 2007).

185

Research has revealed that understandings of disability and illness vary significantly across cultures and across time. While most cultures ascribe to notions of a 'normal' or 'ideal' body or mind, the meanings attached to different illnesses and impairments and the social responses that are deemed appropriate are not universal. In many sub-Saharan African countries, disability in children is associated with maternal wrongdoing and witchcraft, and in the contexts of poverty, negative cultural attitudes and a lack of support, families may 'hide' or abandon disabled children who are considered 'abnormal' (Kabzems and Chimedza, 2002). However, impairment does not always lead to exclusion and research has shown how many individuals are supported and included within their families and communities (Barnes and Mercer, 2003; Braathen and Kvam, 2008).

The importance of understanding the cultural beliefs and meanings associated with particular illnesses and impairments, alongside the social hierarchies that influence vulnerabilities to ill health and the broader geo-political context, is clearly evident when analysing HIV interventions in sub-Saharan Africa. Since the disease was first recognized in the 1980s, Southern Africa has been the region most affected by the epidemic; HIV prevalence rates among the adult population ranged from 11 per cent in Malawi to 26 per cent in Swaziland in 2009 (UNAIDS, 2010). The costs and pricing policies of transnational pharmaceutical corporations, as well as donor discourses and ideologies, prevented access to life-prolonging antiretroviral treatment in many African countries until the mid-2000s and led to high numbers of AIDS-related deaths. Jones (2004) argues that the almost exclusive focus of donor agencies in the 1980s and 1990s on prevention activities to halt the spread of the disease, rather than on the treatment and care of people living with HIV, is linked to multi-layered colonial metaphors and the racial stereotyping of African people within Western development discourses. The epidemic was viewed predominantly through the lens of sexual practices and interventions focused on the problematic behaviour of particular 'risk groups', while the political, economic, social and cultural contexts of HIV transmission were overlooked (Oppong and Kalipeni, 2004).

As a result, HIV prevention interventions have tended to be based on Western models of sexual behaviour change that have had little impact in many African countries. Some argue that such approaches have contributed to increased vulnerability to infection and HIV- and AIDS-related stigma. The ABC approach (Abstinence, Be faithful, use Condoms), which has been used in many African countries, most notably in Uganda, often promoted moralistic messages about sexual behaviour and emphasized abstinence and condom use. Such HIV prevention messages, however, failed to take account of the high value placed on fertility, religious beliefs and patterns of sexual networking in many African contexts (Thornton, 2008). They also undermined local cultural understandings about well-being, health and illness (Liddell et al., 2005).

In addition, prevention activities have often been targeted exclusively towards women and did not take account of power imbalances in gender relations and other social and cultural factors that influence vulnerability to HIV infection (Bujra, 2002). Young women aged 15–24 years are up to three times more likely to be infected than young men of the same age in Eastern and Southern African countries due to a combination of biological, economic, social and cultural factors (UNAIDS, 2010). Young women's low socio-economic status means that they may seek or be coerced into transactional sexual relationships with older men who support them financially. They occupy a weak bargaining position to negotiate safer sex, in the context of strong cultural taboos about the discussion of sexual matters between genders and generations (UNAIDS et al., 2004). Women's greater biological susceptibility to HIV transmission than men through heterosexual intercourse and widespread gender-related violence further increase their vulnerability. More women than men are living with HIV in sub-Saharan Africa (60 per cent of adults living with HIV are women), a trend which has not been seen in other world regions, except the Caribbean (where just over 50 per cent of adults with HIV are women) (UNAIDS, 2010). However, significant declines in new infection rates among young people, particularly young women, have been documented in several sub-Saharan African countries in recent years (UNAIDS, 2010).

Dominant donor discourses that emphasized prevention activities throughout the 1990s argued that health systems in sub-Saharan Africa were too 'undeveloped' to be able to provide effective antiretroviral treatment (Jones, 2004). The rapid scaling up of antiretroviral therapy in many sub-Saharan African countries in recent years, in accordance with the MDGs and universal access targets, has revealed the fallacy of these assumptions. Rights-based HIV activism, such as the Treatment Action Campaign led by people living with HIV in South Africa, helped to secure cheaper access to generic drugs through the legal system and contributed to increased access to antiretroviral therapy in many African countries from the mid-2000s onwards (Leclerc-Madlala, 2005). By 2009, 37 per cent of those requiring treatment in sub-Saharan Africa received antiretroviral therapy (ART), which corresponds to the global figure of 36 per cent ART coverage (World Health Organization (WHO), 2010), although large disparities in access to treatment persist, especially in remote rural locations. 187

Increased access to antiretroviral therapy has had a dramatic effect on mortality rates; in sub-Saharan Africa, 20 per cent fewer people died of AIDS-related causes in 2009 than in 2004 (UNAIDS, 2010). Furthermore, HIV prevalence rates have stabilized or declined in many sub-Saharan African countries in recent years. The need to integrate prevention, treatment, and care and support activities into a holistic continuum in order to tackle the epidemic and meet the MDG targets has been increasingly recognized in global health policy and development discourses (World Health Organization (WHO), 2002). Furthermore, the care and support of people living with HIV is finally receiving greater attention in policy arenas (UK Consortium on AIDS and International Development, 2008).

Development interventions on public health issues have increasingly recognized the need to adopt a 'cultural lens' and seek to understand sociocultural representations of health and illness within particular communities, negotiate with social hierarchies, and draw on local forms of communication and expression to engage people. Such approaches seek to engage with the 'webs of significance' that people create; that is, development practitioners analyse the ways people interact with and understand illness through cultural values, relationships, behaviour, and social and political structures (Vincent, 2005; Gould, 2007). Recent initiatives to tackle HIV have sought, for example, to promote greater dialogue and collaboration between healthcare professionals and traditional healers, whose services have been in high demand in many affected communities in Sub-Saharan Africa (Liddell et al., 2005; Wreford, 2008). Such HIV interventions have drawn on the knowledge of traditional healers and used local communication methods, such as rites, dances, dramas and chants, in order to raise awareness about HIV, confront stigma, increase access to treatment, and support families and community members in caring for people living with HIV (Somma and Bodiang, 2004).

188

KEY POINTS

- Despite the centrality of health in global development goals, processes of globalization and the macroeconomic policy environment often restrict access to healthcare for the poorest people, particularly women and children living in remote rural locations.
- Poverty and disability are mutually reinforcing concepts, which contribute to vulnerability and exclusion.
- Medical and charitable models of disability constructed disabled people as passive and dependent on the charity of others, rather than recognizing their human rights and the structural inequalities that prevent their full participation in society.
- Social models of disability and human rights approaches emphasize the need to empower disabled people, reduce barriers to participation, and ensure disabled people are represented in development processes at the local, national and international levels.
- Understandings of disability, health and illness are historically and geographically contingent, varying according to the economic, geo-political, sociocultural and spatial context.

- Behaviour change interventions to prevent the spread of the HIV epidemic in sub-Saharan Africa have had limited success, due to a failure to engage with local understandings of illness and well-being, to recognize the social hierarchies that influence vulnerabilities to infection, and to address broader geo-political power imbalances.
- There has been growing recognition of the need to take account of cultural understandings of health and illness, negotiate gender relations and other social hierarchies, and draw on local forms of communication to engage people in development interventions.

FURTHER READING

McEwan and Butler's (2007) article in *Geography Compass* provides a good overview of the relationship between disability and development. Yeo and Moore's (2003) article in *World Development* discusses the connections between disability and poverty and the representation of disabled people in development institutions, while Mwendwa et al.'s (2009) article in the *Journal of International Development* discusses the challenges of mainstreaming the rights of disabled persons in national development frameworks. Tony Evans' article, 'A human right to health?' (2002), in *Third World Quarterly*, provides a useful human rights perspective on health within the context of globalization and Jones' (2004) article in *Third World Quarterly* offers a post-colonial perspective on donor discourses surrounding access to HIV treatment in Africa. For further reading on HIV in Africa, see Kalipeni et al.'s (2004) book, *HIV and AIDS in Africa: Beyond Epidemiology*, Baylies and Bujra's (2000) book, *AIDS, Sexuality and Gender in Africa* and Thornton's *Unimagined Community* (2008).

189

4.4 SEXUALITIES AND DEVELOPMENT

Sexualities, Poverty and Development

Sexuality is often perceived as a private affair that has little to do with development (Corrêa and Jolly, 2008). Some regard sexuality as a distraction from the 'real issues' of development – how can we talk about people's intimate private relationships when people's basic needs are not being addressed? Sexuality is not explicitly mentioned in the Millennium Development Goals and is often seen as an 'add-on' rather than as integral to the development concerns of poverty and marginalization (Corrêa and Jolly, 2008: 5). Sexuality does represent, however, an implicit focus of many development interventions and targets, such as improving women's reproductive health and reducing the incidence of early pregnancies, sexually transmitted diseases including HIV, and gender-based violence.

Mainstream development agencies, such as the World Bank, conceptualize sex and sexuality predominantly as a depoliticized health issue – a problem to be prevented and/or improved through medical intervention (Camargo, 2006). In common with approaches to other questions of the body, such as disability (see Chapter 4.3), medical discourses have dominated the development agenda in relation to sexuality. Feminist and post-structuralist perspectives that emerged in social theory from the 1970s onwards, however, argue against the notion of a 'natural' body and suggest that our bodies are constructed through discourses, social systems and cultural norms. Geographers have argued that bodies are constituted through space at a range of scales and have emphasized that the interconnections between bodies and places are political (Longhurst, 2005).

The shift towards multidimensional understandings of poverty within development policy and practice (see Chapters 1.1 and 1.4) enables a greater engagement with questions of the body and sexuality. Strongly influenced by Sen's (1999) concepts of development as 'freedom', and poverty as a series of 'un-freedoms' that restrict human capabilities to provide for ourselves and shape our lives, the goal of development is increasingly perceived in terms of enhancing human well-being. Sexual fulfilment and autonomy often enhance people's well-being, while violence and discrimination related to sexuality represent forms of poverty and the deprivation of human agency and capabilities. Thus, sexuality does not concern only sex and intimate relations between individuals but, rather, 'the social rules, economic structures, political battles and religious ideologies that surround physical expressions of intimacy and the relationships within which such intimacy takes place' (Corrêa and Jolly, 2008: 5).

Violations of sexual rights and poor sexual and reproductive health are thus integral to development and represent both a cause and consequence of poverty (Cornwall and Jolly, 2006). The links between sexuality and poverty can be analysed according to Robert Chambers' web of poverty (see Figure 4.4.1) (Cornwall and Jolly, 2006). The examples demonstrate that many aspects of development and poverty reduction are related to dimensions of exclusion and disadvantage based on sexuality. Development efforts thus need to focus on ensuring the rights of people to a pleasurable and safer sex life, free of prejudice, risk or censure (Corrêa and Jolly, 2008).

191

Sexualities, Violence and Marginalization

While development agencies have been reluctant to address questions of sexuality, neoconservative actors, faith-based organizations and political groups have taken strong positions on issues of sex and sexuality. Neoconservative interests, for example, have promoted abstinence from sexual relations to prevent the spread of HIV, and the denial of contraception to young people and non-married women. They have advocated the criminalization of abortion, repression of homosexuality and the withdrawal of funding from those working with sex workers (Corrêa and Jolly, 2008).

Religious and political discourses about the sexual orientation of lesbian, gay, bisexual and transgender people have become increasingly vociferous in many countries in recent years. In sub-Saharan Africa, this has resulted in widespread stigmatization and violence directed

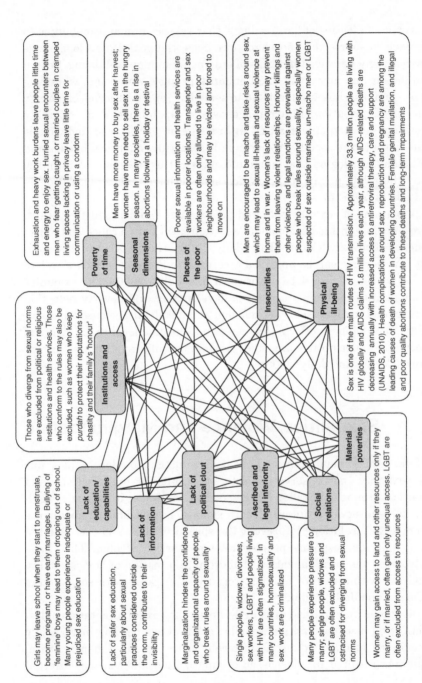

Figure 4.4.1 Disadvantages within the Web of Poverty, with examples related to sexuality (adapted from Cornwall and Jolly, 2006, p.4)

The following are the text boxes shown in the figure:

Exhaustion and heavy work burdens leave people little time and energy to enjoy sex. Hurried sexual encounters between men who fear getting caught, or married couples in cramped living spaces lacking in privacy leave little time for communication or using a condom

Poverty of time

Men have more money to buy sex after harvest; women have more need to sell sex in the hungry season. In many societies, there is a rise in abortions following a holiday or festival

Seasonal dimensions

Poorer sexual information and health services are available in poorer locations. Transgender and sex workers are often only allowed to live in poor neighbourhoods and may be evicted and forced to move on

Places of the poor

Men are encouraged to be macho and take risks around sex, which may lead to sexual ill-health and sexual violence at home and in war. Women's lack of resources may prevent them from leaving violent relationships. Honour killings and other violence, and legal sanctions are prevalent against people who break rules around sexuality, especially women suspected of sex outside marriage, un-macho men or LGBT

Insecurities

Those who diverge from sexual norms are excluded from political or religious institutions and health services. Those who conform to the rules may also be excluded, such as women who keep *purdah* to protect their reputations for chastity and their family's 'honour'

Institutions and access

Sex is one of the main routes of HIV transmission. Approximately 33.3 million people are living with HIV globally and AIDS claims 1.8 million lives each year, although AIDS-related deaths are decreasing annually with increased access to antiretroviral therapy, care and support (UNAIDS, 2010). Health complications around sex, reproduction and pregnancy are among the leading causes of death of women in developing countries. Female genital mutilation, and illegal and poor quality abortions contribute to these deaths and long-term impairments

Physical ill-being

Girls may leave school when they start to menstruate, become pregnant, or have early marriages. Bullying of 'feminine' boys may lead to them dropping out of school. Many young people experience inadequate or prejudiced sex education

Lack of education/ capabilities

Lack of safer sex education, particularly about sexual practices considered outside the norm, contributes to their invisibility

Lack of information

Marginalization hinders the confidence and organizational capacity of people who break rules around sexuality

Lack of political clout

Single people, widows, divorcees, sex workers, LGBT and people living with HIV are often stigmatized. In many countries, homosexuality and sex work are criminalized

Ascribed and legal inferiority

Many people experience pressure to marry; single people, widows and LGBT are often excluded and ostracised for diverging from sexual norms

Social relations

Women may gain access to land and other resources only if they marry, or if married, often gain only unequal access. LGBT are often excluded from access to resources

Material poverties

against sexual minorities. In Uganda, a new anti-homosexuality bill was proposed in parliament in 2009 that increases the penalties for 'homosexual acts' from 14 years in prison to a life sentence. Neoconservative religious and political leaders often draw on a discourse of anti-colonialism to justify their stance; they assert that homosexuality was imported to Africa by colonialism and claim it has been reinforced through economic exploitation in the post-independence era. They perceive homosexuality as a threat to African cultural values. Cross-cultural research with a range of ethnic groups has, however, challenged such assertions (Jolly, 2000). The Gikuyu ethnic group in Kenya, for example, practiced 'woman-to-woman marriage' as a means of enabling children to be brought into households and in order to solve disputes over the inheritance of land and property following a husband's death (Njambi and O'Brien, 2000). Similarly, many African languages have specific words to describe gay people, suggesting that same-sex relationships have a long history in many cultures.

Alongside increasingly repressive discourses surrounding sexuality in some countries, there has been growing recognition of people's sexual rights, evidenced in the introduction of progressive legislation on abortion, civil partnerships among same-sex couples, and non-discrimination on the basis of sexuality. South Africa was the first country in Africa to legalize same-sex marriage. Globalization and transnational flows of people, knowledge and ideas are leading to transformations in gender and sexual relations at both the local and global scale (Corrêa and Jolly, 2008). Digital networks connect people and cultures around the world (see Chapter 3.4) and rapidly transmit news of violations of sexual rights through global media technologies. This helps to disseminate information, raise awareness and facilitate transnational advocacy and activism to promote and protect people's sexual rights.

A 'sexualities and development lens' not only draws attention to the rights of sexual minorities, but also seeks to challenge dominant norms of heterosexuality and patriarchal privilege. The concept of 'heteronormativity' highlights the normative and restrictive nature of constructions of heterosexuality, in which it is assumed that individuals' sexual identities conform to a social norm of heterosexual love, sex and reproduction (Hubbard, 2008). Heteronormativity can, therefore, be defined as the assumptions, naturalization and enforcement of heterosexuality as the norm (Corrêa and Jolly, 2008). Heterosexuality is culturally hegemonic in many contexts, resulting not only in the marginalization of sexual minorities, but also in the institutionalization of 'heteronormativity' in

193

many aspects of public life (Hubbard, 2008), including development discourses and interventions (Camargo, 2006).

Development policy and practice reproduce dominant social and cultural norms around sexuality and marriage, resulting in the restriction of opportunities available to women, men and transgender people. Those who do not conform to 'compulsory heterosexuality' (Rich, 1980) face barriers to accessing services and resources in a wide range of sectors, including healthcare, education and training, employment, housing, agriculture, and social institutions (Chronic Poverty Research Centre (CPRC), 2010). Young unmarried mothers, non-married women, widows, commercial sex workers and those who have experienced rape, forced marriage, human trafficking and other forms of gender-based violence, are often stigmatized on the basis of gender and sexuality. They have limited access to education, livelihood options and assets, resulting in chronic poverty and insecurity (CPRC, 2010). Normative ideas about marriage and sexual relations may result in forced marriage and harmful cultural practices such as female genital mutilation/cutting, which may have long-term consequences for women's and girls' physical and emotional well-being. Non-married women and widows may experience discrimination in seeking sexual and reproductive health services, in being recognized as the next of kin for non-married partners (Corrêa and Jolly, 2008), in safeguarding asset inheritance, and in accessing property, land, credit and services in their own right without the permission of a husband or son (Deere and Doss, 2006; Peterman, 2011).

194

Rights-based Approaches and Sexualities

Rights-based approaches to development appear to offer new perspectives and opportunities to promote and protect sexual rights in a more positive framework than merely viewing sexuality as a sexual and reproductive health problem (Corrêa and Jolly, 2008). The focus of such approaches on non-discrimination, access to information, and on active and informed participation in all decisions affecting the individual, enable a focus on sexual rights as well as sexual and reproductive health rights. This raises questions about the role of the state in promoting, protecting and respecting sexual rights. As Corrêa and Jolly (2008) point out, state intervention and punishment are the major source of violations against sexual minorities around the world. Hence, much of the focus of activism of sexual minority groups to date has been on campaigning for legal reforms to decriminalize safe sex relations and sex work, and to extend social and employment rights to lesbian, gay, bisexual and transgender (LGBT) people and sex workers.

The association of 'sexual rights' with the label LGBT and the rights of sexual minorities is, however, problematic. The categories 'gay', 'lesbian', 'bisexual', 'transgender' are terms that emerged in specific cultural contexts (predominantly in the global North) and they do not adequately convey the diversity of sexual identities and practices that occur globally (Brown et al., 2010). People practising same-sex relations in the global South may not identify as 'gay' or 'lesbian' or adopt these labels to claim their rights. These categories can be exclusionary when they are used to construct as 'deviant' people whose sexual practices do not fit with dominant Western understandings of LGBT identities. Jackson (2007) observes that Western gay and lesbian identities privilege sexuality over gender, viewing these as separate, in contrast to non-Western cultures.

Research in non-Western societies, however, has revealed the centrality of gender to understanding eroticisms and sexual desire. The *hijras* (eunuch-transvestites) of India, for example, dress as women and perform at births and weddings, representing an institutionalized third gender role. Despite the religious, ascetic ideal of renouncing sexual desire, younger *hijras* often engage in sexual relations with men and in sex work (Nanda, 2007). Nanda (2007) suggests that although this results in conflicting values and tensions in the community, the contradictions of their cross-gender role and sexual practices are accommodated within Indian society. This example highlights the complex ways that gender and sexuality may be entwined in particular cultural contexts. Studies have also explored the influence of globalization on diverse gendered and sexual identities. Jackson (2007) identified a proliferation in the labelling of distinctive types of gendered/sexed being, termed *phet* or 'eroticized gender' identities, in public discourses in Thailand over recent decades. This multiplicity of gendered/sexed identity labels challenges the often one-dimensional representations and categorizations of homosexuality in the global North.

The association of sexual rights with the rights of LGBT people reproduces the assumed 'naturalness' of heterosexuality and prevents a focus on heteronormative restrictions. It also means that discussion of the sexual rights of heterosexual men is problematic, due to dominant negative stereotypes of men as sexually promiscuous, patriarchal

195

oppressors (Heise, 2007; Corrêa and Jolly, 2008). This reveals the dangers of basing rights claims and identity politics on essentialized identity categories that do not reflect the constantly shifting nature of individuals' identification within particular spatial and temporal contexts. Corrêa and Jolly (2008) call for an inclusive notion of sexual rights that does not relate exclusively to particular groups of people, but rather analyses the intersection of sexuality with other identities and axes of social difference.

KEY POINTS

- Sexuality, poverty and development are inextricably linked, despite mainstream development agencies' reluctance to engage with such 'intimate' questions of the body to date.
- A sexualities and development lens draws attention to the marginalization of sexual minorities and seeks to challenge the institutionalization of 'heteronormativity', defined as the assumptions, naturalization and enforcement of heterosexuality as the norm.

196

- Rights-based approaches to development may offer opportunities to promote and protect people's sexual rights, sexual and reproductive health rights, and challenge sexuality-related discrimination, violence and poverty.
- Such approaches need to adopt an inclusive notion of 'sexual rights' based on analysis of the intersection of sexuality with gender and other social differences in specific cultural contexts.

FURTHER READING

Andrea Cornwall, Sonia Corrêa and Susie Jolly's book *Development with a Body: Sexuality, Human Rights and Development* (2008) represents a key text for exploring recent work on sexualities, human rights and development in a global context. Similarly, Peter Aggleton's and Richard Parker's (2010) *Routledge Handbook of Sexuality, Health and Rights* and Richard Parker and Peter Aggleton's (2007) *Culture, Society and Sexuality* are both interesting, comprehensive collections of theoretical and empirical work on gender and sexuality from a global perspective. Jolly's article '"Queering" Development: Exploring the Links between Same-Sex Sexualities' (2000) in *Gender and Development* examines the links between development and sexual minorities. In *Geography Compass*, Gavin Brown et al.'s (2010) article provides a useful review of literature on sexualities in/of the global South, while Phil Hubbard's article 'Here, there, everywhere: the ubiquitous geographies of heteronormativity' (2008) provides an accessible introduction to recent literature on heteronormativity.

197

4.5 AGEING AND DEVELOPMENT

Population Ageing and Development

The 'older population' of the world is increasing rapidly as a result of sustained gains in longevity and declines in fertility over the last century. Indeed, by 2050 the global population of older people (defined as aged 60 or over) is projected to reach over 2 billion, increasing from 11 per cent of the total population in 2009 (737 million) to 22 per cent (United Nations, 2009). Although often constructed as a threat to future development, population ageing represents one of the most notable achievements of the last century (Lloyd-Sherlock, 2004). Improvements in health and reductions in mortality have led to significant increases in life expectancy, with a projected increase from 68 years in 2005–2010 to 81 in 2095–2100 (United Nations, 2010). Such improvements in longevity are occurring alongside declining fertility rates in many world regions, which will lead to a projected drop of a third in the proportion of children and, by 2050, the number of older people globally is projected to exceed the number of children (aged 0–14 years) for the first time in history (United Nations, 2002a).

This shift from high to low levels of fertility and mortality, which eventually results in a larger population of older people than younger age groups, is referred to as the 'demographic transition' (United Nations, 2002b). Although the demographic transition is taking place on a global scale, significant variations in population ageing exist between world regions, countries and within countries, which have particular implications for development. In many high income countries, older people already outnumber young people and the 'oldest old' (those aged 80 and over) are the fastest growing portion of many national populations (Powell, 2010). While the highest proportions of older people as a percentage of the population currently live in the global North (one in five people in Europe is 60 or more years old, compared to one in ten in Asia, Latin America and the Caribbean, and one in 19 in Africa), just under two-thirds of the world's older population live in the global South (54 per cent live in Asia) (United Nations, 2009).

Improvements in the well-being and longevity of older people are associated with particular economic, social, cultural and political challenges, which are integral to wider processes of development, globalization and inequality. The increase in the older population in the twenty-first century will be greatest and most rapid in the global South (Zelenev, 2008), where countries are already facing enormous challenges associated with economic restructuring, industrialization, urbanization, changing household and family structures, environmental degradation and climate change. Concern has been expressed that some countries 'will grow old before they grow rich' (Powell, 2010: 3).

Ageing, however, has been largely neglected by mainstream development agencies to date. The United Nations Millennium Development Goals and poverty reduction strategies driven by the World Bank and International Monetary Fund, for example, focus largely on health and development concerns affecting younger age groups – such as child and maternal mortality rates, HIV and other infectious diseases and education – rather than the chronic non-infectious diseases and impairments or financial and social issues that affect the well-being of many older people (Aboderin, 2008). The alarmist tone of mainstream development agencies' responses to population ageing and the lack of attention paid to the well-being of older people reveals the dominance of narrow neoliberal agendas that focus on developing human capital, productivity and economic growth, underpinned by assumptions about a lack of productivity in old age and a failure to recognize older people's contributions to development (Lloyd-Sherlock, 2004; Aboderin, 2008).

Reflecting the limited attention to ageing within development discourses, research has only recently begun to investigate the connections between ageing and development and the implications for the well-being of older people in the global South. The growing interdisciplinary field of 'social gerontology' that developed in the social sciences in recent decades examines a broad range of issues in relation to older people's health, healthcare, welfare and cultural life (Andrews et al., 2009). Most studies, however, address the concerns of ageing populations in the global North, where older people have considerably more access to formal care provision, pensions and welfare support than in the global South and are more likely to benefit from advances in healthcare and technology that enhance their quality of life and longevity. Older people

199

in the global South are often perceived as particularly vulnerable to poverty, ill health, disability and abuse.

However, older people's active contributions to society, strong familial responsibilities towards older relatives, and the respect they often command within age hierarchies in many cultures and social institutions highlight the dangers of constructing older people as a passive, homogeneous vulnerable group. Older people are a diverse group whose experiences and living conditions are shaped by gender, class, age, health and disability, ethnicity, religion, rural and urban location, among other factors. The 'feminization of ageing' has been highlighted as a particular concern in the global South. The older population is comprised of more women than men due to women's greater longevity and rising life expectancy among surviving older women (Zelenev, 2008). Women are often more vulnerable to poverty, violence and abuse in older age than men, are more likely to live alone or in skipped generation households (comprised solely of older people and children), to engage in physically demanding work in subsistence agriculture and domestic and care work in rural areas, to have limited access to physical assets, and to have low levels of literacy which restrict their livelihood options and participation in the labour market (United Nations, 2005).

200

The Life-Course, Care and Intergenerational Relations

The socially constructed, relational nature of 'age' has been increasingly recognized in the social sciences in recent years (Hockey and James, 2003; Hopkins and Pain, 2007). In parallel with critiques of the use of strict age-based definitions of children and youth in international development and rights discourses (see Chapter 4.2), commentators have highlighted the problematic nature of the United Nations' chronological age-based definition of older people as all those aged 60 years or more (Lloyd-Sherlock, 2004). Understandings of older age and generational relations may vary significantly in different socio-economic, cultural and political contexts. Zelenev raises the question,

> Does a specific age – such as 60 or even 65 – represent a realistic threshold (contrary to a purely statistical approach) for defining a certain population cohort as 'older persons'? Or are other criteria more appropriate for contemporary society, given the conditions in which people live? (2008: 5)

A life-course approach offers a useful way of conceptualizing the ways that people live their lives through time (Rigg, 2007). People pass through a series of socially expected transitions, life stages or transformations from infancy to old age that varies in different places and from one generation to another. Transformations in people's social position over the life-course comprise socially expected (often highly gendered) transitions and embodied changes associated with particular ages – such as initiation rites marking the shift from childhood to youth, entry into the labour market, marriage, childbirth and parenthood, grandparenthood, reduced work responsibilities and often increasing frailty in older age. People's lives are also shaped by less predictable events over time, such as illness or impairment, death of a family member, displacement due to conflict or environmental disasters (Bowlby et al., 2010). These life events may represent significant disruptions or reinforcements of existing social ties, roles and identities in an individual's biography.

Furthermore, while stages of the life-course are associated with particular opportunities and restrictions, people also live through historical eras which may have a profound influence on such opportunities and restrictions, as Rigg notes:

> Consumption pressures, changing mores, better education, easing restrictions of female mobility, widening opportunities for employment and so on will ensure that the vistas of opportunity open to a son or a daughter will be different from those that were available to their fathers and mothers, let alone their grandparents. (2007: 56)

This reveals the importance of analysing not only the life stage that a person occupies, but also the generational cohort to which they belong and intergenerational relations (Monk and Katz, 1993; Hopkins and Pain, 2007; Rigg, 2007).

Generational transfers and intergenerational caring relations can be theorized using the framework of a 'generational bargain' (Collard, 2000). The bargain is that the most economically active 'middle generation' makes transfers to the young with the expectation that resources will be reciprocated to them in old age when they require care and support, while also fulfilling their obligations to support their older parents. Collard (2000: 456) suggests that the intergenerational bargain relies on each generation making 'such transfers as are consistent with each cohort having a good life-prospect', which can break down if the middle generation is unable to make the necessary transfer of resources to the young and old.

Research suggests that the 'generational bargain' is coming under increasing pressure in many low- and middle-income countries due to societal transformations associated with a range of global processes. These include globalization, neoliberal economic restructuring, the HIV epidemic – and the consequences of reduced public health spending, user fees and policies that emphasize home-based care (Ogden et al., 2006) – rapid urbanization, high levels of transnational and rural–urban migration, greater emphasis on education, changing family structures and the individualization of kinship responsibilities (Kabeer, 2000). Such changes affect the ability of younger generations to provide care and support for older people in a diverse range of contexts.

In China, for example, the combination of a rapidly ageing population, the change to a market economy that emphasizes reliance on individual effort and the reduction of social welfare provision, the birth control policy of one child per family, and high levels of migration among working-age adults, is placing strains on traditional patterns of care for older people within families and communities (Silverstein et al., 2006). The majority of older people remain in rural regions, while working-age adults migrate to urban areas and usually send remittances to support their parents and children. Studies highlight the growing gap in care provision for older people in poorly developed rural areas and the need for governmental intervention, as longevity increases alongside reduced family sizes due to the 'one-child policy' (Joseph and Phillips, 1999; Woo et al., 2002). Silverstein et al. (2006), however, suggest that traditional family structures are adapting to these social changes. The research found that three-generation households and skipped-generation households (where older people and grandchildren are supported by remittances from the working-age generation who have migrated to urban areas) are more beneficial to the well-being of older people in rural Chinese society than single-generation households.

In Eastern and Southern Africa, three decades of the HIV epidemic have taken a considerable toll on the ability of families and communities to care for large numbers of people living with a chronic life-limiting illness, orphaned children and youth, and older people whose adult children have died (Evans, 2010). The loss of the parental 'middle generation' has led to the emergence of new household forms, such as 'skipped generation households' and 'child- and youth-headed households' (where siblings live independently without a co-resident adult relative) (Samuels and Wells, 2009; Evans, 2011). Data from Demographic and Health Surveys from 24 countries in sub-Saharan Africa indicate that 41 per cent of older adults (aged 60 or over) live with a grandchild under the age of 15 years (Zimmer and Dayton, 2005). Of these grandparents, almost 14 per cent live with one or more grandchildren without any co-resident adult children and most of these households are headed by grandmothers living with young children in rural areas (Zimmer and Dayton, 2005).

The number of skipped generation households is expected to increase in the future because of the continuing impacts of AIDS-related orphanhood and the intensification of negative shocks such as conflict, natural disasters and emergencies associated with climate change (Samuels and Wells, 2009). Older people may be disproportionately vulnerable during crises because they are more likely to have chronic illnesses and sensory, physical and cognitive impairments; are at risk of abuse and neglect; and there is a lack of understanding of their rights and entitlements (Samuels and Wells, 2009). Little research to date has investigated the livelihoods and coping strategies of such skipped generation households, the role of community-based support structures, and emergency preparedness and responses.

203

It is important to recognize, however, the active contributions that older people make to society, including the transfer of wisdom, knowledge, cultural values and skills to younger generations (Lloyd-Sherlock, 2004). Research suggests that in the context of stigma and changing kinship responsibilities, grandparents – particularly grandmothers – play a crucial role in caring for widows living with HIV and children who have been orphaned by AIDS (Evans and Thomas, 2009; Nyambedha et. al., 2003). Children and elderly grandparents living in skipped generation households often share caring and domestic responsibilities and develop close, loving relationships that enhance the emotional well-being of both children and older people (Clacherty, 2008; Evans and Becker, 2009).

Older People's Participation and Rights

The important contributions that older people make to their families and communities, and hence to development itself, has been acknowledged to some extent in development policy and practice in recent years, due in large part to strong advocacy by HelpAge International and other non-governmental organizations (NGOs). If older people's contributions are valued and they are seen as active participants in development processes, this requires a shift in the focus of policy from a welfare approach to one which seeks to enhance the capacity of older people to make contributions and to increase the opportunities for them to do so (Lloyd-Sherlock, 2004; Zelenev, 2008). These ideas are encompassed in the term 'active ageing'. Although this approach has been broadly welcomed, Lloyd-Sherlock (2004) notes that overemphasis on the active participation of older people could potentially divert attention from the high levels of vulnerability and dependence that some older people experience.

A number of notable UN milestones reveal the shift towards 'active ageing' and a rights-based agenda for older people in recent years. The first World Assembly on Ageing was held in Vienna in 1982 and resulted in the Vienna International Plan of Action on Ageing, which placed older people on the international development agenda for the first time. The UN Principles for Older Persons adopted in 1991 provided guidance in securing the human rights of older people in relation to five quality of life characteristics: independence, participation, care, self-fulfilment and dignity (United Nations, 2002a). With the theme of 'towards a society for all ages', 1999 was designated the International Year of Older Persons. This demonstrates growing recognition of the relational nature of older people's situation that 'cannot be considered separately from the scope of long-term opportunities that society allows them' and an understanding of the need for a life-course perspective (Zelenev, 2008: 3).

204

The Second World Assembly on Ageing held in Madrid in 2002 resulted in the Political Consensus and the Madrid International Plan of Action on Ageing, which remains the principal guiding policy framework in relation to ageing and development to date, firmly located within the UN's social development paradigm (Aboderin, 2008). The Madrid Plan of Action is based on three overarching themes: a policy approach to ageing that is integral to the development agenda; the empowerment of older persons and full realization of their rights and potential; and public recognition of the opportunities and challenges of an ageing society (Zelenev, 2008: 7). While these UN milestones reveal a growing shift towards recognition of the rights, contributions and entitlements of older people, older people's views and experiences continue to be overlooked in mainstream development programmes, reinforced by negative perspectives on the consequences of global ageing for future development.

- The older population (defined as those aged **60** years or over) is increasing rapidly globally due to sustained gains in longevity and declines in fertility. The dynamics of population ageing differ within and between countries and world regions, representing a considerable challenge to development in the global South.
- The well-being of older people and their participation in development processes have largely been neglected to date. Neoliberal development agendas fail to acknowledge the significant contributions that older people make to their families and communities.
- A life-course approach reveals the relational nature of age and is useful in analysing the complex transitions and life-phases that individuals experience over time.
- The generational bargain that the most economically active 'middle generation' will provide care and support the young and old is coming under pressure in many countries in the global South due to a range of global processes.
- UN discourses on older people have shifted from a welfare approach to an 'active ageing' approach that seeks to enhance the opportunities for older people to contribute to development and move towards a 'society for all ages'.

205

The collection edited by Peter Lloyd-Sherlock *Living Longer: Ageing, Development and Social Protection* (2004) provides a comprehensive introduction to debates on ageing and development, with chapters covering a wide range of country contexts, including Brazil, China, South Africa, Ghana, Argentina, Mexico and Thailand. Isabella Aboderin's short essay in Desai and Potter's *The Companion to Development Studies* (2008) provides a useful overview of ageing and development debates. Jason Powell's 2010 article in *Ageing International* discusses the phenomenon of global ageing and the social and economic processes influencing this from a regional perspective. Hopkins and Pain's 2007 article in *Area* provides a helpful discussion about relational approaches to age and the life-course.

Section 5
Contemporary Issues in Development

INTRODUCTION

We have seen enough in *Key Concepts in Development* to know that the disciplines of development geography, and development studies more generally, represent dynamic fields that are changing in response to world events and changes in global economic, political and social circumstances. While it is not possible to chart all such dynamic contemporary processes in this final section of the book, a number of such pressing themes and associated issues are discussed. The section starts with an overview of the intersections between culture and human rights, and then proceeds to the consideration of civil society, social capital and Non-Governmental Organizations (NGOs). In the final two chapters, the perspective remains essentially global, covering the implications of global migration and transnationalism, and the possibilities of global taxation meeting the pressing development needs of the global population.

The complex relationships existing between culture, development and human rights are discussed in Chapter 5.1 and the account analyses how these play out in relation to rights-based approaches to development. Understandings of 'culture' have shifted over time according to different ideological and theoretical approaches to development. Culture has become increasingly prominent in recent development agendas, as has the discourse of human rights, underpinned by the international legal framework of human rights led by the United Nations. The chapter traces the ways that different understandings of culture and the rights discourse have informed development interventions. It examines the contested nature of each of these concepts and analyses the potential, tensions and challenges associated with rights-based approaches to development in relation to 'culture'. The polarized nature of the universalism–cultural relativism debate demonstrates the need for a more dynamic understanding of culture in order to fulfil people's economic, social and cultural rights and to foster human flourishing and well-being.

Chapter 5.2 explores an important set of interrelated concepts that stem from the belief that people must play a central role in the development interventions that impact upon their lives. The growth of people-centred development as a new orthodoxy within development studies has largely arisen from the grassroots work of Non-Governmental Organizations (NGOs), and it has shaped international development agendas over the last thirty years. Beginning with a brief overview of the emergence of the concept of participation in development policy, the chapter explores the relationship between participation and empowerment, and it evaluates its contribution over time and space. In order to highlight the social relationships that underpin interconnections between people-centred development and civil society, the chapter moves on to explore the contributions of social capital and civic engagement to development policy since the 1990s. The latter half of the chapter traces the evolution of the concept of civil society, and it offers critical analysis of its role in constructing participatory spaces for marginalized communities. Concluding with an evaluation of recent transformations in civil society that have propelled NGOs and other non-state actors into the mainstream, the chapter argues that issues of transparency, accountability and impartiality remain key to engendering participation at the grassroots.

The focus in Chapter 5.3 is the migration of people in contemporary times. Both internal and international mobility are treated in the account, though internal mobility is much larger in volume, while international mobility is considered to be more problematic in contemporary times. Particular attention is paid to a recent form of international movement conceptualized as transnationalism. This is a form of cross-border mobility that is being practised more often these days in response to globalization. These global-to-local forces that are underway are also rendering national boundaries less meaningful in terms of people's identity formation and territorial affiliation(s). The developmental potential of global migration for the source and destination societies is then examined, with the migration–development nexus of global interrelationships being singled out. First, there is the increasing influence of migrant-donated remittances in the development and growth of the home communities that emigrant donors have left. Both economic (monetary) and social remittances are circulating, freely. Secondly, a selective return migration of middle-class professionals appears to be gaining pace, which promises to be a 'brain gain' to offset earlier 'brain drains'.

The argument that there are potential global solutions to the pressing global issues that the world faces is presented in Chapter 5.4, the final chapter. This involves the idea of establishing a global tax on all currency transactions, as was first advocated in 1972 by James Tobin, an American economist. It is estimated that trillions of United States dollars are traded daily on foreign exchange markets around the world, although it is thought that only some 5 to 10 per cent of this is necessary to finance trade. The rest amounts to financial speculation in order to make profits. James Tobin suggested that all such transactions should be subject to taxation of between 0.1 and 0.25 per cent. Although this is a small proportion, it is estimated that such a tax would generate around US$250 billion per annum for development purposes, in particular the alleviation of poverty and inequality. This figure represents over five times the total amount that is presently given in the form of aid around the world. It is argued that such a form of taxation would also serve to reduce the volatility that is characteristic of the international financial market.

5.1 CULTURE AND HUMAN RIGHTS

Changing Approaches to Culture in Development Discourses

Since the mid-1990s, the importance of culture has been increasingly acknowledged in development discourses. This has resulted in what has been termed a 'cultural turn' in development policy and practice. 'Culture' is, however, a contested concept, associated with multiple meanings which have changed over time and which have influenced development policy and practice. This chapter traces the changing relationship between culture and development, before exploring the rise of rights-based approaches to development and the potential, tensions and challenges of the rights discourse in relation to culture.

Early understandings defined 'culture' as the actions of humans on nature, such as the cultivation of land, production of crops and animals, or as the symbolic behaviour of humans, which established class hierarchies and privileged elite lifestyles (Crang, 1998). During the eighteenth and nineteenth centuries, however, a notion of culture emerged as a process of social development and 'civilization', based on dominant Enlightenment values and moralities. Imperial expansion and colonization were underpinned by racial ideologies that generalized a distinction between 'civilized' and 'uncivilized' peoples across entire nations and world regions and resulted in non-Europeans being labelled as 'primitive' and 'inferior' (Schech and Haggis, 2000).

This understanding of culture was based on a binary opposition between 'traditional' and 'modern' that devalued traditional cultural values. Early approaches to development were informed by such understandings of culture. Modernization theory from the 1950s onwards, for example, was based on assumptions that Third World countries would follow a linear trajectory of development from a 'traditional' to a 'modern' society (see Chapters 1.1 and 2.1). Culture was seen as a barrier to progress and it was assumed that traditional cultural values and practices would 'die out' or be 'bred out' of a people, as non-Western peoples would eventually adopt the cultural values of Western Europe and North America (Schech and Haggis, 2000: 19).

Alongside such ethnocentric, destructive approaches to culture, anthropological accounts were perhaps more positive, in that they recognized the plurality and diversity of cultures around the world. However, non-Western cultures were romanticized and constructed as 'Other' to Western cultures. Culture was seen primarily in terms of 'exotic authenticity', as anthropologists strove to document the meanings, values, social practices and ways of life of particular 'tribes' (Schech and Haggis, 2000). This led to exoticized, stereotypical representations of non-Europeans and their 'traditional' ways of life, such as the idea of the 'noble savage' who was perceived as being closer to nature and existing outside modernity.

Within both of these dominant perspectives, culture was viewed as a discrete, bounded entity and non-Western people were constructed as inferior and 'Other' in relation to the Western norm. Since the 1990s, however, post-colonial and post-development critiques of modernization and neoliberal development paradigms have deconstructed the cultural assumptions and values that underpin development (Escobar, 1995; Kothari, 2006). Such perspectives have revealed that the notion of progress implicit within development discourses was based on an ethnocentric world view of modernity. 'Development' is understood to operate as a discourse of power/knowledge within which the relations between the First and Third Worlds are constructed, imagined and operationalized (Said, 1978; Hall, 2002; Schech and Haggis, 2000; McEwan, 2001).

Such developments within post-colonial and post-development theories have been accompanied by a wider 'cultural turn' in the social sciences from the 1970s onwards, which has led to more dynamic understandings of 'culture'. The importance of culture to the production of knowledge has been increasingly recognized by cultural studies proponents and post-structuralist theorists such as Michel Foucault. These perspectives challenge the view of culture as a static, single entity, but rather regard culture as being shaped by multiple flows, exchanges and interactions. Processes of globalization challenge binary models of 'modernity/tradition', 'core/periphery' and the dominant values underlying modernization and Marxist development theories. From this perspective, culture can be defined as 'a network of representations – texts,

213

images, talk, codes of behaviour and the narrative structures organising these – which shapes every aspect of social life' (Frow and Morris, 1993: viii, in Schech and Haggis, 2000).

Alongside these shifts in thinking about culture, Radcliffe (2006a: 3) argues that a range of other factors have influenced the increasing prominence of culture in recent development agendas: the failure of previous development paradigms; perceptions of globalization's threat to cultural diversity; activism around social difference (gender, ethnicity, anti-racism); development success stories in East Asia, where questions have been asked about the role of cultural values and work ethics in achieving economic success; and a perceived need for social cohesion.

Culture is increasingly used as a tool for development by mainstream development actors and is often equated with terms such as social capital. Neoliberal development policymakers, for example, view the encouragement of a robust civil society and social trust as a key means of fostering economic development and labour market participation (Radcliffe, 2006a; see also Chapter 5.2). Perspectives that treat culture as a catch-all term for all the different dimensions of social capital, however, risk viewing social capital as separate from the power relations, inequalities and axes of social difference that contextualize it (Radcliffe, 2006a).

This raises the question of whether culture, seen as a creative process, can be mobilized to achieve social justice or whether culture is seen more as a product or a tool of analysis to target interventions to increase economic growth (McEwan, 2006). McEwan's (2006) case study of the Amazwi Abesifazane memory cloths programme in KwaZulu-Natal, South Africa, suggests that development projects that bring together cultural and economic approaches have radical transformative potential. In this case the process of African women, who have experienced economic and political discrimination and violence, participating in cultural activities and collectively producing knowledge, helps to bring about gender justice and can enhance their well-being and economic empowerment – on both an individual and a collective basis. Although neoliberal perspectives may adopt a more narrow understanding of culture as a product or tool that helps to achieve economic growth, McEwan argues that culture can be seen more holistically as an end in itself and as a goal of development that has the potential to bring about social justice.

214

Rights-based Approaches to Development

Throughout the chapters in Section 4, the growing prominence of human rights discourses in relation to the development agenda was noted. Indeed, some argue that since the late 1990s, the rights discourse has become the new orthodoxy in development policies and programmes. Rights-based approaches to development have their legal basis in international and regional human rights instruments. Key United Nations milestones in the shift towards rights-based development are shown in Figure 5.1.1.

The UN Declaration on the Right to Development (UNDRD) describes the right to development as 'an inalienable human right' and affirms the importance of people to development. Article 2 of the UNDRD, for example, declares that the 'human person' (rather than the nation state) 'is the central subject of the development process'. Tsikata (2007) suggests that rights-based approaches to development are based on a consensus around several basic elements: the link between development and human rights; greater accountability of states and international actors; an emphasis on empowerment, participation and non-discrimination; and attention to vulnerable groups.

215

A number of advantages of rights-based approaches to development (RBD) have been identified. These include the fact that there is an emphasis on economic, social and cultural rights as well as political and civil rights, and that the fulfilment of these rights implies a claim on national and international resources (Tsikata, 2007). RBD can be seen as enhancing accountability and legitimacy, since human rights instruments are signed by governments who have duties to respect, protect and

---

- Declaration on Human Rights (1948)
- International Covenant on Civil and Political Rights (1966)
- International Covenant on Economic, Social and Cultural Rights (1966)
- Convention on Elimination of Discrimination Against Women (1979)
- Declaration on the Right to Development (1986)
- Convention on the Rights of the Child (1989)
- Convention on the Rights of Disabled Persons (2006)
- Declaration on the Rights of Indigenous Peoples (2007)

Figure 5.1.1   Key United Nations milestones in the development of the international human rights legal framework (Office of the United Nations High Commissioner for Human Rights, 2012)

fulfil their citizens' rights. The shift in emphasis from a 'needs-based' charity model to an approach which seeks to redress injustice and bring about institutional change is also seen as more empowering for marginalized groups. RBD have been mobilized in anti-colonial struggles and new social movements, and human rights instruments concerning particular social groups (for example, women, children, indigenous people) have provided a useful basis for legal arguments and seeking social justice.

Competing understandings of the relationship between human rights and development are, however, evident among development actors. The World Bank, for example, views the attainment of human rights as a goal of development, while the United Nations Development Programme sees human rights as critical to achieving development but not as a goal of development in itself (Manzo, 2003). Rights-based approaches have also been subject to a number of critiques, as Tsikata discusses (2007). First, there has been a lack of clarity about the differences between rights-based approaches and how they relate to other development alternatives, such as participatory development, gender and development and so on. Second, RBD are 'state-centric', as human rights instruments define the nation state as the primary site for accountability and responsibility for fulfilling the rights of its citizens. This 'state-centric' approach appears to contradict the dominant neoliberal agenda that prioritizes increased global interdependence and often results in a weakened role for the state, with significant power instead being accorded to global financial institutions such as the World Bank and the International Monetary Fund and transnational corporations.

RBD imply that citizens have legal rights and can potentially make a claim against their governments to fulfil their economic and social rights. However, in the context of neoliberal restructuring and economic liberalization within much of the global South, decisions about the economy and public spending priorities that would improve social protection are often beyond the control of nation states. Indeed, the privatization of essential services such as water, education and health, and cost-recovery measures under structural adjustment programmes which reduce access to basic services for the poorest groups, could be seen as violations of people's economic and social rights (Tsikata, 2007). Yet governments in the global South are often unable to fulfil these economic and social rights. Meanwhile, global financial institutions, multilateral and bilateral agencies, transnational corporations, Western governments and international NGOs, who are acknowledged as the

216

main 'drivers' of development, are difficult to hold to account. Further criticisms of RBD include the limited support for the Declaration on the Right to Development by key donor countries including the UK, US, Germany, Japan, Sweden, Denmark; and concerns that the legalistic approach of RBD will result in a neglect of the poorest people and a devaluing of grassroots work (Tsikata, 2007).

Culture and Rights-based Development

A number of tensions emerge when rights-based approaches to development are considered in relation to the notion of culture. The rights discourse is premised on the idea that there are fundamental universal human rights that affect all human beings around the world, regardless of culture, and that these can be defined, protected, respected and fulfilled through the legal mechanisms of international human rights instruments. This universalist approach directly contradicts more cultural relativist positions that argue that the meanings associated with the idea of people's rights and obligations are socially- and culturally-constructed, and hence vary according to the historical and geographical context. Critics of the rights discourse **217** have argued that the concept of universal human rights is based on Western liberal notions of subjecthood that emerged in Europe during the Enlightenment period in the eighteenth century (Schech and Haggis, 2000). At this time, new discourses of science and universal reason, linked to colonial expansion and racial ideologies, were replacing previous world views. Some commentators have thus argued that the notion of universal human rights, as defined and implemented through the United Nations legal framework, is an ethnocentric concept that emerged from a distinctly 'Western' or 'Judeo-Christian' cultural imperialist discourse (Preis, 2002).

Furthermore, the individualistic nature of the legal discourse associated with human rights conflicts with the communitarian values evident in many countries in the global South. Here, people are viewed as having reciprocal rights and responsibilities to their families and communities, rather than viewing an individual as a rights-holder who can make particular claims against the state. Indeed, disenfranchisement with the universalist and individualistic nature of the UN rights discourse led to the establishment of African regional charters on human rights, such as the African Charter on Human and People's Rights

(1981) and the African Charter on the Rights and Welfare of the Child (1990). Alongside identifying individual rights, these regional charters recognize the sociocultural responsibilities of individuals to their families, communities, ethnic group, nation and region. For example, the African Charter on the Rights and Welfare of the Child (1990) contains articles that focus on a child's responsibility to 'preserve and strengthen positive African cultural values', 'to preserve and respect the family' and 'to serve the nation and promote African unity'.

Critics have also suggested that RBD's emphasis on the individual can lead to inadequate attention being paid to *collective* oppressions that particular social groups may experience based on class, gender, race, religion, kinship and other social relations. Feminists have argued that the universal 'subject' of human rights conventions often takes a man/boy as the norm, leading to gender-blind omissions. In order to address more gender-specific concerns, the African Charter on the Rights and Welfare of the Child (1990), for example, explicitly addresses issues such as girls' unequal access to education.

Despite these critiques of the ethnocentrism of the rights discourse, some commentators have refuted the assumed 'Western heritage' of the concept of human rights and argued that the values associated with recognizing an individual's rights and entitlements to well-being can be found in all major religions and cultural contexts (Tomalin, 2006). Cultural relativism – the idea that 'culture' determines people's rights and obligations and hence these can only be defined in relation to a particular cultural, ideological and political context – has been criticized for confusing human rights with human dignity, and for not distinguishing between rights and duties. Furthermore, cultural relativists' refusal to accept some notion of common basic needs or entitlements that are necessary to ensure everyone's well-being can be seen as absolving them of taking a moral stance on crucial development issues, such as poverty, marginalization and violence. Olson and Sayer (2009) discuss the value of 'normative thinking' and call for geographers (and other social scientists) to take a subjective, political and ethical stance in relation to what constitutes 'human flourishing' or 'the human good'. Drawing on Amartya Sen's and Martha Nussbaum's notions of 'capabilities' ('the range of things people need to be able to have and do to be able to flourish'), Olson and Sayer (2009: 192) argue that 'universal' should not be equated with 'uniform' and a capabilities approach does not deny that there is variation according to cultural context: 'We are all capable, needy, dependent, vulnerable social beings, though the ways in which we are varies [sic] both individually and according to our place in the world'.

As these ideas imply, the universalism versus cultural relativism debate is highly polarized and in many ways can hinder development. This is most evident regarding interventions to address harmful cultural practices affecting women in the global South, such as Female Genital Mutilation/Cutting (FGM/C) which is practised mainly in north-east Africa, in some areas in western Africa, southern parts of the Arabian peninsula, and among some migrants from these areas to Europe, North America and Australia (Almroth et al., 2001). From a cultural relativist stance, FGM/C can be seen as a cultural tradition that is important to particular ethnic and religious groups as a significant initiation rite in girls' transition to womanhood. It may be viewed as necessary by men and women within particular communities in securing a girl's marriage prospects and those who refuse to undergo circumcision may be ostracized (Almroth et al., 2001). FGM/C rights-based development interventions that seek to eliminate this practice may be criticized for not understanding the importance of this practice to local communities and for glossing over significant differences in practices among the diverse ethnic groups that adhere to FGM/C (Gruenbaum, 1996). FGM/C rights-based interventions may also be criticized as being driven by Western donor concerns that 'lack respect' for particular cultures and perpetuate colonial and modernist discourses that construct culture and tradition as 'backward'. On the other hand, a rights-based, usually biomedical, approach views FGM/C as a harmful cultural practice which represents a violation of girls' and women's human rights, especially those of bodily integrity and sexuality, and can lead to psychological trauma, long-term physical impairments and health concerns or even death (Parker, 1999).

219

These polarized perspectives raise the question of who defines 'culture' and 'tradition' and whose voices are heard. As discussed in Chapter 4.4 in relation to sexuality, notions of 'culture' and 'tradition' are often appropriated by powerful actors to impose their views on societies. Post-colonial feminists have argued that unless rights-based interventions on FGM/C and other harmful cultural practices affecting women in the global South are led by women and men (and children) from communities where these customs are practised – and are connected to broader structural issues of education, health and poverty reduction programmes – such interventions are in danger of being based on neocolonial attitudes that lack understanding for 'non-Western' cultures (Gruenbaum, 1996; Parker, 1999). Mohanty (1988) critiques Western feminist discourse on 'Third-World women' that constructs them as a homogeneous 'powerless' group who are the victims of male violence around the world. Such representations of women, as 'archetypal victims', objectify them and deny their agency, while simultaneously constructing men as static 'subjects-who-perpetrate-violence'. Mohanty argues that analyses of 'male violence', for example, must be theorized and interpreted *within* specific societies in order to understand it better and effectively organize to challenge it.

Preis (2002) argues that the stalemate of the universality–relativity debate is due to the fact that both stances draw on an unproblematic, outmoded notion of 'culture' as a static, homogeneous, bounded unit. As discussed earlier, culture is increasingly conceived of as a 'porous array' of everyday practices, shared meanings, symbols and discourses that are multi-vocal and constantly shifting (Rosaldo, 1989, cited in Preis, 2002). Development interventions which start from a more dynamic understanding of cultural difference – and seek to engage with the web of meanings, cultural values, practices and social relations evident in specific contexts – appear to stand a better chance of fulfilling people's economic, social and cultural rights, enhancing their well-being and fostering their capabilities.

220

KEY POINTS

- Understandings of culture have shifted over time according to different theories and ideologies of development. Modernist perspectives viewed culture as a discrete bounded entity that hindered 'progress' towards a 'modern' (Western) society. Post-colonial and post-development perspectives have revealed the ethnocentric cultural assumptions and values that underpin such notions of development.
- Culture can be seen as the representations and everyday interactions, practices and values that shape every aspect of social life. It is a fluid process that is constantly being transformed and reproduced across space by multidirectional connections and cultural interactions within the context of globalization.
- The importance of culture is increasingly recognized in development agendas, although different actors often adopt different approaches.

These range from more narrow understandings of culture as a product or tool to achieve economic growth, to more progressive understandings that seek to mobilize culture to achieve social justice.

- Rights-based approaches to development have become increasingly prominent since the late 1990s. Key elements are the link between development and human rights, greater accountability of states and international actors, an emphasis on empowerment, participation and non-discrimination, and attention to vulnerable groups.

- Criticisms of rights-based development include the fact that the 'state-centric' approach establishes the nation state as the primary site for accountability and responsibility for fulfilling people's rights, which contradicts the dominant neoliberal paradigm and contemporary era of globalization. The universalist and individualistic nature of the international human rights legal framework has also been criticized for not taking account of cultural differences and the communitarian values evident in much of the global South.

- Cultural relativist arguments that people's rights and obligations can only be defined in relation to particular cultural, ideological and political contexts have also been subject to criticisms for failing to address important development concerns that affect people around the world. Notions of 'culture' and 'tradition' are often appropriated **221** by powerful actors to impose their views on societies.

- This raises the question of the potential of rights-based approaches to challenge sociocultural norms and institutional discrimination. Development interventions need to engage with the constantly shifting web of meanings, cultural values, practices and social relations in particular places in order to fulfil people's economic, social and cultural rights.

FURTHER READING

Schech and Haggis' *Culture and Development* (2000) provides a critical introduction to the relationship between culture, development and human rights, drawing on useful case studies to illustrate the arguments. Similarly, Radcliffe's edited book, *Culture and Development in a Globalizing World* (2006b) gives a helpful overview of recent approaches to culture and development from a range of global contexts. Schech and Haggis' collection, *Development: a Cultural Studies Reader* (2002), contains extracts from classic texts relating to culture and development by post-colonial and post-development theorists, such as Edward Said,

Stuart Hall and Arturo Escobar. Tsikata's chapter in Cornwall et al.'s *Feminisms in Development* (2007) provides a helpful overview of rights-based approaches to development and the tensions and challenges from a feminist perspective. Manzo's (2003) article in *Geoforum* and Tomalin's (2006) article in *Progress in Development Studies* give useful insights into the potential and tensions of rights-based development.

5.2 CIVIL SOCIETY, SOCIAL CAPITAL AND NON-GOVERNMENTAL ORGANIZATIONS (NGOS)

Participatory Development and Empowerment

The emergence of participatory development has brought about significant transformations in the ways in which development is constructed and articulated, and it has become firmly embedded in twenty-first century notions of legitimacy, civic engagement and citizenship. Grounded in the concepts of social exclusion and empowerment, participation advocates the involvement of local people in the development projects that impact upon their lives. Participatory development promises to deliver social inclusion through programmes that are designed to listen to, and act upon, the voices of local marginalized groups in society. Interest in participation has accompanied development theory and practice since the 1970s, and it originated as a radical backlash against top-down, expert-led modernist strategies that were disempowering for local communities (Mohan, 2008). Stemming from the work of Paul Freire on participatory research and participatory planning in physical development projects of the 1970s, the concept was further operationalized through Participatory Rural Appraisal (PRA) by Robert Chambers (see Chapter 3.1). In the 1990s, a growing body of literature on different perspectives on participatory development began to frame academic and policy discourse. Originally based on the principle that local development projects should be 'people-driven' and inclusionary, more recent interpretations of participation see the concept firmly embedded within more ambitious global goals of good governance, citizenship, human rights (see Chapter 5.1) and civil society. Participatory development is now widely used in a broad range of development projects worldwide but, despite widespread adoption by multilateral agencies and NGOs alike, there have been a number of problems associated with participatory approaches.

The term 'participation' is rather ambiguous, and it is open to a wide range of different interpretations and definitions. While some commentators focus on the importance of power sharing and cooperation, others take a more epistemological approach that advocates mutual learning as a way of understanding the issues that impact upon people's lives (Chambers, 1997) or a more transformative agenda that produces lasting social change (Hickey and Mohan, 2005). In reality, many development projects never exceed tokenism or what has been called 'co-option', whereby members of a community are enlisted onto expert-led committees but fail to make a substantial contribution to key decision making. Other critics have argued that participation has been used to justify the predetermined actions of external agencies like the World Bank and IMF in order to give legitimacy to their programmes. As such, the extent to which the development process has become truly participatory is contested as policies often lack the power fundamentally to change inequitable and unjust power relations at the global level (Mohan, 2008). Furthermore, the communities that engage in participatory projects are often seen as socially homogeneous, and agencies can easily bypass intra-community conflict and listen to the voices of the powerful minority over the majority. As discussed in Section Four, issues relating to gender, ethnicity, generation or disability may be paramount in deciding whose voices are heard. Despite these criticisms, there has still been widespread adoption of participation in grassroots development policy and praxis, due to the overriding consensus that it has the capacity to empower communities to play a role in their own development trajectories.

As mentioned earlier, fundamentally, participatory development is about facilitating the empowerment of marginalized communities. At its simplest, empowerment refers to any process by which people's control over their lives in increased. Back in the 1990s, empowerment was largely focused around enabling poor communities to claim their own political and economic spaces at the local level, and it was a particularly important component of gender and development programmes (see

Chapter 4.1). More recently, empowerment is seen as a wider process for facilitating self-reliance, well-being, political action and engagement in civil society at a range of spatial scales. Transformations in ICT, such as the Internet, have assisted the mobilization of virtual global communities to share experiences and advocate for change (see Chapter 3.4). Yet decades of policies aimed at empowering vulnerable communities, particularly in gender mainstreaming, have not really transformed power relations. Critics argue that empowerment can be just another form of 'managed intervention' in a neoliberal era where global structural inequalities remain stable (Lewis, 2002) (see Section 1). To address its fundamental aims, empowerment needs to do more than just 'invite' marginalized communities to participate (McEwan, 2005), it needs help them 'acquire' the skills and assets needed to 'reclaim' their own spaces and actively engage in strategies that fundamentally challenge inequitable global relations (Cornwall, 2002). In order to help communities reclaim political and economic space, attention has also been paid to understanding the role of social relationships and networks in engendering participation.

225

Understanding Social Relationships and Social Capital in Development

The rise and fall of social capital as a panacea for development tells an interesting story about the ways in which theoretical paradigms become quickly absorbed into policy and praxis without critical reflection. Social capital was one of the most popular development concepts of the 1990s, and it was universally embraced by development agencies and practitioners working with communities in both the global South and North. Social capital is a rather ambiguous and intangible concept that refers to the rules, norms, obligations, reciprocity and trust embedded in social relations, social structures and society's institutional arrangements which enable its members to achieve their individual and community objectives. Social networks encompass a diverse set of relationships and associations around a shared set of values or interests that may include: kinship or neighbourhood based groups; migrant networks; gender, political or religious based networks; or savings or worker related movements. The popularity of social capital can largely be attributed to Robert Putnam's (1993) study of regional government in Italy, where he argued that local participation in civic associations fostered greater levels of citizenship, accountability and responsibility in society, and efficiency in the economy. In essence, social capital refers to the different qualities that stem from people's social relationships, and it is argued that these qualities can have important impacts upon other aspects of life for both individuals and societal groups (Bebbington, 2008).

There have been a number of different interpretations which have framed key debates over social capital's contribution to development studies (Bebbington, 2007). Uphoff (1999) differentiates social capital according to whether it is cognitive or structural. Cognitive social capital refers to the importance of intangible qualities such as trust, which are inextricably linked to behaviours, experiences and attitudes. Structural social capital focuses on the structure of social relationships, their associations and networks, whether they are informal or formal, or built upon weak or strong ties. Furthermore, bonding social capital refers to the links between like-minded people or 'people like us' while bridging social capital is based on the building of connections between people from different social, class or ethnic groups.

226   According to many commentators, it is structural rather than cognitive social capital that has been enthusiastically adopted as a framework for explaining poverty and vulnerability in development studies. As discussed in Chapter 3.1, development agencies highlighted the importance of social capital in helping vulnerable communities to access resources and services, a view that was promoted via the livelihood assets framework popular at the time and resulted in its mainstreaming by the World Bank (Moser, 1998).

Since its heyday in the 1990s, social capital has undergone a substantial critique for a number of weaknesses (Bebbington, 2004). First, the concept is seen to be too broad to offer any meaningful insight into the social fabric of people's lives. Secondly, it fails to explore the role of power in shaping social relations and networks, and it is often seen to be gender neutral. From a neoliberal perspective, facilitating communities to increase their stocks of social capital is a relatively low cost option that aligns responsibility for local development with individuals and community groups, rather than the state. Thirdly, policies aimed at bridging social capital were often too focused on asset-based livelihood frameworks that proclaimed 'more social capital' as the ultimate goal, a view that neglected the negative impacts of people's inclusion in some social networks or associations. In his work on 'habitus' – which refers to the implicit assumptions, habits, the 'taken for granted' ideas and ways of operating that underpin social networks – Bourdieu (1977) argued that social capital needed to be understood within wider political and cultural relations. As such, social networks come with a set of cultural markers, or cultural capital, that can be exclusionary as well as inclusionary – a factor that was often bypassed in development projects. Although the power of social capital as a tool for poverty alleviation is now regarded as overstated, it has been a valuable tool in focusing attention on the role played by social relationships and associations in structuring people's everyday livelihoods. Furthermore, and in the context of development, some have argued that there is a strong synergy between social capital and civil society associations in local development (Mohan and Stokke, 2000).

Civil Society, Collective Action and NGOs

While the state has often been seen as an impediment to participatory development, it is argued that meaningful participation at the grass-roots requires an alternative set of relationships, actors and agencies. Civil society is an arena of collective social interactions that is situated between the household, market and the state, and it encompasses a diverse range of NGOs, groups, networks and associations (McIlwaine, 2007). Civil society organizations can be further differentiated according to type, size, function, scale of operation and place. Central to the notion of civil society is its relationship with the nation state and it is often seen as a means of limiting the power of the state and challenging its legitimacy. While civil society operates at a range of spatial scales, McIlwaine argues that it is theoretically flawed to speak of a 'global civil society' in the absence of a global state; instead she identifies a transnational civil society that consists of a mix of overlapping groups and actors that operate across national borders.

227

Though it is argued that a strong civil society encourages the citizenship, democracy, cooperation, tolerance and accountability required to foster development and social inclusion, two main theoretical viewpoints have emerged. First, there is a liberal democratic approach that views civil society as a beneficial force for good, a non-critical stance that has been adopted by many development agencies. Civil society is important to the neoliberal agenda as it fosters democracy and undertakes important service delivery functions in place of the state. An alternative and more radical perspective comes from a Marxist or Gramscian tradition, focusing on the notion that civil society represents a site of resistance and counter hegemony in the capitalist economic system.

In the 1990s, development agencies championed civil society as a way of facilitating participatory development, but over time it has become increasingly open to criticism. Civil society is extremely heterogeneous and encompasses a diverse range of interest groups that compete for power over limited resources. Civil Society Organizations (CSOs) may be further differentiated along social axes based on class, religion, gender, ethnicity or disability, among others. Widely criticized for failing to reach poor and marginal groups, it is important to note that civil society is not inherently radical as it includes the interest groups of wealthy elites as well as those from poorer communities, a situation that creates an arena of inherent conflict and inclusion/exclusion. However, more radical interpretations of civil society have focused upon the informal collective action between individuals or groups that develops into social movements. New social movements, as they were labelled in the 1990s, referred to the growth of grassroots community and self-help groups that sought to challenge or resist powerful interest groups or regulations. According to McEwan (2005), social movements can provide 'action spaces' for marginal communities to create alternative ideologies and plans for social change, although their informality can often limit their effectiveness. Despite the growth of grassroots collective action in human rights and worker solidarity, it is Non-Governmental Organizations (NGOs) that have been identified as the main agents of civil society and they have become an important stage for addressing global development agendas.

228

'Non-Governmental Organization' is a broad term applied to a range of non-profit, non-state organizations that range from large Northern NGOs, like Oxfam or Save the Children, to local co-operatives and self-help organizations in the global South (Desai, 2008). Originally based on providing direct intervention to poor communities in the global South, NGOs were regarded as magic bullets for development in the 1990s. By the millennium, their failure to engender widespread progress in the global South prompted Northern NGOs to address the fact that international political processes and power relations – circumstances that led them to expand their roles into advocacy and activism – impeded their efforts. Participatory approaches to development were also increasingly critical of expert-led projects; Northern NGOs were sought to build new partnerships with indigenous Southern NGOs to manage projects at the grassroots. These fundamental changes to civil society have transformed the political landscape of development. International funding has been increasingly channelled towards the big international NGOs (BINGOs), a situation that undermines informal organizations and social movements. Nelson (2006) notes that many Northern NGOs do not work with smaller grassroots organizations, and she argues that the concentration of funds among larger organizations creates unfair competition.

As a result of their growing power base, BINGOS have increasingly been accused of tokenism, bureaucracy, non-democracy and wasting funds on staff costs and expenses. Furthermore, the role of Northern NGOs as 'ambassadors' and Southern NGOs as the 'representatives of the poor' has increasingly been problematized (Mercer, 2002). Assumptions that indigenous NGOs always represent the interests of the poor are contentious as many organizations are staffed by local elites who bring with them their own agendas and political biases (McIlwaine, 2007). As such, NGOs are criticized for failing to address structural issues underlying poverty and inequality in both local and international arenas (Mohan, 2002). Recent partnerships between BINGOs and MNCs, whether in coffee or clothing, have raised further questions over their independence, impartiality and autonomy.

Despite these misgivings, the reality is that NGOs are now key agents in a global development business. Although some critics have labelled them as the 'human face' of neoliberalism, BINGOs like Oxfam have the capacity to influence international agendas, raise public awareness of injustice and human rights abuses, and campaign against damaging state and corporate legislation. By acting as catalysts for gender equality or anti-slavery, they have brought about transformations in global policy by mobilizing large numbers of people in both the North and South. Although civil society has provided new spaces for social mobilization and resistance, the extent to which it has the capacity significantly to transform the lives of the majority of people in the global South is questionable. Although NGOs have transformed development agendas in the twenty-first century, their overall legacy in grassroots participation and empowerment remains to be seen.

KEY POINTS

- The concepts of participation and empowerment have been widely adopted by development agencies worldwide since the 1990s, and they promise to listen to, and act upon, the voices of local marginalized groups in society.
- The extent to which the development process has become truly participatory or empowering is contested, as policies often lack the power fundamentally to change inequitable and unjust social relations at the global level.
- Grounded in the notions of civic engagement and association, social capital was seen as a panacea for development in the 1990s but its popularity as a tool for poverty alleviation has diminished due to its ambiguity and breadth.
- Civil society has been championed as a way of facilitating participatory development, and it has created new spaces for marginal communities to mobilize and campaign for rights, resources and equity.
- Although informal social movements and grassroots organizations have been indentified as providing more radical spaces for action and resistance, NGOs have been identified as the main agents of civil society in the twenty-first century. NGOs have become an important stage for addressing the development issues that frame participatory development.

FURTHER READING

There is a substantial literature on the issues raised in this chapter but sound introductions to the interrelated concepts of participation, social capital and civil society can be found in Desai and Potter's *Companion to Development Studies* (2008): Giles Mohan on participatory development (Chapter 1.10); Anthony Bebbington on social capital (Chapter 2.15); and Vandana Desai on NGOs (Chapter 10.6). Anthony Bebbington offers further critique of the concept of social capital in a series of reports for *Progress in Development Studies*, while Cathy McIlwaine (2007) provides a comprehensive and illuminating review of local and global civil society in *Geography Compass*, 1 (16) and Cheryl McEwan (2005) explores the gendering of new spaces of citizenship in *Political Geography*, 24 (8).

5.3 MIGRATION, TRANSNATIONALISM AND DEVELOPMENT

This chapter deals with the main characteristics and features of the migration of people in contemporary times, and the consequences of migrants' decisions for the source and destination societies and their economies. Both internal and international mobility is discussed and, in addition to discussing the main types of movement, the developmental consequences of migration are given specific attention.

First, migration in its many varied forms is detailed. As a primary factor of production, migrant labour must obviously be considered for its developmental impacts and consequences. Particular attention is then paid to a recent form of international movement conceptualized as transnationalism, because this flexible form of cross-border mobility is being practised more and more often in response to the globalizing world. The global-to-local forces underway that are impacting millions of lives are also rendering national boundaries less meaningful in terms of such mobile people's identity formation and territorial affiliation(s). Multiple citizenship is replacing unitary citizenship for many, as dual passports become advantageous for transnationally mobile professionals and global workers (Stalker 2000; Faist and Kivisto, 2007).

The migration–development nexus of interrelationships is next examined. This is because the increasing influence of migrant-donated remittances in the development and growth of the home communities they have left is currently viewed as a very important development factor (Newland, 2007). Both economic (monetary) and social remittances are discussed, because their growing value and broadening scope of impacts are becoming more appreciated than in times past.

Migration

Human migration involves the movement of a person (a migrant) between two places for a certain period of time. It is often considered a relatively permanent relocation as compared to temporary spatial mobility, which includes all kinds of movement such as commuting, temporary working away from home, circulating 'back and forth' and visiting. Commonly, the migrant's migration decision is motivated by 'hope' that the move will bring positive returns to themself, or themselves, and/or provide better opportunities for their children.

Internal migration

Internal migration within national political boundaries has always been the largest kind of population redistribution enumerated since demographic statistics have been collected and compared at global scales. Its character is often differentiated by the source and destination of such flows, with rural-to-urban migration almost always being the most prevalent internal migration stream. Urban-to-urban and urban-to-suburban movement has occasionally predominated in advanced, highly urbanized economies such as the US. Most significantly, migration has been a fundamental factor in economic development precisely because capitalist growth and accumulation depends upon the ready availability of migrant labour. With urban-industrialization processes evolving under successive phases of capitalist expansion from the eighteenth century onwards, in-migration of a much-needed labour force from less-developed rural areas has contributed to the rapid growth of the world's urban centres in the global North and South (Todaro 1976; Skeldon 1997).

232

Concerning urbanization patterns in the global South, Michael Lipton (1977) has argued convincingly of an 'urban bias' in development theory and practice. To Lipton, modernization's messages and advocacy of conventional economic development theory and practice, such as urban industrialization, adoption of modern technological innovations and the like, have always discriminated against the rural poor of the global South – in this case, by making them urban poor. With rural development ignored, or treated as a secondary concern across the global South, many have had to in-migrate to their nearby cities in search of work, to make a living, or simply survive. Once

there, these newcomers live in urban squalor and poverty, in burgeoning squatter settlements with few resources, no infrastructure and few
social services. Josef Gugler (1982) would soon add a caveat to Lipton's
arguments, charging that 'overurbanization' was another reason why
the poor stayed poor in the global South. In his view, much of the
blame for such urban migrant poverty could be directed at the South's
urban elites who were only too eager to have the majority of resources
of their developing societies invested in their largest cities, or 'centres
of power and privilege'.

Migration has consequences for development (or the lack thereof) in
rural sources too, and an important set of migration–development relationships occur both within countries and across borders, that have
both negative and positive aspects. While out-migration can cause disruptive and devastating labour losses, in-migration can swell the
number of unemployed, so that urban informal sectors have to absorb
the surpluses. Consequently, continuous excesses of uncontrolled occu-
pancy and irregular, spontaneous squatter settlements prevail to make
the residential landscapes of global South cities extremely disorderly
and divisive, relatively powerless, yet informally autonomous (Hardoy
and Satterthwaite, 1989). A fuller set of migration–development relationships will receive attention later, because cross-border as well as
internal migration processes are accompanied by a substantial set of
development impacts that appear to be more positive than the earlier
outcomes just mentioned (Skeldon, 1997).

International migration

International migration occurs when migrants cross national borders,
with immigration being a relatively permanent move to reside in a different country than the migrant's original home. Emigration is the
relatively permanent move out of the home country. International circulation refers to a more temporary move and subsequent return-move
between the migrant's source home country and their destination,
thereby completing a migration circuit 'back and forth' across borders.
The 2009 UN Human Development Report estimated that by mid-2010
there would be around 214 million international migrant workers and
their families, voluntarily residing outside their country of birth. This
figure excludes the world's 15–16 million refugees, those whose movement across a border has been forced by fear of persecution or violence.

233

It does include, however, an estimated total of between 20 and 30 million unauthorized, or irregular migrants who do not possess work permits or residency permits, or who have illegally/clandestinely entered and stayed in the country whose border they crossed (International Organization of Migration (IOM), 2005; 2008).

Transnationalism

In contemporary times, both temporary and relatively permanent international 'cross-border' movements can take on more diverse and complex characters, with migrants undertaking what has come to be labelled transnational migration (Vertovec, 2009). Conceived as a transformative spatial and mobile option for an increasing number of international migrants, transnationalism constitutes the social, economic and cultural experiences and practices of living 'between two or more life-worlds'. Globalization's influences have also contributed, so that over time and through their life-course transnational migrants undertake repetitive mobilities; circulate regularly; pursue skill acquisition, occupational advancement and wealth; and exchange information, knowledge, remittances, goods in kind, technologies and innovations via IT and other communication media, or personally on visits. In short, many live highly mobile lives which are strategically flexible and cosmopolitan in terms of their career and family goals.

234

Transnationalism's 'cross-border', multi-local spatial contexts span origin home environments and destination locales. The latter can be overseas diasporas of earlier waves of international migrants replenished by new-immigrant waves. Or, they can be new immigrants from non-traditional sending countries who soon form their own diasporic communities and build their own transnational networks and interactions. Of salience to many transnational migrants' security and social safety net is their reliance on family connections and obligations (Chamberlain, 2006). They benefit from belonging to multi-local, transnational networks of kith and kin, as well as retaining attachments to more than one national territory: their 'homeland' and their 'home away from home' (Conway 2007b). Regular return visiting, the maintenance of cross-border ties via international communications, regular donations of remittances to extended family members, maintenance of cross-border ties with friends and business partners, are all common practices of transnational migrants. Also part of many transnational migrants' strategies are the obligatory transfers of remittances to family, and their social and economic (monetary) investments in housing, land, community projects, international business partnerships and altruistic efforts. Such transfers and investments ensure their future lives and livelihoods remain 'flexible' and appropriately practical as they take advantage of their multiple transnational social links and networks (Conway, 2007b; Vertovec, 2009).

The Migration–Development Nexus

Remittances

There is an upsurge of interest in the migration–development nexus of relationships, because estimates of foreign currency deposits (though conservative under-estimations of the full range of remittances, pocket transfers, gifts in kind, cash exchanges and such) have demonstrated the rapid growth in size and importance of remittance flows from migrant donors to their countries of origin, during the last twenty-five years (World Bank, 2011). Indeed, a 2008 IOM estimate indicated flows of remittances were US$440 billion worldwide, of which US$330 billion went to developing countries.

235

Alleviating poverty in the global South, remittances are person-to-person flows that meet the immediate needs of family recipients, but also contribute to savings and investment when sustained. With remittances being spent locally to buy goods and services, this has a multiplier effect in the recipients' communities. Remittances represent a direct investment in human capital as well as needed consumption and, with further migration being financed as well, the reproduction of flows of remittances can be assured. Remittances can also be altruistic transfers to community and family to fulfil obligations, without repayment. On the negative side, however, remittances may create migration-dependency, encourage conspicuous consumption of luxury imports, and contribute locally to wealth inequalities – where 'haves' and 'have nots' among recipient households are distinguished by their overseas connections and family member's propensities, rather than their own industry and work effort while staying home (Cohen, 2005; Conway and Cohen, 1998; 2003; Newland, 2007).

Return migrants as 'agents of change'

'Counter-diasporic migration' is Russell King and Anastasia Christou's (2009) conceptual label for the return of second-generation, transnational migrants to Greece, their ancestral homeland, which illuminates the many ambiguities and cultural challenges such contemporary returnees have faced. Also, challenging what had been the conventional wisdom that Caribbean return migrants made few developmental impacts back home, Conway and Potter (2007) convincingly argued that despite their relatively small numbers, return migrants were making positive social and economic benefits and were contributing as significant 'agents of change'.

Social remittances

Continuing their revisions of earlier conventional ideas about remittances being more than mere material inputs 'back home', Peggy Levitt and Deepak Lamba-Nieves (2011) have widened the scope of social remittances' impacts to include the contributions of diasporic returnees as meaningful organizational actors. Consequently, this recognition of return migrants' considerable stocks of social and human capital has developmental implications for social remittances as vehicles for 'people-centred' organizational management and capacity building in global South origins (see Chapter 2.2). Migration-development relationships that occur at micro-scales such as these, therefore, appear to show promise for the future, in that migrant families and local communities appear to be the major beneficiaries. Regions and more geographically marginal areas, however, may not be so fortunate as investment prospects for social and economic remittances (Cohen, 2005; Newland, 2007).

Migration: Remittances and Beyond

It is no longer in doubt that there has been an increasing influence of migrant-donated remittances in the development and growth of the home communities they have left (International Organization of Migration (IOM) 2005; 2008). Migration and development relations are currently viewed as very important for global South development prospects (Faist, 2008). Remittances have always been sent back to family dependents back in the villages or small rural towns by city-ward

236

migrants, so that the labour loss was offset somewhat, though not if rural out-migration was excessive. At the global scale, not only are economic remittances making more substantial economic and social impacts in global South origin communities than international aid transfers (Newland, 2007), remittances are providing poor relatives with basic needs to help raise them above poverty levels, helping rebuild communities after natural disasters and crises have devastated their homelands, and generally helping families survive, and even prosper in many cases (Cohen, 2005; De Haas, 2005). Return migrants, whether temporary or relatively permanent are contributing social remittances, bringing professional skills and innovations, and bringing much-needed social capital and sociocultural resources back home (Gmelch, 1992; 2006; Conway, 2007a).

Summing up the current conventional wisdom about the migration–development nexus, Kathleen Newland offers this important caveat:

> The debate about the relationship between migration and development goes far beyond the trade-off between remittances and the brain drain. Diasporas have more to offer their countries of origin than remittances; in the long run, their skills, investments, and social networks may have more important effects. (2007: 6)

237

KEY POINTS

- Migration and development relations are currently viewed as very important for global South development prospects.
- Remittances are person-to-person monetary flows that meet the immediate needs of family recipients, but also contribute to savings and investment when sustained.
- Transnationalism refers to multiple ties and interactions linking people across the borders of nation states.

FURTHER READING

Peter Stalker's *Workers without Frontiers* (2000) is a very readable assessment of the new era of international migration that has accompanied globalization. Stephen Castles and Mark Miller's *The Age of Migration* (2009) has more comprehensive global coverage and is also a worthwhile read. Steven Vertovec's *Transnationalism* (2009) is the most concise and thorough explanation of the multidisciplinary nature of transnational migration experiences and practices. For remittances, Kathleen Newland's 'A new surge of interest in migration and development' (2007), on the Migration Information Source website, is a most accessible and readable article.

5.4 TOBIN-TYPE TAXES

Since the early 1970s, some analysts of the world economy have put forward proposals for the introduction of globally-based taxes in order to fight world poverty and underdevelopment. Just as importantly it is argued that, at the same time, such taxes would serve to reduce the volatility of international financial markets. In other words, what some people have argued is needed is for strong forms of global redistribution, representing a global response to the problems of global poverty and underdevelopment.

In 1972 James Tobin, then Professor of Economics at Yale University, suggested exactly that – the need for a global taxation on financial speculation, speculation being regarded as where another currency is bought over a short-term period in order to make a profit. Tobin put this argument forward in the Janeway Lectures that he gave at Princeton University. Born in 1918 and educated in economics at Harvard University from 1935, James Tobin had a long-term interest in financial markets and investment decision making extending back to the 1960s (Simon, 2006). It was in this context that Tobin suggested the need for global currency speculation to be taxed (see, for example, Tobin, 1978; 1996).

Tobin referred to such a tax as 'throwing sand in the wheels' of international financial markets, which would serve to reduce their overall volatility. At first this suggestion was ignored both by professional economists and policymakers, who were generally against any market interference, believing in the liberal and neoliberal view that markets should be left to regulate themselves (Simon, 2006). This was the predominant view held in the 1970s and 1980s among those operating the financial markets and among central bankers. Tobin was seen as advocating the ideas of John Maynard Keynes, who had suggested the general idea of transaction taxes in the 1930s. The implications of the tax for redistribution have led to it sometimes being referred to as the 'Robin Hood tax' or the 'Financial or Currency Transaction' tax.

The Basic Mechanism of Tobin-type Taxes

Commenting on his proposed tax, Tobin (1996: 154) stated:

> It would be an internationally agreed uniform tax, administered by each government over its own jurisdiction. Britain, for example, would be responsible for taxing all inter-currency transactions in Eurocurrency banks and brokers located in London, even when sterling was not involved.

It is estimated that between US$1.5 and 2.0 trillion are traded daily on foreign exchange markets around the world. This represents a large market – and one that is potentially very volatile. It is estimated that only 5 to 10 per cent of the total sum traded is necessary to finance global trade. The remainder effectively amounts to speculative trading, that is making profits from short-term changes in currency rates. It is reckoned that in two-thirds of all currency transactions, the money is moved into a foreign currency for less than seven days. Tobin-type taxes involve a levy of around 0.10 to 0.25 per cent on such global financial activities. Initially in proposing such a tax, Tobin suggested, 'let's say, 0.5 per cent of the volume of the transaction'.

240

Initially at least, it seemed that Tobin himself appeared to regard the funds raised by such taxation as a mere by-product of producing greater financial stability. However, it is estimated that this would presently yield between US$ 100 and 300 billion per year. Many sources assume that at present around US$ 250 billion per annum would be raised, that is, over five times the total amount that is given in aid around the world. Although formidable issues would have to be faced in collecting and allocating such monies, it is generally argued that revenues should be collected by national central banks and then deposited with a United Nations body such as the United Nations Development Programme (UNDP) or United Nations Educational, Scientific and Cultural Organization (UNESCO). Tobin originally suggested the World Bank or the International Monetary Fund should carry out such a function.

The US$250 billion that could be raised each year by a Tobin tax only makes full sense when we consider it alongside what might actually be achieved with such tranches of money. For example, it has long been estimated that as little as US$8 billion per year would be enough to establish universal primary education on a global basis. Meanwhile, the United Nations Development Programme has calculated that US$80 billions are needed to eliminate the worst forms of global poverty. Further, the Jubilee 2000 campaign argued that US$160 billion per annum would be the cost of wiping out the global South's unpayable debts.

Support for Tobin-style Taxes

James Tobin commented in 1995 that his initial idea 'did not make much of a ripple. In fact, one could say that it sank like a rock. The community of professional economists simply ignored it'. But in 1978 Tobin formalized his proposal, and in 1981, he was awarded the Nobel Prize for Economics for his work on global taxation. Tobin formally retired in 1988 and died in 2002 at the age of 84.

A Tobin-style tax was staunchly advocated in the mid-1990s by President François Mitterand of France, shortly before his death. At the start of the 2000s, the British Non-Government Organization, War on Want ran a very strong and extensive campaign supporting the introduction of a Tobin-style tax. At the same time, the Canadian parliament voted two-to-one in favour of introducing a Tobin tax. Anti-globalists also find it relatively easy to align with Tobin's proposals as there is the strong argument that they would serve to dampen down some of the most volatile and destabilizing aspects of financial globalization.

However, it appears that, in general, the very politicians who espouse globalization are those who dismiss out of hand a globalized tax to tackle global world poverty. Thus, in 1995, the then Managing Director of the International Monetary Fund, Michel Casessus is reported as having commented that 'financing an attack on poverty should be left to governments'. Notably, the possibility of global taxation was not even mentioned in the United Kingdom Government's 2000 White Paper dealing with the links between globalization and poverty reduction (DFID, 2000b).

As a result of the financial crash of 2008 onwards, however, the idea of a Tobin tax has been resurrected in a number of quarters. In 2009, the approach was still being actively supported by the Governments of France and Brazil. At the G20 Summit in Scotland in November 2009 the then British Prime Minister, Gordon Brown, specifically raised the idea of a transaction tax. In addition Angela Merkel, the Chancellor of Germany, expressed her support for such a tax in December 2009.

241

A number of commentators have argued that the real constraint on the introduction of Tobin-style taxes as a platform for world development and stability remains the lack of an overall political will in the places that matter – Washington, London, Tokyo, Frankfurt (Potter et al., 2008). In all too many cases, the call for such redistributive mechanisms has been met by the response that taxation is the concern of the sovereign state and, therefore, cannot be regarded as a global issue.

KEY POINTS

- The idea of establishing a global tax on currency transactions was strongly advocated by the American economist James Tobin in 1972.
- The basic idea is to levy a tax of between 0.1 and 0.25 per cent on all transactions between currencies.
- Although a small percentage, it is estimated that globally such a tax would generate around US$250 billion per annum for development purposes, in particular the alleviation of poverty.
- A major consideration is that a Tobin tax would also serve to promote greater financial stability by damping down financial markets, rather than the extreme volatility that so often seems to characterize them.
- While the Tobin tax has been advocated by NGOs such as War on Want, in the political domain considerable resistance clearly remains to the introduction of global forms of taxation.

242

FURTHER READING

One of the most accessible summaries of the Tobin tax and the wider work of James Tobin is provided in David Simon's biographical essay on James Tobin, which appeared in the same author's edited collection under the title, *Fifty Key Thinkers on Development* (2006). An overview of the tax is to be found in Chapter 4 of Rob Potter et al.'s text *Geographies of Development* (2008). The War on Want 'It's time for Tobin' campaign aimed at introducing the Tobin tax is to be found on the website (www.waronwant.org/past-campaigns/tobin-tax), from which you can download the 23-page booklet under the title, *The Currency Transaction Tax: Rate and Revenue Estimates*, published by the United Nations University, War on Want and the North–South Institute (2008).

BIBLIOGRAPHY

Aboderin, I. (2008) 'Ageing', in V. Desai and R.B. Potter (eds), *The Companion to Development Studies*, 2nd edn. London: Hodder Education. pp. 418–23.

Afshar, H. and Barrientos, S. (1999) *Women, Globalization and Fragmentation in the Developing World*. London: Macmillan.

Aggleton, P. and Parker, R. (2010) *The Routledge Handbook of Sexuality, Health and Rights*. Abingdon: Routledge.

Aguilar, J.V. and Cavada, M. (2002) *Ten Plagues of Globalization*, trans. K. Ogle. Washington, DC: EPICA.

Aitken, S. (2001) 'Global crises of childhood: rights, justice and the unchildlike child', *Area*, 33 (2): 119–27.

Almroth, L., Alroth-Berggren, V., Hassanein, O., El Hadi, N., Al-Said, S., Hasan, S., Lithell, U-B. and Bergstroem, S. (2001) 'A community based study on the change of practice of female genital mutilation in a Sudanese village', *International Journal of Gynecology and Obstetrics*, 74: 179–85.

Amanor, K.S. and Moyo, S. (2008) *Land and Sustainable Development in Africa*. London: Zed Books.

Amin, S. (1976) *Unequal Development: An Essay on the Social Formation of Peripheral Capitalism*. New York: Monthly Review Press.

Amin, S. (1990) *Delinking: Towards a Polycentric World*. London: Zed Books.

Amin, S. (2007) *A Life Looking Forward: Memoirs of an Independent Marxist*. London: Zed Books.

Andrews, G., Milligan, C., Phillips, D. and Skinner, M. (2009) 'Geographical gerontology: mapping a disciplinary intersection', *Geography Compass*, 3 (5): 1641–59.

Andreyev, I. (1977) *The Non-Capitalist Way*. Moscow: Progress Publishers.

Annan, K. (2000) 'The politics of globalization', in P. O'Meara, H.D. Mehlinger and M. Krain (eds), *Globalization and the Challenges of a New Century: A Reader*. Bloomington, IN: Indiana University Press. pp. 125–30.

Ansell, N. (2004) 'Secondary schooling and rural youth transitions in Lesotho and Zimbabwe', *Youth and Society*, 36 (2): 183–202.

Ansell, N. (2005) *Children, Youth and Development*. London: Routledge.

Bacon, C. (2005) 'Confronting the coffee crisis: can fair trade, organic and speciality coffees reduce small-scale farmer vulnerability in Northern Nicaragua?', *World Development*, 33 (3): 497–511.

Baran, P.A. (1957) *The Political Economy of Growth*. New York: Monthly Review Press.

Baran, P.A. and Sweezy, P.M. (1966) *Monopoly Capital: An Essay on the American Economic and Social Order*. Harmondsworth: Penguin Books.

Barnes, C. and Mercer, G. (2003) *Disability*. Cambridge: Polity Press.

Bass, L. (2004) *Child Labor in Sub-Saharan Africa*. Boulder, CO: Lynne Rienner.

Baylies, C. and Bujra, J. (eds) (2000) *AIDS, Sexuality and Gender in Africa: Collective Strategies and Struggles in Tanzania and Zambia*. Abingdon and New York: Routledge.

Bebbington, A. (2004) 'Social capital and development studies 1: critique, debate, progress?', *Progress in Development Studies*, 4 (4): 343–9.

Bebbington, A. (2007) 'Social capital and development studies II: can Bourdieu travel to policy?', *Progress in Development Studies*, 7 (1): 155–62.

Bebbington, A. (2008) 'Social capital and development', in V. Desai and R.B. Potter (eds), *The Companion to Development Studies*. London: Hodder. pp. 132–6.

Bhat, B. (2010) 'Gender, education and child labour: a sociological perspective', *Educational Research and Reviews*, 5 (6): 323–8.

Black, R. and White, H. (2004) (eds) *Targeting Development: Critical Perspectives on the Millennium Development Goals*. London and New York: Routledge.

Blaikie, P. (2000) 'Development, post-, anti-, and populist: a critical review', *Environment and Planning A*, 32: 1033–50.

Boas, T., Dunning, T. and Bussell, J. (2005) 'Will the digital revolution revolutionise development? Drawing together the debate', *Studies in Comparative International Development*, 40 (2): 95–110.

Boserup, E. (1970) *Women's Role in Economic Development*. London: George Allen & Unwin.

Bourdieu, P. (1997) *Outline of a Theory of Practice*. Cambridge: Cambridge University Press.

Bourdillon, M. (2004) 'Children in Development', *Progress in Development Studies*, 4 (2): 99–113.

Bowlby, S., McKie, L., Gregory, S. and MacPherson, I. (2010) *Interdependency and Care Over the Lifecourse*. Oxford: Routledge.

Boyden, J. (1997) 'Childhood and the Policy Makers: A Comparative Perspective on the Globalization of Childhood', in A. James and A. Prout, *Constructing and Reconstructing Childhood*. London: Falmer Press. pp. 190–229.

Braathen, S. and Kvam, M. (2008) 'Can anything good come out of this mouth? Female experiences of disability in Malawi', *Disability and Society*, 23 (5): 461–74.

Bradley, C. (1993) 'Women's power, children's labor', *Cross-Cultural Research*, 27 (1–2): 70–96.

Brecher, J. and Costello, T. (1998) *Global Village to Global Pillage: Economic Reconstruction from the Bottom Up*, 2nd edn. Cambridge, MA: South End Press.

Brohman, J. (1996) *Popular Development: Rethinking the Theory and Practice of Development*. Oxford: Blackwell.

Brooker, P. (1992) *Modernism/Postmodernism*. London and New York: Longman.

Brookfield, H. (1975) *Interdependent Development*. London: Methuen.

Brown, G., Browne, K., Elmhirst, R. and Hutta, S. (2010) 'Sexualities in/of the Global South', *Geography Compass*, 4 (10): 1567–79.

Bujra, J. (2002) 'Targeting men for a change: AIDS discourse and activism in Africa', in F. Cleaver (ed.) *Masculinities Matter! Men, Gender and Development*. London: Zed Books: pp. 209–34.

Burnell, P. (2008) 'Foreign aid in a changing world', in V. Desai and R.B. Potter (eds), *The Companion to Development Studies*. London: Arnold. pp. 503–7.

Camargo, K. (2006) 'The failure of the World Bank to address sexuality', *ID21 Insights* 75. Institute of Development Studies, University of Sussex.

Carney, D. (ed.) (1998) *Sustainable Rural Livelihoods: What Contribution Can We Make?* London: Department for International Development.

Carr, M. and Chen, M. (2004) 'Globalization, social exclusion and work: with special reference to informal employment and gender', *International Labour Review: Special Issue on More Equitable Globalization*, 143: 1–2.

Castells, M. (2001) *The Internet Galaxy: Reflections on the Internet Business and Society*. Oxford: Oxford University Press.

Castles, S. and Miller, M.J. (2009) *The Age of Migration: International Population Movements in the Modern World*, 4th edn. Basingstoke: Palgrave MacMillan.

Chamberlain, M. (2006) *Family Love in the Diaspora: Migration and the Anglo-Caribbean Experience*. New Brunswick, USA; London; and Jamaica: Transaction Publishers and Ian Randle.

Chambers, R. (1983) *Rural Development: Putting the Last First*. London: Longman.

Chambers, R. (1997) *Whose Reality Counts? Putting the First Last*. London: Intermediate Technology Publications.

Chambers, R. and Conway, G. (1992) 'Sustainable rural livelihoods: practical concepts for the 21st century', *IDS Discussion Paper* 296. Brighton: Institute of Development Studies.

Chant, S. (2007a) 'Dangerous equations? How female-headed households became the poorest of the poor: causes, consequences and cautions', in A. Cornwall, E. Harrison and A. Whitehead (eds), *Feminisms in Development: Contradictions, Contestations and Challenge*. London: Zed Books.

Chant, S. (2007b) *Gender, Generation and Poverty: Exploring the 'Feminisation of Poverty' in Africa, Asia and Latin America*. Cheltenham: Edward Elgar.

Chant, S. (2008) 'The informal sector and employment', in V. Desai and R.B. Potter (eds), *The Companion to Development Studies*. London: Arnold. pp. 216–24.

Chant, S. and McIlwaine, C. (1995) *Women of a Lesser Cost: Female Labour, Foreign Exchange and Philippine Development*. London: Pluto Press.

Chant, S. and McIllwaine, C. (2009) *Geographies of Development in the 21st Century: An Introduction to the Global South*. London: Edward Elgar.

Chant, S. and Pedwell, C. (2008) *Women, Gender and the Informal Economy: An Assessment of ILO Research and Suggested Ways Forward*. Geneva: International Labour Organization. Available at http://www.ilo.org/global/What_we_do/Publications/WorkingPaper/lang_en/docName_WCMS_091228/index.htm [last accessed 1/11/10].

Chari, S. and Corbridge, S. (eds) (2008) *The Development Reader*. London and New York: Routledge.

Chen, M., Vanek, J. and Heintz, J. (2006) 'Informality, gender and poverty', *Economic and Political Weekly*, 27 May: 2131–9.

Chilcote, R.H. (1984) *Theories of Development and Underdevelopment*. Boulder, CO and London: Westview Press.

Cho, G. (1995) *Trade, AID and Global Interdependence*. London: Routledge.

Chronic Poverty Research Centre (2010) *Stemming Girls' Chronic Poverty: Catalysing development change by building just social institutions*. Chronic Poverty Research Centre, available at www.chronicpoverty.org [last accessed 10/1/11].

Clacherty, G. (2008) *Living with our Bibi. A qualitative study of children living with grandmothers in the Nshamba area of north western Tanzania*. South Africa: World Vision and REPSSI.

Cohen, J.H. (2005) 'Remittance outcomes and migration: theoretical contests, real opportunities', *Studies in Comparative International Development*, 40: 88–112.

245

Collard, D. (2000) 'Generational transfers and the generational bargain', *Journal of International Development*, 12: 453–62.

Conway, D. (2007a) 'The importance of remittances for the Caribbean's future transcends their macroeconomic influences', *Global Development Studies*, 4: 3–4: 41–76.

Conway, D. (2007b) 'Caribbean transnational migration behaviour: reconceptualising its "strategic flexibility"', *Population, Space and Place*, 13: 415–31.

Conway, D. and Cohen, J.H. (1998) 'Consequences of migration and remittances for Mexican transnational communities', *Economic Geography*, 74: 26–44.

Conway, D. and Cohen, J.H. (2003) 'Local dynamics in multi-local, transnational spaces of rural Mexico: Oaxacan experiences', *International Journal of Population Geography*, 9: 141–61.

Conway, D. and Heynen, N. (2005) 'The ascendency of neoliberalism and emergence of globalization', in D. Conway and N. Heynen, *Globalization's Contradictions: Geographies of Discipline, Destruction and Transformation*. Aldershot: Ashgate. pp. 17–34.

Conway, D. and Potter, R.B. (2007) 'Caribbean transnational return migrants as agents of change', *Geography Compass*, 1: 25–45.

Corbridge, S. (1997) 'Beneath the pavement only soil: the poverty of post-development', *Journal of Development Studies*, 33: 138–48.

Cornwall, A. (2002) 'Making spaces, changing places: situating participation in development', *IDS Working Paper* 170, Brighton: Institute of Development Studies.

Cornwall, A. and Jolly, S. (2006) 'Introduction: sexuality matters', *IDS Bulletin*, 37 (5): 1–11.

Cornwall, A., Corrêa, S. and Jolly, S. (eds) (2008) *Development with a Body: Sexuality, Human Rights and Development*. London: Zed Books.

Cornwall, A., Harrison, E. and Whitehead, A. (eds) (2007) *Feminisms in Development: Contradictions, Contestations and Challenges*. London: Zed Books.

Corrêa, S. and Jolly, S. (2008) 'Development with a body: making the connections between sexuality, human rights and development', in A. Cornwall, S. Corrêa and S. Jolly (eds), *Development with a Body: Sexuality, Human Rights and Development*. London: Zed Books. pp. 1–21.

Cowen, M.P. and Shenton, R. (1995) *Doctrines of Development*. London: Routledge.

Cox, H. (1999) 'The Market as God: living in the new dispensation', *The Atlantic Monthly*, 283 (3): 4.

Cracknell, D. (2004) 'Electronic banking for the poor – panacea, potential and pitfalls', *Small Enterprise Development*, 15 (4): 8–24.

Crang, M. (1998) 'Locating culture', in M. Crang (1998) *Cultural Geography*. London: Routledge. pp. 1–13.

Dag Hammarskjöld Foundation (1975) *What Now? Another Development*. Uppsala: Dag Hammarskjöld Foundation.

Dag Hammarskjöld Foundation (1977) *Another Development: Approaches and Strategies*. Uppsala: Dag Hammarskjöld Foundation.

Daly, H.E. (1973) *Economics, Ecology, Ethics: Essays toward a Steady-State Economy*. San Francisco, CA: W.H. Freeman & Co.

Daly, H.E. (1990) 'Sustainable growth: an impossibility theorem', *Development – Journal of Society for International Development*, 3 (4): 45–7.

Bibliography

Daly, H.E. (1991) 'Notes towards an environmental macroeconomics', in N. Girvan and D. Simmons (eds), *Caribbean Ecology and Economics*. Barbados: Caribbean Conservation Association. pp. 9–24.

Daly, H.E. (1996) *Beyond Growth: The Economics of Sustainable Development*. Boston, MA: Beacon Press.

Danaher, K. (1994) *50 Years is Enough: The Case against the World Bank and the International Monetary Fund*. Cambridge, MA: South End Press.

Dean Nielsen, H. (2009) *Moving Toward Free Primary Education: Policy Issues and Implementation Challenges*. Social and Economic Working Paper, UNICEF Policy and Practice, United Nations Children's Fund (UNICEF), the World Bank, and the Education for All-Fast Track Initiative (EFA FTI): November 2009. Available at http://www.unicef.org/socialpolicy/files/Postscript_Formatted_SFAI_SOA_Review_11_December_2009.pdf [last accessed 20/11/10].

Debray, R. (1974) *A Critique of Arms*. Paris: Seuil.

Deere, C. and Doss, C. (2006) *Gender and the Distribution of Wealth in Developing Countries*, Research Paper No 2006/115. Helsinki: United Nations University World Institute for Development Economics Research (UNU-WIDER).

De Haas, H. (2005) 'International migration, remittances and development: myths and facts', *Third World Quarterly*, 26: 1269–84.

Department for International Development (DFID) (1999) *Sustainable Livelihoods and Poverty Elimination*. London: Department for International Development.

Department for International Development (DFID) (2000a) *Disability, Poverty and Development*. London: Department for International Development.

Department for International Development (DFID) (2000b) *Eliminating World Poverty: Making Globalization Work for the Poor*, White Paper on International Development. London: Department for International Development.

Desai, V. (2008) 'The role of non-governmental organizations (NGOs)', in V. Desai and R.B. Potter (eds), *The Companion to Development Studies*. London: Hodder. pp. 525–30.

Desai, V. and Potter, R.B. (2008) (eds) *The Companion to Development Studies*, 2nd edn. London and New York: Hodder Education.

Dicken, P. (2007) *Global Shift: Mapping the Changing Contours of the World Economy*, 5th edn. London: Sage.

Doha Development Agenda (DDA) (WTO 2001) www.wto.org/english/tratop_e/dda_e/dda_e.htm [last accessed 20/10/11]

Eade, D. (1997) *Capacity Building: An Approach to People-centred Development*. Oxford Oxfam (UK and Ireland); Atlantic Highlands, NJ: Humanities Press International.

Easterly, W. and Pfutze, T. (2008) 'Where does the money go? Best and worst practices in foreign aid', *Journal of Economic Perspectives*. 22 (2): 1–36.

Edwards, M. (1996) 'New approaches to children and development: introduction and overview', *Journal of International Development*, 8 (6): 813–27.

Ekins, P. (1992) *A New World Order: Grassroots Movements for Global Change*. London and New York: Routledge.

Ekins, P. and Max-Neef, M. (1992) *Real-Life Economics: Understanding Wealth Creation*. London and New York: Routledge.

Elliott, J.A. (2006) *An Introduction to Sustainable Development*, 3rd edn. London and New York: Routledge.

Ellis, F. (2000) *Rural Livelihoods and Diversity in Developing Countries*. Oxford: Oxford University Press.

Escobar, A. (1995) *Encountering Development. The Making and Unmaking of the Third World*. Princeton, NJ: Princeton University Press.

Esteva, G. (1992) 'Development', in W. Sachs (ed.), *The Development Dictionary*. London: Zed Books. pp. 6–25.

Evans, R. (2010) 'Children's caring roles and responsibilities within the family in Africa', *Geography Compass*, 4 (10): 1477–96.

Evans, R. (2011) '"We are managing our own lives...": Life transitions and care in sibling-headed households affected by AIDS in Tanzania and Uganda', *Area*, 43 (4): 384–96.

Evans, R. and Becker, S. (2009) *Children Caring for Parents with HIV and AIDS: Global Issues and Policy Responses*. Bristol: The Policy Press.

Evans, R. and Thomas, F. (2009) 'Emotional interactions and an ethic of care: caring relations in families affected by HIV and AIDS', *Emotions, Space and Society*, 2, 111–19.

Evans, T. (2002) 'A human right to health?', *Third World Quarterly*, 23 (2): 197–215.

Faist, T. (2008) 'Migrants as transnational development agents: an inquiry into the newest round of the migration-development nexus', *People, Space and Place*, 14: 21–42.

Faist, T. and Kivisto, P. (2007) *Dual Citizenship in Global Perspective: From Unitary to Multiple Citizenship*. Basingstoke: Palgrave MacMillan.

Fanon, F. (1967) *The Wretched of the Earth (Les Damnés de la Terre [Fr]*, first published in 1961). Harmondsworth: Penguin Books.

Fisher, W.F. and Ponniah, T. (2003) *Another World is Possible: Popular Alternatives to Globalization at the World Social Forum*. London and New York: Zed Books.

Food and Agriculture Organization of the United Nations (FAO) (2010) *The State of Food and Agriculture 2010–2011: Women in Agriculture – Closing the Gender Gap for Development*. Geneva: FAO.

Frank, A.G. (1967) *Capitalism and Underdevelopment in Latin America: Historical Studies of Chile and Brazil*. New York and London: Monthly Review Press.

Frank, A.G. (1969) *Latin America: Underdevelopment or Revolution*. New York: Monthly Review Press.

Frank, A.G. (1979) *Dependent Accumulation and Underdevelopment*. New York: Monthly Review Press.

Freeman, C. (2000) *High Tech and High Heels in the Global Economy: Women, Work and Pink-collar Identities in the Caribbean*. London: Duke University Press.

Friedmann, J. (1992) *Empowerment: The Politics of Alternative Development*. Cambridge and Oxford: Blackwell.

Friere, P. (2000) *Pedagogy of the Oppressed*, 30th anniversary edn [first published in 1970]. New York: Continuum.

Furlong, A. and Cartmel, F. (2007) *Young People and Social Change: New Perspectives*. Maidenhead: Open University Press.

George, S. (1988) *A Fate Worse than Debt*. New York: Grove Press.

George, S. (1992) *The Debt Boomerang: How Third World Debt Harms Us All*. Ann Arbor, MI: University of Michigan Press.

George, S. (1999) *A Short History of Neoliberalism*, Paper presented at the Conference on Economic Sovereignty in a Globalizing World, 24–26 March, Global

Policy Forum. Available at http://www.globalpolicy.org/globaliz/econ/histneo1.htm [last accessed 16/4/03].

Gereffi, G. (1994) 'The organization of buyer-driven global commodity chains: how US retailers shape overseas production networks', in G. Gerrefi and M. Korzenewicz (eds), *Commodity Chains and Global Capitalism*. London: Praeger.

Giddens, A. (1990) *The Consequences of Modernity*. Cambridge: Polity Press.

Giddens, A. (2003) *Runaway World: How Globalization is Reshaping our Lives*. New York: Routledge.

Giddens, A. and Pierson, C. (1998) *Conversations with Anthony Giddens: Making Sense of Modernity*. Stanford, CA: Stanford University Press.

Gmelch, G. (1992) *Double Passage: the Lives of Caribbean Migrants Abroad and Back Home*. Ann Arbor, MI: University of Michigan Press.

Gmelch, G. (2006) 'Barbadian migrants abroad and back home', in D. Plaza and F. Henry (eds), *Returning to the Source: the Final Stage of the Caribbean Migration Circuit*. Jamaica, Barbados, Trinidad and Tobago: The University of the West Indies Press. pp. 49–73.

Goodland, R., Daly, H. and El Serafy, S. (1992) *Population, Technology and Lifestyle: The Transition to Sustainability*. Washington, DC: Island Press.

Goodman, M. (2004) 'Reading fair trade: political ecological imaginary and the moral economy of fair trade foods', *Political Geography*, 23 (7): 891–915.

Gould, H. (2007) 'What's culture got to do with HIV and AIDS?', *Findings*, 7. Healthlink Worldwide. Available at http://www.healthlink.org.uk/PDFs/findings7_hiv_culture.pdf [last accessed 29/10/11].

Goulet, D. (1971) *The Cruel Choice: A New Concept on the Theory of Development*. London and New York: Routledge.

Goulet, D. (1996) 'A new discipline: development ethics', *Working Paper*, 231. University of Notre Dame, IN: The Kellogg Institute.

Gourou, P. (1947) *Les Pays Tropicaux: Principes d'une Geographie Humaine et Economique*. Paris: Presses Universitaires de France.

Graham, S. (2002) 'Bridging urban digital divides? Urban polarization and information and communications technologies (ICTs)', *Urban Studies*, 39 (1): 33–56.

Greenaway, D. and Milner, C. (2008) 'Trade and industrial policy in developing countries', in V. Desai and R.B. Potter (eds), *The Companion to Development Studies*. London: Arnold. pp. 196–201.

Gruenbaum, E. (1996) 'The cultural debate over female circumcision: the Sudanese are arguing this one out for themselves', *Medical Anthropology Quarterly*, New Series, 10 (4): 455–75.

Gugler, J. (1982) 'Overurbanization reconsidered', *Economic Development and Cultural Change*, 31: 173–89.

Gwynne, R.N. (2008) 'Free trade and fair trade', in V. Desai and R.B. Potter (eds), *The Companion to Development Studies*. London: Arnold. pp. 201–6.

Hale, A. and Opondo, M. (2005) 'Humanising the cut flower chain: confronting the realities of flower production for workers in Kenya', *Antipode*, 37 (2): 301–22.

Hall, S. (2002) 'The West and the Rest: Discourse and Power', in S. Schech and J. Haggis (eds), *Development: A Cultural Studies Reader*. Oxford: Blackwell Publishing. pp. 56–64.

Hall, S. and Gieben, B. (1992) *Foundations of Modernity*. Cambridge: Polity.

Hancock, G. (1989) *Lords of Poverty: The Power, Prestige and Corruption of the International Aid Business*. London: Macmillan.

Haq, Mahbub ul (1999) *Reflections on Human Development*. Delhi and Oxford: Oxford University Press.

Hardoy, J.E. and Satterthwaite, D. (1989) *Squatter Citizen: Life in the Urban Third World*. London: Earthscan Publishers.

Harriss, J. (2005) 'Great promise, hubris and recovery: a participant's history of development studies', in U. Kothari (ed.), *A Radical History of Development Studies: Individuals, Institutions and Ideologies*. Cape Town: David Philip; London and New York: Zed Books. pp. 17–46.

Harvey, D. (1973) *Social Justice and the City*. London: Arnold.

Harvey, D. (1990) *The Condition of Postmodernity: An Enquiry into the Origins of Cultural Change*. Cambridge, MA: Blackwell.

Harvey, D. (2005) *A Brief History of Neoliberalism*. Oxford: Oxford University Press.

Heeks, R. (2008) 'Current analysis and future research agenda on "gold farming": real world production in developing countries for the virtual economies of online games', *Development Informatics: Working Papers, Institute for Development Policy and Management, University of Manchester*, 32: 1–85. Available at http://www.sed. manchester.ac.uk/idpm/research/publications/wp/di/index.htm [last accessed 21/05/11].

Heise, L. (2007) 'Violence, sexuality and women's lives', in R. Parker and P. Aggleton (eds), *Culture, Society and Sexuality: A Reader*, 2nd edn. London: Routledge. pp. 275–97.

Heward, C. and Bunwaree, S. (eds) (1999) *Gender, Education and Development: Beyond Access to Empowerment*. London: Zed Books.

Hickey, S. and Mohan, G. (2005) 'Relocating participation within a radical politics of development', *Development and Change*, 36 (2): 237–62.

Hill, M. and Tisdall, K. (1997) *Children and Society*. Harlow: Addison Wesley Longman.

Hockey, J. and James, A. (2003) *Social Identities Across the Life Course*. Basingstoke: Palgrave MacMillan.

Hopkins, P. and Pain, R. (2007) 'Geographies of age: thinking relationally', *Area* 39 (3): 287–94.

Hubbard, P. (2008) 'Here, there, everywhere: the ubiquitous geographies of heteronormativity', *Geography Compass*, 2 (3): 640–58.

Huws, U. (2007) 'Defragmenting: towards a critical understanding of the new global division of labour', *Work Organisation, Labour and Globalisation*, 1 (2): 1–4.

Independent Commission on International Development Issues (1980) *North–South: A Programme for Survival*. London: Pan Books.

Inkeles, A. (1969) 'Making men modern: on the causes and consequences of individual change in six developing countries', *American Journal of Sociology*, 75 (2): 208–25.

International Forum on Globalization (2002) *Alternatives to Economic Globalization: A Better World is Possible*. San Francisco, CA: Barrett-Koehler.

International Fund for Agricultural Development (IFAD) (2010) *Rural Poverty Report 2011*. Rome: IFAD.

International Labour Organization (ILO) (2004) *Fair Globalization: Creating Opportunities for All*. Geneva: International Labour Organization, World

Bibliography

Commission on the Social Dimension of Globalization. Available at http://www.ilo. org/public/english/wcsdg/globali/globali.htm [last accessed 18/5/05].

International Labour Organization (ILO) (2010a) *World Employment Trends 2010*. Geneva: International Labour Office.

International Labour Organization (ILO) (2010b) *Accelerating Action against Child Labour: Global Report under the follow-up to the ILO Declaration on Fundamental Principles and Rights at Work*, Report I (B). Geneva: International Labour Office.

International Organization of Migration (IOM) (2005) *World Migration Report 2005*. Geneva: International Organization of Migration.

International Organization of Migration (IOM) (2008) *Global Estimates and Trends*. Geneva: International Organization of Migration.

Jackson, P. (2007) 'An explosion of Thai identities: global queering and re-imagining queer theory', in R. Parker and P. Aggleton (eds), *Culture, Society and Sexuality: A Reader*. London: Routledge. pp. 341–57.

Jacobs, S. (2008) 'Livelihood strategies and their environmental impacts', in V. Desai and R.B. Potter (eds), *The Companion to Development Studies*, 2nd edn. London: Arnold. pp. 334–41.

Jacobs, S. (2009) 'Gender and land reforms: comparative perspectives', *Geography Compass*, 3 (5): 1675–87.

Jacque, L.L. (2010) 'The currency wars', *Le Monde Diplomatique*, 3 December.

James, A. and Prout, A. (eds) (1997) *Constructing and Reconstructing Childhood*. London: Falmer Press.

Jennings, J., Aitken, S., Lopez Estrada, S. and Fernandez, A. (2006) 'Learning and earning: relational scales of children's work', *Area*, 38 (3): 231–9.

Jodha, N.S. (1988) 'Poverty debate in India: a minority view', *Economic and Political Weekly*, 23: 45–7.

Jolly, S. (2000) '"Queering" development: exploring the links between same-sex sexualities', *Gender and Development*, 8 (1): 78–88.

Jones, P. (2004) 'When "development" devastates: donor discourses, access to HIV/ AIDS treatment in Africa and rethinking the landscape of development', *Third World Quarterly*, 25 (2): 385–404.

Joseph, A. and Phillips, D. (1999) 'Ageing in rural China: impacts of increasing diversity in family and community resources', *Journal of Cross-Cultural Gerontology*, 14 (2): 153–68.

Kabeer, N. (1994) *Reversed Realities: Gender Hierarchies in Development Thought*. London: Verso.

Kabeer, N. (2000) 'Inter-generational contracts, demographic transitions and the "quantity–quality" trade-off: parents, children and investing in the future', *Journal of International Development*, 12 (4): 463–82.

Kabeer, N. (2008a) 'Gender, labour markets and poverty: an overview', *IPC Poverty in Focus*, 13: 3–5. Available at http://www.undp-povertycentre.org/pub/IPCPoverty InFocus13.pdf [last accessed 1/10/11].

Kabeer, N. (2008b) *Mainstreaming Gender in Social Protection for the Informal Economy*. London: Commonwealth Secretariat.

Kabzems, V. and Chimedza, R. (2002) 'Development assistance: disability and education in Southern Africa', *Disability and Society*, 17 (2): 147–57.

Kalipeni, E., Craddock, S., Oppong, J. and Ghosh, J. (2004) *HIV and AIDS in Africa: Beyond Epidemiology*. Oxford: Blackwell Publishing.

Kaplinsky, R. (2000) 'Globalisation and unequalisation: what can be learned from value chain analysis', *Journal of Development Studies*, 37 (2): 117–46.

Katz, C. (2004) *Growing up Global: Economic Restructuring and Children's Everyday Lives*. Minneapolis, MN: University of Minnesota Press.

Kelly M. (2005) 'The response of the educational system to the needs of orphans and children affected by HIV/AIDS', in G. Foster, C. Levine and J. Williamson (eds), *A Generation at Risk: The Global Impact of HIV/AIDS on Orphans and Vulnerable Children*. New York: Cambridge University Press. pp. 66–92.

Kesby, M., Gwanzura-Ottemoller, F. and Chizororo, M. (2006) 'Theorising *other*, "other childhoods": issues emerging from work on HIV in urban and rural Zimbabwe', *Children's Geographies*, 4 (2): 185–202.

King, R. and Christou, A. (2010) 'Cultural geographies of counter-diasporic migration: perspectives from the study of second-generation "returnees" to Greece', *Population, Space and Place*, 16: 103–19.

Korten, D. (1987) 'Third generation NGO strategies: a key to people-centered development', *World Development*, 15: 145–59.

Korten, D. (1990) *Getting to the 21st Century – Voluntary Action and the Global Agenda*. West Hartford, CT: Kumarian Press.

Korten, D.C. (1996) 'Sustainable development: conventional versus emergent alternative wisdom', Paper prepared for the Office of Technology Assessment, US Congress, Washington, DC, by D.C. Korten, The People Centered Development Forum, New York.

Korten, D. and Klauss, R. (1984) *People Centered Development: Contributions toward Theory and Planning Frameworks*. West Hartford, CT: Kumarian Press.

Kothari, U. (2005) 'A radical history of development studies: individuals, institutions and ideologies', in U. Kothari (ed.), *A Radical History of Development Studies: Individuals, Institutions and Ideologies*. Cape Town: David Philip; London and New York: Zed Books. pp. 1–14.

Kothari, U. (2006) 'An agenda for thinking about "race" in development', *Progress in Development Studies*, 6 (1): 9–23.

Leach, M., Mearns, R. and Scoones, I. (1999) 'Environmental entitlements: dynamics and institutions in community-based natural resource management', *World Development*, 27 (2): 225–47.

Le Mare, A. (2008) 'The impact of air trades on social and economic development: A review of the literature, *Geography Compass*, 2 (6): 1922–42.

Leclerc-Madlala, S. (2005) 'Popular responses to HIV/AIDS and policy', *Journal of Southern African Studies*, 31 (4): 845–56.

Lenin, V.I. (1963) 'Imperialism: the highest stage of capitalism', in *Lenin's Selected Works, Volume 1*. Moscow: Progress Publishers.

Lenin, V.I. (1972) 'The right of nations to self-determination', in *Lenin's Collected Works, Volume 20*, Moscow: Progress Publishers.

Levitt, P. and Lamba-Nieves, D. (2011) 'Social remittances revisited', *Journal of Ethnic and Migration Studies*, 37: 1–22.

Lewis, D. (2002) 'Civil society in African contexts: reflections on the usefulness of a concept', *Development and Change*, 33: 569–86.

Bibliography

Liddell, C., Barrett, L. and Bydawell, M. (2005) 'Indigenous representations of illness and AIDS in Sub-Saharan Africa', *Social Science and Medicine*, 60: 691–700.

Lipton, M. (1977) *Why Poor People Stay Poor: Urban Bias in World Development*. Cambridge, MA: Harvard University Press.

Lloyd-Evans, S. (2008a) 'Geographies of the contemporary informal sector in the global South: gender, employment relationships and social protection', *Geography Compass*, 2 (6): 1885–1906.

Lloyd-Evans, S. (2008b) 'Child labour', in V. Desai and R.B. Potter (eds), *The Companion to Development Studies*, 2nd edn. London: Hodder Education. pp. 225–9.

Lloyd-Evans, S. and Potter, R.B. (2009) 'Third world cities', in R. Kitchen and N. Thrift (eds), *The International Encyclopedia of Human Geography*. Oxford: Elsevier. pp. 247–55.

Lloyd-Sherlock, P. (2004) 'Ageing, development and social protection: generalisations, myths and stereotypes', in P. Lloyd-Sherlock (ed.), *Living Longer: Ageing, Development and Social Protection*. London: Zed Books. pp.1–17.

Longhurst, R. (2005) 'The body' in D. Atkinson, P. Jackson, D. Sibley and N. Washbourne, *Cultural Geography: A Critical Dictionary of Key Concepts*. London and New York: I.B. Tauris. pp. 91–6.

Mackinnon, D. and Cumbers, A. (2007) *An Introduction to Economic Geography: Globalisation, Uneven Development and Place*. Harlow: Pearson-Prentice Hall.

Manzo, K. (2003) 'Africa in the rise of rights-based development', *Geoforum*, 34: 437–56.

Mawhinney, M. (2003) *Sustainable Development: Understanding the Green Debates*. Oxford: Blackwell.

McAfee, K. (1991) *Storm Signals*. London: Zed Books.

McEwan, C. (2001) 'Postcolonialism, feminism and development: intersections and dilemmas', *Progress in Development Studies*, 1 (2): 93–111.

McEwan, C. (2005) 'New spaces of citizenship? Rethinking gendered participation and empowerment in South Africa', *Geoforum*, 34 (4): 469–82.

McEwan, C. (2006) 'Mobilizing culture for social justice and development: South Africa's *Amazwi Abesifazane* memory cloths program', in S. Radcliffe (ed.), *Culture and Development in a Globalizing World: Geographies, Actors and Paradigms*. London and New York: Routledge. pp. 203–27.

McEwan, C. and Butler, R. (2007) 'Disability and development: different models, different places', *Geography Compass*, 1 (3): 448–66.

McIlwaine, C. (2007) 'From local to global to transnational civil society: re-framing development perspectives on the non-state sector', *Geography Compass*, 1 (6): 1252–81.

McIlwaine, C. and Datta, K. (2003) 'From feminising to engendering development', *Gender, Place and Culture*, 10 (4): 369–82.

McIntyre, D. (2007) *Learning from Experience: Health Care Financing in Low- and Middle-Income Countries*. Geneva: Global Forum for Health Research. Available at www.globalforumhealth.org [last accessed 1/7/08].

McMichael, P. (2009) 'Contemporary contradictions of the global development project: geopolitics, global ecology and the "development climate"', *Third World Quarterly*, 30 (1): 247–62.

253

Meintjes, H. and Giese, S. (2006) 'Spinning the epidemic: the making of mythologies of orphanhood in the context of AIDS', *Childhood*, 13 (3): 407–30.

Mercer, C. (2002) 'NGOs, civil society and democratization: a critical review of the literature', *Progress in Development Studies*, 2: 5–22.

Mitlin, D. and Satterthwaite, D. (2007) 'Strategies for grassroots control of international aid', *Urbanization and Environment*, 19 (2): 483–500.

Mittleman, J. (1995) 'Rethinking the international division of labour in the context of globalisation', *Third World Quarterly*, 16 (2): 273–96.

Mohan, G. (2002) 'The disappointments of civil society: the politics of NGO intervention in northern Ghana', *Political Geography*, 21: 125–54.

Mohan, G. (2008) 'Participatory development', in V. Desai and R.B. Potter (eds), *The Companion to Development Studies*. London: Hodder. pp. 45–50.

Mohan, G. and Stokke, K. (2000) 'Participatory development and empowerment: the dangers of localism', *Third World Quarterly*, 21 (2): 247–68.

Mohan, G., Brown, E., Milward, B. and Zack-Williams, A. (2000) *Structural Adjustment: Theory, Practice and Impacts*. London and New York: Routledge.

Mohanty, C. (1988) 'Under Western Eyes: feminist scholarship and colonial discourses', *Feminist Review*, 30: 65–88.

Momsen, J. (2002) 'Myth or math: the waxing and waning of the female-headed household', *Progress in Development Studies*, 2 (2): 145–51.

Momsen, J. (2004) *Gender and Development*. London: Routledge.

Monbiot, G. (2004) *Manifesto for a New World Order*. New York: W.W. Norton.

Monbiot, G. (2007) *Heat: How to Stop the Planet from Burning*. Cambridge, MA: South End Press.

Monk, J. and Katz, C. (1993) 'When in the world are women?', in C. Katz and J. Monk (eds), *Full Circles: Geographies of Women over the Lifecourse*. London: Routledge. pp. 122–37.

Moriset, B. and Malecki, E.J. (2009) 'Organisation versus space: the paradoxical geographies of the digital economy', *Geography Compass*, 3 (1): 256–74.

Morris, J. (1991) *Pride Against Prejudice: Transforming Attitudes to Disability*. Philadelphia: New Society Publishers.

Moser, C. (1998) 'The asset vulnerability framework: reassessing urban poverty reduction strategies', *World Development*, 26 (1): 1–19.

Murray, W.E. (2006) *Geographies of Globalization*. Abingdon: Routledge.

Murray, W.E. and Overton, J.D. (2011) 'Neoliberalism is dead, long live neoliberalism? Neostructuralism and the international aid regime of the 2000s', *Progress in Development Studies*, 11: **307**–19.

Mwendwa, T., Murangira, A. and Lang, R. (2009) 'Mainstreaming the rights of persons with disabilities in national development frameworks', *Journal of International Development*, 21: 662–72.

Nanda, S. (2007) 'The *hijras* of India: cultural and individual dimensions of an institutionalized third gender role', in R. Parker and P. Aggleton (eds), *Culture, Society and Sexuality: A Reader*. London: Routledge. pp. 237–49.

Narlikar, A. (2005) *The World Trade Organization: A Very Short Introduction*. Oxford: Oxford University Press.

Nast, H. and Pile, S. (1998) 'Introduction: makingplacesbodies', in H. Nast and S. Pile (eds), *Places through the Body*. London: Routledge. pp. 1–19.

Bibliography

Nederveen Pieterse, J. (2002) 'After post-development', *Third World Quarterly*, 21: 175–91.

Nelson, P. (2006) 'The varied and conditional integration of NGOs in the aid system: NGOs and the World Bank', *Journal of International Development*, 18: 701–713.

New Internationalist (2003) 'Capitalism is the extraordinary belief that the nastiest of men for the nastiest of motives will somehow work for the benefit of all.' Attributed to British economist John Maynard Keynes by Reuters in the *New Internationalist*, Issue 362, 5 November.

Newland, K. (2007) 'A new surge of interest in migration and development', *Migration Information Source*. Available at www.migrationinformation.org [last accessed 27/7/08].

Nieuwenhuys, O. (1994) *Children's Lifeworlds: Gender, Welfare and Labour in the Developing World*. London: Routledge.

Njambi, W. and O'Brien, W. (2000) 'Revisiting woman–woman marriage: notes on Gikuyu women', *National Women's Studies Association Journal*, 12 (1): 1–23.

Nkrumah, K. (1965) *Neocolonialism: the Last Stage of Imperialism*. London: Thomas Nelson & Sons, Ltd.

Nkrumah, K. (1969) *Handbook of Revolutionary Warfare*. New York: International Publishers.

Norris, P. (2001) *Digital Divide: Civic Engagement, Information Poverty and the Internet*. Cambridge: Cambridge University Press.

Norwine, J. and Gonzalez, A. (1988) (eds) *The Third World: States of Mind and Being*. London: Unwin-Hyman.

Nyambedha, E., Wandibba, S. and Aagaard-Hansen, J. (2003) 'Changing patterns of orphan care due to the HIV epidemic in Western Kenya', *Social Science and Medicine*, 57: 301–11.

Nyerere, J.K. (1968) *Ujamaa: Essays on Socialism*. Dar es Salaam: Oxford University Press.

OECD (1996) *Shaping the Twenty-First Century*. Paris: Organisation for Economic Cooperation and Development.

Office of the United Nations High Commissioner for Human Rights (2012) Universal Human Rights Instruments. Available at www.ohchr.org/english/law/index.htm#core [last accessed 03/01/2012].

Ogden, J., Esim, S. and Grown, C. (2006) 'Expanding the care continuum for HIV/AIDS: bringing carers into focus', *Health Policy and Planning*, 21 (5): 333–42.

Oliver, M. (1990) *The Politics of Disablement*. Basingstoke: Macmillan and St Martin's Press.

Olson, E. and Sayer, A. (2009) 'Radical geography and its critical standpoints: embracing the normative', *Antipode*, 41 (1): 180–98.

Oppong, J. and Kalipeni, E. (2004) 'Perception and misperceptions of AIDS in Africa', in E. Kalipeni, S. Craddock, J. Oppong and J. Ghosh (eds), *HIV and AIDS in Africa: Beyond Epidemiology*. Oxford: Blackwell. pp. 47–57.

Overa, R. (2006) 'Networks, distance and trust: telecoms development and changing trading practices in Ghana', *World Development*, 34 (7): 1301–15.

Oxfam (2004) *Trading Away Our Rights: Women Working in Global Supply Chains*. Oxford: Oxfam International.

Oxfam (2009) *Paying the Price for the Economic Crisis*. Oxfam International Discussion Paper. Oxford: Oxfam.

Panelli, R., Punch, S. and Robson, E. (eds) (2007) *Global Perspectives on Rural Childhood and Youth: Youth Rural Lives*. London: Routledge.

Parker, M. (1999) 'Female circumcision and cultures of sexuality', in T. Skelton and T. Allen (eds), *Culture and Global Change*. London and New York: Routledge. pp. 201–11.

Parker, R. and Aggleton, P. (eds) (2007) *Culture, Society and Sexuality. A Reader*, 2nd edn. Abingdon and New York: Routledge.

Pearson, R. (2007) 'Beyond women workers: gendering corporate social responsibility', *Third World Quarterly*, 28 (4): 731–49.

Perrons, D. (2004) *Globalisation and Social Change: People and Places in a Divided World*. London: Routledge.

Peterman, A. (2011) 'Widowhood and asset inheritance in sub-Saharan Africa: empirical evidence from 15 countries', *CRPC Working Paper No. 183*, Chronic Poverty Research Centre, University of Manchester.

Porter, D.J. (1995) 'Scenes from childhood', in J. Crush (ed.), *Power of Development*, London: Routledge. pp. 63–86.

Potter, R.B. and Conway, D. (2011) 'Development', in J.A. Agnew and D.N. Livingstone (eds), *The Sage Handbook of Geographical Knowledge*. London: Sage. pp. 595–609.

Potter, R.B. and Lloyd-Evans, S. (1998) *The City in the Developing World*. Harlow: Longman.

Potter, R.B. and Lloyd-Evans, S. (2009) 'The Brandt Commission', in R. Kitchen and N. Thrift (eds), *The International Encyclopedia of Human Geography, Volume 1*. London: Elsevier. pp. 348–54.

Potter, R.B. and Unwin, T. (1988) 'Developing areas research in British geography', *Area*, 20: 121–6.

Potter, R.B., Binns, T., Elliott, J.A. and Smith, D. (2008) *Geographies of Development: an Introduction to Development Studies*, 3rd edn. Harlow, London and New York: Pearson-Prentice-Hall.

Powell, J. (2010) 'The power of global aging', *Ageing International*, 35: 1–14.

Power, M. (2001) 'Geographies of disability and development in Southern Africa', *Disability Studies Quarterly*, 21 (4): 84–97.

Power, M. (2003) *Rethinking Development Geographies*. London and New York: Routledge.

Power, M. (2008) 'Enlightenment and the era of modernity', in V. Desai and R.B. Potter (eds), *The Companion to Development Studies*, 2nd edn. London: Hodder Education. pp. 71–5.

Preis, A. (2002) 'Human rights as cultural practice: an anthropological critique', in S. Schech and J. Haggis (eds), *Development: a Cultural Studies Reader*. Oxford: Blackwell Publishing. pp. 132–43.

Preston, P.W. (1996) *Development Theory: an Introduction*. Oxford: Blackwell.

Pretty, J. (2002) 'Re-generating agriculture', in V. Desai and R.B. Potter (eds), *The Companion to Development Studies*, 1st edn. London: Arnold. pp. 170–5.

Punch, S. (2001) 'Household division of labour: generation, gender, age, birth order and sibling composition', *Work, Employment and Society*, 15 (4): 803–23.

Punch, S. (2004) 'The impact of primary education on school-to-work transitions for young people in rural Bolivia', *Youth and Society*, 36 (2): 163–2.

Bibliography

Putnam, R. (1993) *Making Democracy Work: Civic Traditions in Modern Italy.* Princeton, NJ: Princeton University Press.

Radcliffe, S. (2006a) 'Culture in development thinking: geographies, actors and paradigms', in S. Radcliffe (ed.), *Culture and Development in a Globalizing World: Geographies, Actors and Paradigms.* London and New York: Routledge. pp. 1–29.

Radcliffe, S. (ed.) (2006b) *Culture and Development in a Globalizing World: Geographies, Actors and Paradigms.* London and New York: Routledge.

Rakodi, C. (2002) *Urban Livelihoods: A People Centred Approach to Reducing Poverty.* London: Earthscan Publications.

Raynolds, L.T., Murray, D.L. and Wilkinson, J. (2007) *Fair Trade: The Challenge of Transforming Globalization.* Abingdon: Routledge.

Redclift, M.R. (1987) *Sustainable Development: Exploring the Contradictions.* London: Routledge.

Redclift, M. (2008) 'Sustainable development', in V. Desai and R.B. Potter (eds), *The Companion to Development Studies*, 2nd edn. London: Arnold. pp. 279–82.

Rich, A. (1980) 'Compulsory heterosexuality and lesbian existence', *Signs*, 5: 631–60.

Rigg, J. (2006) 'Land, farming, livelihoods and poverty: rethinking the links in the rural South', *World Development*, 34 (1): 180–202.

Rigg, J. (2007) *An Everyday Geography of the Global South.* London: Routledge.

Rigg, J. (2008) 'The millennium development goals', in V. Desai and R.B. Potter (eds), *The Companion to Development Studies.* London: Hodder Education. pp. 37–45.

Roberts, S. (1995) 'Small place, big money: the Cayman Islands and the international financial system', *Economic Geography*, 71: 237–56.

Robinson, G. (2004) *Geographies of Agriculture: Globalization, Restructuring and Sustainability.* Harlow: Pearson-Prentice Hall.

Rodney, W. (1974) *How Europe Underdeveloped Africa.* Washington, DC: Howard University Press.

Rogers, P.P., Jalal, K.F. and Boyd, J.A. (2008) *An Introduction to Sustainable Development.* London: Earthscan.

Sachs, W. (1992) *The Development Dictionary.* London: Zed Books.

Sachs, W. (1993) *Global Ecology: A New Arena of Political Conflict.* London and New Jersey: Zed Books.

Sadler, D. (2004) 'Anti-corporate campaigning and corporate "social" responsibility: towards alternative spaces of citizenship', *Antipode*, 36 (5): 851–70.

Safa, H. (1981) 'Runaway shops and female employment: the search for cheap labour', *Signs*, 7 (2): 418–33.

Said, E. (1978) *Orientalism.* New York: Vintage.

Samuels, F. and Wells, J. (2009) 'The loss of the middle ground: the impact of crises and HIV and AIDS on "skipped-generation" households', *ODI Project Briefing No. 33*: November 2009. London: Overseas Development Institute. Available at www.odi.org.uk [last accessed 10/10/10].

Sassen, S. (ed.) (2002) *Global Networks, Linked Cities.* London: Routledge.

Schech, S. and Haggis, J. (2000) *Culture and Development: A Critical Introduction.* Oxford: Blackwell.

Schech, S. and Haggis, J. (2002) *Development: A Cultural Studies Reader.* Oxford: Blackwell.

257

Scholte, J.A. (2000) *Globalization: A Critical Introduction*. Basingstoke: Palgrave.

Schumacher, E.F. (1973) *Small is Beautiful: Economics as if People Mattered*. New York and London: Harper & Row.

Schuurman, F. (2000) 'Paradigms lost, paradigms regained? Development studies in the twenty-first century', *Third World Quarterly*, 21: 7–20.

Schuurman, F. (2008) 'The impasse in development studies', in V. Desai and R.B. Potter (eds), *The Companion to Development Studies*, 2nd edn. London: Hodder Education. Chapter 1.3.

Scott, A. (1994) *Divisions and Solidarities: Gender, Class and Employment in Latin America*. London: Routledge.

Sen, A. (1984) *Poverty and Famines: An Essay in Entitlement and Deprivation*. Oxford: Clarendon Press.

Sen, A. (1987) 'Gender and Co-operative Conflicts', *Working Paper No. 18*. Helsinki: World Institute for Development Economics Research (WIDER). Available at http://www.wider.unu.edu/Offline/2009/previous-series/1987/en_GB/wp-18/ [last accessed 21/2/10].

Sen, A. (1999) *Development as Freedom: Human Capability and Global Need*. Oxford: Oxford University Press.

Serra, N. and Stiglitz, J.E. (2008) *The Washington Consensus Reconsidered*. Oxford: Oxford University Press.

Shelley, T. (2007) *Exploited: Migrant Labour in the New Global Economy*. London: Zed Books.

Shrestha, N.R. and Conway, D. (2005) 'Globalization's cultural challenges: homogenization, hybridization and heightened identity', in D. Conway and N. Heynen (eds), *Globalization's Contradictions: Geographies of Discipline, Destruction and Transformation*. Aldershot: Ashgate. pp. 196–211.

Sidaway, J. (2008) 'Post-development', in V. Desai and R.B. Potter (eds), *The Companion to Development Studies*, 2nd edn. London: Hodder Education. Chapter 1.4.

Silverstein, M., Cong, Z. and Shuzhuo, L. (2006) 'Intergenerational transfers and living arrangements of older people in rural China: consequences for psychological wellbeing', *Journal of Gerontology: Series B Psychological Sciences*, 61 (5): S256–S266.

Simon, D. (2006) (ed.) *Fifty Key Thinkers on Development*. London and New York: Routledge.

Skeldon, R. (1997) *Migration and Development*. Harlow: Addison Wesley Longman.

Smith, A., Stening, A. and Willis, K. (eds) (2007) *Social Justice and Neoliberalism: Global Perspectives*. London: Zed Books.

Smith, J. (2001) 'Globalizing resistance: The Battle of Seattle and the future of social movements', *Mobilization: an International Quarterly*, 6: 1–19.

Solodovnikov, V. and Bogoslovsky, V. (1975) *Non-capitalist Development*. Moscow: Progress Publishers.

Somma, D.B. and Kessler Bodiang, C. (c. 2004) *The Cultural Approach to HIV/AIDS Prevention*. Swiss Agency for Development and Cooperation/Swiss Centre for International Health. Geneva: Swiss Tropical Institute. Available at www.sdc-health.ch/priorities_in_health/communicable_diseases/hiv_aids/cultural_approach_to_hvi_aids_prevention [last accessed 29/08/11].

Bibliography

de Soto, H. (1989) *The Other Path: The Economic Answer to Terrorism*. New York: HarperCollins.

Sparke, M. (2007) 'Geopolitical fears, geoeconomic hopes and the responsibilities of geography', *Annals, Association of American Geographers*, 97 (2): 338–49.

Stalker, P. (2000) *Workers without Frontiers: The Impact of Globalization on International Migration*. Boulder, CO: Lynne Rienner.

Standing, G. (1999) 'Global feminisation through flexible labour: a theme revisited', *World Development*, 27: 535–50.

Stephens, S. (1995) 'Children and the Politics of Culture in "Late Capitalism"', in S. Stephens (ed.), *Children and the Politics of Culture*. Princeton, NJ: Princeton University Press. pp. 3–50.

Stiglitz, J.E. (2010) *Free Fall: America, Free Markets and the Sinking of the World Economy*. New York: W.W. Norton & Co.

Stiglitz, J. and Charlton, A. (2005) *Fair Trade for All: How Trade Can Promote Development*. Oxford: Oxford University Press.

Stohr, W.B. (1981) 'Development from below: the bottom-up and periphery-inward paradigm', in W.B. Stohr and D.R.F. Taylor (eds), *Development from Above or Below? The Dialectics of Regional Planning in Developing Countries*. New York: Wiley. pp. 39–72.

Sturgeon, T.J. and Gereffi, G. (2009) 'Measuring success in the global economy: international trade, industrial upgrading, and business function outsourcing in global value chains', *Transnational Corporations*, 18 (2): 1–35.

Thirlwall, A.P. (2006) *Growth and Development: with Special Reference to Developing Economies*, 8th edn. Basingstoke and New York: Palgrave Macmillan.

Thirlwall, A.P. (2008) 'Development and economic growth', in V. Desai and R.B. Potter (eds), *The Companion to Development Studies*. London: Hodder Education. pp. 37–45.

Thomas, J.J. (2002) 'Decent work in the informal sector: Latin America', *Employment Sector Working Papers in the Informal Economy*, 12. Geneva: International Labour Organization (ILO).

Thornton, R. (2008) *Unimagined Community: Sex, Networks and AIDS in Uganda and South Africa*. Berkeley and Los Angeles: University of California Press.

Thrift, N.J. (1983) 'On the determination of social action in space and time', *Society and Space, Environment and Planning, D*. 1 (1): 23–5.

Thrift, N. (1986) 'The geography of international economic disorder', in R.J. Johnston and P.J. Taylor (eds), *A World in Crisis?* London: Basil Blackwell.

Thrift, N.J. (2002) 'A hyperactive world', in R.J. Johnston, P.J. Taylor and M.J. Watts (eds), *Geographies of Global Change: Remapping the World*, 2nd edn. Oxford, Malden, MA, Melbourne and Berlin: Blackwell Publishing.pp. 29–42.

Thrift, N.J. (2005) 'The rise of soft capitalism', *Knowing Capitalism*. Thousand Oaks, CA: Sage.

Tobin, J. (1978) 'A proposal for international monetary reform', *Eastern Economic Journal*, 4: 153–9.

Tobin, J. (1996) 'A currency conversion tax: why and how', *Open Economics Review*, 7: 493–9.

Todaro, M.J. (1976) *Internal Migration in Developing Countries*. Geneva: International Labour Organization (ILO).

Tomalin, E. (2006) 'Religion and a rights-based approach to development', *Progress in Development Studies*, 6 (2): 93–108.

Toye, J. (1987) *Dilemmas of Development*. Oxford: Blackwell.

Tsikata, D. (2007) 'Announcing a new dawn prematurely? Human rights feminists and the rights-based approaches to development', in A. Cornwall, E. Harrison and A. Whitehead (eds), *Feminisms in Development: Contradictions, Contestations and Challenges*. London: Zed Books. pp. 214–226.

UK Consortium on AIDS and International Development (2008) 'What do we really mean by "HIV care and support"? Progress towards a comprehensive definition', HIV Care and Support Working Group. London: UK Consortium on AIDS and International Development. Available at www.aidsconsortium.org.uk [last accessed 29/08/11].

ul Haq, M. (1995) *The UN and the Bretton Woods Institutions: New Challenges for the Twenty-first Century*. Basingstoke: Macmillan.

ul Haq, M., Jolly, R., Streeten, P. and Haq, K. (2005) *The UN and the Bretton Woods Institutions: New Challenges for the Twenty-first Century*. London and Basingstoke: Macmillan.

UNAIDS, UNFPA (United Nations Population Fund) and UNIFEM (United Nations Development Fund for Women) (2004) *Women and HIV/AIDS: Confronting the Crisis*. Geneva: UNAIDS; New York: UNFPA/UNIFEM.

UNAIDS (2010) 'Global Report', *UNAIDS Report on the Global AIDS Epidemic 2010*. Joint United Nations Programme on HIV/AIDS. Available at www.unaids.org [last accessed 25/9/11].

UNICEF (2006) *The State of the World's Children 2007, Women and Children: The Double Dividend of Gender Equality*. New York: UNICEF. Available at http://www.unicef.org [last accessed 25/9/11].

UNICEF (2007) *Progress for Children: A World Fit for Children Statistical Review*. Number 6. New York: UNICEF.

UNICEF (United Nations Children's Fund) (2008) *State of the World's Children 2009*. New York: UNICEF. Available at http://www.unicef.org/sowc09/docs/SOWC09-FullReport-EN.pdf [last accessed 28/01/10].

UNICEF (2012) Convention on the Rights of the Child. Available at www.unicef.org/crc [last accessed 03/01/2012]

United Nations (UN) (2002a) 'Political Declaration and Madrid International Plan of Action on Ageing', Second World Assembly on Ageing, Madrid, Spain, 8–12 April 2002. New York: United Nations. Available at www.un.org [last accessed 16/05/11].

United Nations (2002b) 'World Population Ageing 1950–2050', UN Population Division. Available at www.un.org/esa/population/publications/worldageing19502050/ [last accessed 16/05/11].

United Nations (2005) *Living Arrangements of Older Persons around the World*. Population Studies No. 240, Sales No. E.05.XIII.9. New York: United Nations.

United Nations (2007) *World Youth Report 2007 Young People's Transitions to Adulthood: Progress and Challenges*. New York: United Nations.

United Nations (2009a) *Millennium Development Goals Report 2009*. New York: United Nations. Available at http://www.un.org/millenniumgoals/pdf/MDG_Report [last accessed 8/9/10].

United Nations (2009b) *Population Ageing and Development 2009*. Department of Economic and Social Affairs, United Nations Population Division. Available at www.unpopulation.org [last accessed 16/05/11].

United Nations (2010a) *World Population Prospects 2010 Revision*. Available at www.unpopulation.org [last accessed 16/05/11].

United Nations (2010b) Convention on the Rights of Persons with Disabilities and Optional Protocol. Available at www.un.org/disabilities/documents/convention/convoptprot-e.pdf [last accessed 26/01/11].

United Nations (2011) *UN Enable Factsheet on Persons with Disabilities*. Available at www.un.org/disabilities/documents/toolaction/pwdfs.pdf [last accessed 26/01/11].

United Nations Development Programme (UNDP) (1980) *North–South, A Programme for Survival*. New York: United Nations Development Programme.

United Nations Development Programme (UNDP) (1983) *Common Crisis*. New York: United Nations Development Programme.

United Nations Development Programme (UNDP) (1990) *Human Development Report*. New York and Oxford: Oxford University Press.

United Nations Development Programme (UNDP) (2009) *Human Development Report 2009*. New York: United Nations Development Programme.

United Nations Development Programme (UNDP) (2010) *Human Development Report 2010*. Available at http://hdr.undp.org/un/reports/global/hdr2010/ [last accessed 17/8/10].

United Nations University, War on Want and the North–South Institute (2008) *The Currency Transaction Tax: Rate and Revenue Estimates*. Tokyo, New York, Paris: UNU Press.

UNWEP (1987) *Our Common Future*. New York: United Nations Development Programme.

Unwin, T. and Potter, R.B. (1992) 'Undergraduate and postgraduate teaching on the geography of the Third World', *Area*, 24: 56–62.

Uphoff, N. (1999) 'Understanding social capital: learning from analysis and experience of participation', in P. Dasgupta and I. Serageldin (eds), *Social Capital: A Multifaceted Perspective*. Washington DC: World Bank.

Varley, A. (2008) 'Gender, families and households', in V. Desai and R.B. Potter (eds), *The Companion to Development Studies*, 2nd edn. London: Hodder Education. pp. 346–51.

Vertovec, S. (2009) *Transnationalism*. Oxford and New York: Routledge.

Vincent, R. (2005) 'What do we do with culture? Engaging culture in development', *Exchange Findings*, 3, March. Available at http://www.healthlink.org.uk/PDFs/findings_culture.pdf [last accessed 25/9/11].

Visvanathan, N., Duggan, L., Nisonoff, L. and Wiegersma, N. (eds) (1997) *The Women, Gender and Development Reader*. London: Zed Books.

War on Want (2009) *Trading Away Our Jobs: How Free Trade Threatens Employment Around the World*. Available at http://www.waronwant.org/campaigns/trade-justice/more/inform/16486-trading-away-our-jobs [last accessed 29/5/11].

Wells, K. (2009) *Childhood in a Global Perspective*. Cambridge: Polity Press.

White, H. (2008) 'The measurement of poverty', in V. Desai and R.B. Potter (eds), *The Companion to Development Studies*. London: Hodder Education. pp. 25–30.

Whitehead, A. (2002) 'Tracking livelihood change: theoretical, methodological and empirical perspectives from North-East Ghana', *Journal of Southern African Studies* 28(3): 575–598.

Whitehead, M. (2007) *Spaces of Sustainability: Geographical Perspectives in the Sustainable Society*. Oxford: Routledge.

Williams, G., Meth, P. and Willis, K. (2009) *Geographies of Developing Areas: The Global South in a Changing World*. London: Routledge.

Willis, K. (2005) *Theories and Practices of Development*. London and New York: Routledge.

Woo, J., Kwok, T., Sze, F.K.H. and Yuan, H.J. (2002) 'Ageing in China: health and social consequences and responses', *International Journal of Epidemiology*, 31: 772–5.

World Bank (2007) *World Development Report 2008: Agriculture for Development*. Oxford: Oxford University Press for the World Bank.

World Bank (2008) Development Indicators. Available at http://data.worldbank.org/indicator.

World Bank (2011) *Migration and Remittances Fact Book 2011*. Washington, DC: Migration and Remittances Unit, World Bank. Available at www.worldbank.org/prospects/migrationandremittances [last accessed 19/3/11].

World Commission on Environment and Development (1987) *Our Common Future*. Oxford: Oxford University Press.

World Economic Forum (WEF) (2004) *Global Governance Initiative, Annual Report 2004*. Geneva, Switzerland: World Economic Forum. Available at http://www.weforum.org [last accessed 26/9/05].

World Health Organization (WHO) (2002) *Community Home-Based Care in Resource-Limited Settings: A Framework for Action*. Geneva: World Health Organization. Available at www.who.int/chp/knowledge/publications/comm_home_based_care.pdf [last accessed 25/9/11].

World Health Organization (WHO) (2008) *Towards Universal Access: Scaling Up Priority HIV/AIDS Interventions in the Health Sector*. Progress Report 2008. Geneva: World Health Organization. Available at www.who.org.

World Health Organization (WHO) (2010) *Towards Universal Access: Scaling Up Priority HIV/AIDS Interventions in the Health Sector*. Progress Report 2010. Geneva: World Health Organization. Available at www.who.org.

World Institute for Development Economics Research (2006) *The World Distribution of Household Wealth*. Tokyo: United Nations University.

WTO's Agreement on Trade-related Aspects of Intellectual Property Rights (TRIPS) www.wto.org/english/tratop_e/trips_e/trips_e.htm [last accessed 20/10/11].

Worldmapper: the world as you've never seen it before. Available at http://www.worldmapper.org.

Worsley, P. (1964) *The Third World*. London: Weidenfeld and Nicolson.

Worsley, P. (1979) 'How many worlds?', *Third World Quarterly*, 1, 100–108.

Wreford, J. (2008) 'Myths, masks and stark realities: traditional African healers, HIV/AIDS narratives and patterns of HIV/AIDS avoidance', CSSR Working Paper No. 209, Centre for Social Science Research, University of Cape Town. Available at www.cssr.uct.ac.za/publications/working-paper/2008/209 [last accessed 25/9/11].

Wright, M. (2003) 'Factory daughters and Chinese modernity: a case from Dongguan', *Geoforum*, 34: 291–301.

Wright, R. (2002) 'Transnational corporations and global divisions of labor', in R.J. Johnston, P.J. Taylor and M.J. Watts (eds), *Geographies of Global Change: Remapping the World*, 2nd edn. Oxford: Blackwell. pp. 68–77.

Wroe, M. and Doney, M. (2005) *The Rough Guide to a Better World*. London: Rough Guides Ltd.

Bibliography

Yeo, R. and Moore, K. (2003) 'Including disabled people in poverty reduction work: "Nothing About Us, Without Us"', *World Development*, 31 (3): 571–90.

Young, K. (1997) 'Gender and development', in N. Visvanathan, L. Duggan, L. Nisonoff and N. Wiegersma (eds), *The Women, Gender and Development Reader*. London: Zed Books. pp. 51–4.

Zelenev, S. (2008) 'The Madrid Plan: a Comprehensive Agenda for an Ageing World' in *Review Report 2008 of The Madrid International Plan of Action on Ageing*. New York: United Nations. pp. 1–17. Available at www.un.org [last accessed 16/05/11].

Zimmer, Z. and Dayton, J. (2005) 'Older adults in sub-Saharan Africa living with children and grandchildren', *Population Studies*, 59 (3): 295–312.

INDEX